BP

# NUCLEAR HISTORY PROGRAM

*General Editor* Robert O'Neill

## I
## NUCLEAR WEAPONS AND
## BRITISH STRATEGIC PLANNING, 1955–1958

# NUCLEAR HISTORY PROGRAM

The Nuclear History Program is an international programme of training, research, and discussion concerning the development and deployment of nuclear forces, the elaboration of policies for their management and possible use, and their role in the evolution of relations among the United States, the Soviet Union, and the countries of Europe.

Major funding is provided by the Ford Foundation, the Volkswagen-Stiftung, the John D. and Catherine T. MacArthur Foundation, and the German Marshall Fund. Other donors are also assisting specific projects.

# NUCLEAR WEAPONS AND BRITISH STRATEGIC PLANNING, 1955–1958

MARTIN S. NAVIAS

CLARENDON PRESS · OXFORD
1991

Oxford University Press, Walton Street, Oxford OX2 6DP

Oxford New York Toronto
Delhi Bombay Calcutta Madras Karachi
Petaling Jaya Singapore Hong Kong Tokyo
Nairobi Dar es Salaam Cape Town
Melbourne Auckland

and associated companies in
Berlin Ibadan

Oxford is a trade mark of Oxford University Press

Published in the United States
by Oxford University Press, New York

British Library Cataloguing in Publication Data
Navias, Martin S.
Nuclear weapons and British strategic planning, 1955–
1958.—(The nuclear history program)
1. Great Britain. Nuclear weapons
I. Title  II. Series
355. 033541
ISBN 0–19–827754–7

Library of Congress Cataloging in Publication Data
Navias, Martin S.
Nuclear weapons and British strategic planning, 1955–1958 / Martin
S. Navias.
p.  cm.
Includes bibliographical references and index.
1. Nuclear weapons—Great Britain.  2. Great Britain—Military
policy.  I. Title.
UA647.N42 1991.  355.8'25119'0941—dc20  90–49133
ISBN 0–19–827754–7

Set by Hope Services (Abingdon) Ltd.
Printed in Great Britain by
Biddles Ltd
Guildford & King's Lynn

To the memory of my father

# Acknowledgements

I wish to acknowledge my deep indebtedness to Professor Lawrence Freedman and Dr Michael Dockrill of the Department of War Studies, King's College, London for their constant guidance and support during the long and arduous years of this project. Professor Freedman also went to great trouble in order to secure me the funding without which the research could not have been undertaken.

Throughout this project Dr Nicholas Wheeler very generously provided me with many ideas and much information from his own work. Lady Duncan Sandys and Dr S. Forgan kindly allowed me to read and quote from unpublished manuscripts in their possession. Sir Richard Powell and Colonel L. Post gave me much of their time to discuss various aspects of this study. Mr T. C. G. James of the RAF Air Historical Branch contributed greatly to my understanding of this period in British nuclear strategy. Thanks must also go to Dr John Simpson, Dr John Baylis and Mr Eric Grove who read my earlier drafts and provided me with many valuable insights as well as to Dr Christoph Bluth and Dr Jan Honig for their many comments.

Funding for the research was received from the Nuclear History Project and an Overseas Research Scholarship.

Preliminary versions of some of the material on alliance commitments, national service, and the V-bomber force appeared in a book edited by Dr Anne Deighton entitled *Britain and the First Cold War* (London, 1990), the *Journal of Contemporary History*, 24, No. 2 (1989), and the *Journal of Strategic Studies*, 11, No. 2 (June 1988), respectively. Permission for expanding this material and incorporating it into the book is acknowledged. I am also grateful to the controller of Her Majesty's Stationery Office for permission to reproduce extracts from documents held in the Public Records Office, and the Trustees of the Liddell Hart Centre for Military Archives for permission to quote from papers in their collection.

M. S. N.

# Contents

# Abbreviations

| | |
|---|---|
| BAOR | British Army on the Rhine |
| CAS | Chief of Air Staff |
| CIGS | Chief of Imperial General Staff |
| COSC | Chiefs of Staff Committee |
| DRPC | Defence Research Policy Committee |
| *FRUS* | *Foreign Relations of the United States* |
| IRBM | intermediate range ballistic missile |
| JCAE | Joint Committee on Atomic Energy |
| JIC | Joint Intelligence Committee |
| JPS | Joint Planning Staff |
| LTDP | Long Term Defence Programme |
| MEAF | Middle East Air Force |
| NATO | North Atlantic Treaty Organization |
| RAF | Royal Air Force |
| SAC | Strategic Air Command |
| SACEUR | Supreme Allied Commander in Europe |
| SACLANT | Supreme Allied Commander Atlantic |
| SAGW | surface-to-air guided weapon |
| SEATO | South East Asia Treaty Organization |
| SHAPE | Supreme Headquarters, Allied Powers, Europe |
| TAF | Tactical Air Force |
| WEU | Western European Union |

# Introduction

B y the time Winston Churchill had been replaced as Prime Minister by Anthony Eden in April 1955, the United Kingdom was well on the way towards acquiring the major accoutrements of a nuclear power. Over the next few years the order of battle of Britain's nuclear delivery force was set to expand dramatically with the entry into squadron service of significant numbers of V-bombers. The destructive yield of the ordnance at the United Kingdom's disposal also faced an exponential leap in the not too distant future through the expansion of her existing fission arsenal and by the prospective deployment of fusion warheads.

The British Cabinet decision of the previous year to produce and deploy thermonuclear weapons had certainly signified Britain's intention of maintaining technological pace with the United States and the Soviet Union as well as its determination to build up a sizeable deterrent force. With research into a nuclear capable medium range missile under way and the prospects for co-operation with the United States on strategic nuclear matters improving, there emerged an imperative to clarify further both the strategic objectives of Britain's nuclear arsenal and the degree to which a new balance could be struck between future nuclear and existent conventional forces.

To this end, Minister of Defence Duncan Sandys's famous Defence White Paper of 1957 served to place recent strategic developments into a formulation that more strongly than ever reflected a British willingness to rely on the threatened employment of nuclear weapons in response to enemy aggression. The White Paper emphasized that 'scientific advances must fundamentally alter the whole basis of military planning' and that 'the time has now come to revise not merely the size, but the whole character of the defence plan'. In the context of the new scientific advances, 'The only existing safeguard against major aggression is the power to threaten retaliation with nuclear weapons' and consequently Britain 'must possess an appreciable element of nuclear deterrent power of her own'. Also central to Sandys's thesis was that without a strong economy 'military power cannot in the long run be supported' and major savings in defence spending would have to be secured. The paper was explicit that once the services were redistributed and reshaped and commitments curtailed Her Majesty's government was confident 'that Britain could discharge her overseas responsibilities and make an effective contribution to the defence of the free world with armed forces much smaller than at present'.[1]

This apparent formal elevation of nuclear weapons and nuclear deterrence to central pillars of British strategic policy and the concomitant downgrading of conventional forces and capabilities underscored the similarity between Britain's 1957 strategic formulation and the 1954 American 'New Look'. Indeed, analogous to the American 'New Look' strategy, the British variant as expressed in the 1957 Defence White Paper, and various related private and public documents and statements, was also to integrate nuclear weapons with the requirements of economy and to express this relationship both on the levels of declaratory and deployment policy. The Labour politician and defence intellectual Richard Crossman, for one, did not hesitate to state that 'it was not until 1957 that the New Look strategy was adopted in London'.[2]

In defending the applicability of the label 'New Look' to describe the Sandys doctrine—with that label's stress on 'newness' and its implication of debt to the American policy of the same name—two issues naturally need to be further addressed: specifically, how actually new were the policies adopted by British decision-makers in 1957 in the context of the evolution of British nuclear policy and how derivative was the British variant of the American 'New Look' of 1954?

It is clear that the ideas that Sandys expressed in his 1957 White Paper were in many instances an echo of the equally famous (but still classified) British Global Strategy Paper of 1952—itself a reflection of policy strains extant in British defence thinking since the end of World War II. The heavy demands of the Korean War rearmament programme coupled with growing economic pressures led the Chiefs of Staff Committee (COSC) meeting at Greenwich in September 1952 to agree on the need to impose substantial decreases on defence

---

[1] *Defence: Outline of Future Policy*, Cmnd. 124, paras. 3, 5, 6, 14, 15, and 40.
[2] R. H. S. Crossman, 'The Nuclear Obsession', *Encounter*, 11, No. 1 (July 1958), 6.

spending as well as on the necessity of integrating an analysis of the strategic implications of allied and Soviet nuclear weapons into both force programming and war planning. The committee concluded that while conventional forces were to be retained to guard against threats to Britain's world-wide interests and as a partial deterrent to aggression in Europe, the main emphasis of Britain's global strategy was to be placed on the deterrent and operational capabilities of nuclear weaponry with conventional forces reduced in size.[3] Thus when juxtaposed against the 1952 Global Strategy Paper, Sandys's 'New Look' of 1957 was certainly, in the context of British strategic planning, neither original in seeking substantially to reduce the heavy costs of defence expenditure or unique in adopting a formula that sought to integrate nuclear weapons more fully into British defence policy.

Concomitantly, in using the term 'New Look' when referring to the 1957 defence statement care must be taken not to imply that Britain's policy found its prime inspiration in the American 'New Look' of 1954. Certainly the American economic and strategic predicament bore some similarity to that of the British with the need to balance escalating defence costs with continued containment of growing Soviet power. The 1953 decision by the American Joint Chiefs to cut back heavily on conventional forces and to place greater stress on nuclear weapons[4] was first set out in National Security Council document 162/2 but received its major declaratory expression early the following year when Secretary of State John Foster Dulles stated that the United States' new policy would 'depend primarily upon a great capacity to retaliate instantly, by means and at places of our own choosing'.[5] Significantly, rather than acting as a direct

---

[3] M. Gowing, *Independence and Deterrence: Britain and Atomic Energy 1945–1952* (London, 1974), i. 440–1.

[4] For a discussion of the American 'New Look' see for example W. Schilling, P. Hammond, P. and S. Snyder, *Strategy Politics and Defence Budgets* (New York, 1962), 436–40.

[5] FO 371/109112, J. F. Dulles, 'The Evolution of Foreign Policy', *Department of State Bulletin*, 30 (25 Jan. 1954), 108; also see J. H. Kahan, *Security in the Nuclear Age: Developing US Strategic Arms Policy* (Washington, DC, 1975), 12–13. The statement was later toned down and Dulles maintained that massive retaliation would not be employed in all situations and that in certain circumstances the United States would prefer to accept setbacks rather than risk turning a limited local conflict into a strategic

model for Britain's defence officials, the direction of influence seemed to be the other way around with the American 'New Look' policy perhaps benefiting from British formulations as expressed in the 1952 Global Strategy Paper. As a result of Chief of the Air Staff (CAS) Sir John Slessor's visit to the United States in 1952 the Americans were made well aware of British formulations—though they had, in fact, first reacted negatively believing that the British were attempting more to renege on their commitments than to be adumbrating a new strategic vision.[6] Yet, as has been claimed by a number of commentators, by 1954 the United States had come around to the British approach and, to some degree, at least, the 1954 'New Look' was an acceptance by the United States of the principles underlying the 1952 Global Strategy Paper.[7]

Yet even bearing these considerations in mind, the term 'New Look' as it applies to the British defence policy annunciated in 1957 remains applicable in a restricted sense for two basic reasons. In the first place, while the central ideas had certainly been adumbrated in the 1952 Global Strategy Paper, it was Sandys's policy which—similarly to the American 'New Look' —was actually accompanied by a major shift in the balance between conventional and nuclear forces. The 1952 Global Strategy Paper, after all, failed to make the shift from theory to practice with little alteration resulting in Britain's force posture. For one thing, the need to appease Army and especially Navy sensibilities made it necessary in the 1952 document to mention the so-called 'broken-backed' phase of global war in which fighting would continue on a conventional level following a nuclear exchange: the implication here being that not all conventional forces designated for such a contingency could be disbanded and total reliance would not be placed on nuclear weaponry even for the scenario of global nuclear war. Indeed,

nuclear one. FO 371/109112, J. F. Dulles, 'Foreign Policy and National Security', Statement Before the Senate Foreign Relations Committee, 19 Mar. 1954, *Dept. of State Bulletin*, 30 (1954), 465.

[6] See for example R. Rosecrance, *Defence of the Realm* (New York, 1968), 159; P. Malone, *The British Nuclear Deterrent* (London, 1984), 86; G. H. Snyder, 'The New Look of 1953', in Schilling, Hammond, and Snyder, *Strategy Politics and Defence Budgets*, 389.

[7] See e.g. S. P. Huntington, *The Common Defense: Strategic Programmes in National Politics* (New York, 1961), 118.

while not attempting to deny that the Global Strategy Paper
had throughout the 1950s undoubtedly been a source of underlying influence on British defence policy-making, it was only in
1957 that a major change in the extant equilibrium of nuclear–
conventional forces was to take place and a 'New Look' force
posture reflecting added emphasis on nuclear weapons and
decreased conventional forces was to come in to being.

Secondly, the 1957 White Paper, similarly to the American
'New Look' and unlike the Global Strategy Paper, was an *open
declaratory statement*. While it is true that the essence of the
Global Strategy Paper had been revealed in the public debates
between Slessor, Buzzard, and others during the mid-1950s, an
official pronouncement along the lines of the 1957 White Paper
had ultimately more far-reaching ramifications on the level of
military planning, diplomacy, economics, and politics. For, it
had the important effect of nailing the government's position
more firmly to the mast, making friends and foes alike more
aware of the official position, as well as opening the issue up to
more intense public and broader expert scrutiny and debate. It
allowed less leeway for ambiguity and made a large-scale
retreat from the chosen policy more difficult.

It is in this sense—with a major shift in Britain's order of
battle finally taking place together with an accompanying
strong declaratory commitment to nuclear deterrence—that
'New Look' is employed in this study, to refer to the policies
announced by Sandys in 1957.

As the comments on the 1952 Global Strategy Paper above
suggest, the emphasis and thrust of British development, deployment, and procurement activities associated with nuclear
weapons in the mid-1950s clearly reflected policy choices already
made in an earlier period. The concerns expressed by British
policy-makers with regard to their strategic environment as
well as the motivations underlying their nuclear and conventional
policy choices in the mid-1950s represented the continuation of
trends and tendencies long present in British defence policy.
Therefore the next question to be raised is whether the period
under study may rightfully be described as a 'move to the
British New Look'—with the insinuation that is of policy
continuity and progression ultimately culminating in the strategic design adopted by Duncan Sandys in April 1957.

This is a perspective that has long been recognized in the existing literature on British strategic policy in the first post-war decades. A. J. R. Groom in his major study on the evolution of British nuclear strategy views British Defence White Papers during the mid-1950s as reflecting a steady progression towards the policies enunciated in April 1957.[8] Phillip Darby in his work on British defence policy east of Suez agrees with this perspective and claims that the 1957 willingness to rely so heavily on nuclear weapons can be seen as 'the logical outcome of the attempt to give some intellectual coherence to the strategic ideas of the previous three years'.[9] This is reaffirmed in Laurence Martin's important 1962 article on British defence policy in the second half of the 1950s when he states, 'It should already be clear that the new policy was no complete break with previous trends . . .'.[10] In fact, already in 1957 the former CAS, Sir John Slessor, was unequivocal that the White Paper

introduces no basic revolution in policy, but merely rationalizes and (probably for the first time) explains in admirably intelligible form tendencies which have long been obvious and policies most of which successive British governments have accepted and urged upon their Allies for some years.[11]

Given these continuities in pressures and motivations it may with justification be argued that the British 'New Look' would inevitably have realized itself at some point in the late 1950s and may well have found expression prior to 1957 had it not been for the Suez conflict. Nevertheless, the vexed issue remains of why it had to take a major international and national political and military crisis such as that emanating from the disastrous Suez Campaign of 1956 to make possible in 1957 what was

---

[8] A. J. R. Groom, *British Thinking about Nuclear Weapons* (London, 1974), 207.

[9] P. Darby, *British Defence Policy East of Suez 1947–68* (London, 1973), 95.

[10] L. Martin, 'The Market for Strategic Ideas in Britain: The "Sandys Era"', *American Political Science Review*, 56, No. 1 (1962), 27.

[11] J. Slessor, 'British Defence Policy', *Foreign Affairs*, 35, No. 4 (1957), 551. For similar perspectives see Malone, *The British Nuclear Deterrent*, 104; C. Gordon, 'Duncan Sandys and the Independent Nuclear Deterrent', in I. Beckett and J. Gooch (eds.), *Politicians and Defence* (Manchester, 1981), 142; E. J. Grove, *From Vanguard to Trident: British Naval Policy Since World War II* (London, 1987), 197; W. Rees, 'The 1957 Sandys White Paper: New Priorities in British Defence Policy', *Journal of Strategic Studies* (June 1989), 215–29.

certainly clear to many British policy-makers throughout the post-war period and in 1955 and 1956 in particular. Clearly, the issue of continuity and progression is a more complex one than appears at first and one that needs to be further explored if the dynamics and tendencies of policy-making in the mid-1950s are to be appreciated.

By dissecting defence policy into its various elements and placing them firmly in the context of the bureaucratic struggles of the period, a fuller assessment of the pace of progression, the actual content of these reputedly consistent policies and service attitudes towards them is made possible. As the subject of this study concerns the 1957 British 'New Look' the two areas of focus will be the issues of the nuclear–conventional force balance and the role and objectives of Britain's nuclear deterrent. Furthermore, the book will first focus on these subjects in the context of the pre-1957 period (in this study 1955–6) so as to help throw light on the questions of what was possible and what was unlikely in terms of policies in the years immediately prior to 1957; and secondly it will analyse the issues of the objectives of Britain's nuclear deterrent and the balance between nuclear and conventional forces across the immediate pre- and post-1957 period so as to reach some conclusions as to the impact and consequence of the 1957 Defence White Paper in the context of British defence policies during the mid-1950s.

Specifically, the study will seek to address the questions of whether during the years 1955–6 the Eden administration was actually moving towards the procurement and deployment of an independent deterrent and whether it was succeeding in replacing conventional arms and men with more economical but highly effective nuclear firepower. If it was not, what were the competing strategic visions prevalent in British defence circles during the mid-1950s and what was the role of nuclear weapons within them? And finally, what was the significance of the British 'New Look' in terms of both declaratory and deployment policies in the mid-1950s and what can this tell us about the meaning British policy-makers attached to the difficult and notoriously ambiguous concept of independence for their deterrent?

In analysing the determinants and progress of British nuclear strategy in the years 1955–8 this book makes use of recently released archival material in Britain and the United States as well as interviews with a number of relevant personalities.

The evolution of various significant issues in British nuclear strategic policy from the late 1940s until the mid-1950s will be outlined in Chapter 1. The object will be to highlight the broader context and historical legacy for nuclear strategic policy-making in the mid-1950s. The progress of policy in the areas of independent nuclear capabilities and the need for interdependence with the United States will be discussed as will the evolving strategic debate within the United Kingdom, the impact of thermonuclear weapons on British strategic appraisals and the constraints imposed by economy and service proclivities on nuclear and conventional strategic choices.

It is important to recognize that the mid-1950s also witnessed the consolidation of Britain's alliance commitments outside Europe and the continuing review of NATO's strategy on the Continent. In the Far and Near East Britain found itself fending off allied demands for more troops and less empty promises, while in Europe, the United Kingdom had to convince its allies to review their strategic concepts with the aim of decreasing investment in men and conventional material. In both the European and extra-European theatres, nuclear weapons were attractive instruments of deterrence, war-fighting, and, when used to replace conventional firepower, of economic savings. Chapter 2 will analyse the strength and motivation behind Britain's commitment to these strategies and its success in convincing its allies accordingly. It is contended that such an analysis will provide one indication of the pace at which British nuclear strategy was moving towards a 'New Look' posture in the middle of the 1950s which involved greater reliance on nuclear weapons at the expense of conventional forces.

Such an analysis, however, can provide only one indication of progress towards such a strong nuclear orientated defence policy. On the level of force planning and procurement, the various service departments remained very attached to strategic concepts that seemed to downplay the significance of nuclear weapons on the modern battlefield. When it came to surrendering troops in Europe, the Army proved most recalcitrant; when it came to giving up forces designated for so-called 'broken-backed' warfare the Navy sought to distance itself from strategic concepts that acknowledged the irrelevance of conventional operations. Chapter 3 therefore analyses service attitudes to war-fighting in the thermonuclear age during 1955–6 and the actual inability of the government to match the declaratory drift to massive retaliation with a force posture that reflected this strategy.

The debate over the importance of the Army and Navy in an age of thermonuclear weapons was accompanied by continued ambiguity concerning whether Britain was aiming at deterring the Soviet Union independently of the United States or primarily in conjunction with her. This issue, in turn, directly informed upon operational planning and the type of targets Britain would attempt to destroy in a future nuclear war. Chapter 4 approaches this problem through an analysis of the manner by which medium bomber force requirements were determined, attitudes to the Blue Streak missiles expressed, and the problems of vulnerability and credibility addressed. It is argued that in the years immediately prior to the 1957 White Paper, attention focused less on an independent British nuclear capability than on varying degrees of limited autonomy within the confines of the Anglo-American relationship.

In 1957 the new Minister of Defence, Duncan Sandys, sought finally to mould British defence policy and force structure to reflect the exigencies of war in the thermonuclear age. His termination of national service meant that even relatively, the importance of the deterrent would increase. His stress on the independence of Britain's deterrent gave the impression to some of a new departure in British defence policy—at least in terms of the degree of commitment attributed to this posture. Chapter 5 investigates these issues and analyses the contribution of Duncan Sandys to the substance of Britain's nuclear strategy through a review of the 1957 White Paper negotiations as well as that document's immediate implications for force structuring. It describes the political environment of the post-Suez world in which the Minister had to function and it argues that although Sandys was guided by a strategic vision which recognized the merits of a policy of nuclear deterrence, he was more directly and immediately impressed by the economic necessity of terminating national service. It is further contended that his 'New Look' force posture followed more from the relative decline of conventional forces than from new plans for an increase in the absolute power of Britain's nuclear deterrent.

The announcement of the 1957 White Paper took place against a background of attempts to shift the course of the Anglo-American relationship away from the dangerous path it was taking during and immediately following the Suez crisis. Of central concern to British policy-makers was to create a more favourable perception of British actions within Washington and the securing of an agreement with President Eisenhower and Congress to allow for the amendment of the McMahon Act such that Britain could lay her hands on US nuclear techno-logical know-how. Chapter 6 explores the progress of the Atlantic relationship from the meeting at Bermuda to the changes made to the McMahon Act in 1958. An analysis of British nuclear targeting during this period, Britain's attitude to improving Soviet capabilities, the ongoing negotiations over Thor missile deployments, and the Royal Air Force (RAF) and Navy nuclear ambitions are used as indications that nuclear interdependence was still receiving priority over nuclear inde-pendence.

The conclusion of this book will employ the previous discussion in an attempt to assess a claim made by Clark and Wheeler in their study of British nuclear strategy in the first post-war decade that 'the erosion of British nuclear strategy was to coincide with the articulation of a public doctrine of independ-ence, as in the White Paper of 1957'.[12] It will analyse both the veracity of this contention and then the causes of this irony. By so doing it will help set pointers for analysing the progress of British nuclear strategy in the 1960s and beyond.

[12] I. Clark and N. J. Wheeler, *The British Origins of Nuclear Strategy 1945–1955* (Oxford, 1989), 16.

# I

## The Historical Legacy

WHILE the first decade of British nuclear strategy was characterized by unresolved tensions concerning the military and
political purposes of the deterrent and its implications for
traditional forces and capabilities, it is nevertheless clear that
the general thrust of policy was towards greater emphasis on
nuclear deterrence and reductions in conventional weaponry
and manpower. In this sense, British strategy as it was to be
expressed in the 1957 Defence White Paper represented the
continuation of a momentum that was well in place as a result
of decisions taken in the 1945–55 period.

The backdrop against which policy choices in the mid-1950s
had to be made was one in which the deployment of a British
nuclear deterrent force was seen to be a major goal but the
objectives and role of this force—specifically, the meaning of
independent deterrence in the framework of Anglo-American
defence and foreign relations—had yet to be satisfactorily
resolved. Furthermore, although there was a recognition that
nuclear weapons could replace conventional firepower there
remained differing interpretations as to the new balance to be
struck between the two forces. These latter tensions were, in
turn, to be included in the broader controversy arising out of
the clash between, on the one hand, increasing economic
imperatives for reductions in orders of battle and, on the other,
traditional service strategic proclivities and preferences.

A further complication arose in that during the latter part of
the first decade of British nuclear power the implications of the
advent of thermonuclear weapons had also to be integrated
both into the wider strategic debate in the United Kingdom
and into defence policy itself. The general appreciation that
thermonuclear weapons made war both more terrible and less
likely remained to be translated into policy choices in terms of

force structuring and strategic planning. The beginnings of this specific debate are to be located in the early middle 1950s and were to inform directly upon discussions in the Eden and Macmillan administrations.

Consequently, so as to better place the 1955–8 years in a broader historical and strategic context it is important to outline briefly the evolution of what may be regarded as some of the major themes in British nuclear strategy during the 1945–55 period.

## Nuclear Weapons: Independence and Interdependence with the United States

The military and political benefits of nuclear weapons in the post-war period had been recognized by British scientists and policy-makers as early as 1941 while experience in the various facets of civil and military development had been gained through joint co-operation with the United States in the lead up to the Hiroshima and Nagasaki explosions. The post-war unwillingness of the United States to countenance continued co-ordinated nuclear research and development forced Britain back on a solely indigenous programme. The formal decision was taken in 1947 independently to develop an atomic bomb and to produce a range of medium range bombers capable of delivering nuclear warheads. It is important to recognize that these early British decisions on nuclear weapons production and deployment were located in a specific political and economic environment which was perceived by policy-makers at the time to make the nuclear choice one that was both desirable and even crucial.

While the 1956 Suez crisis was to come to symbolize the termination of the United Kingdom's great power capabilities, already in the immediate post-war period the exigencies of economic depletion and relative military weakness necessitated almost instant contraction as well as serving to adumbrate further retreat from the international stage. The decline in Britain's global eminence had begun early in the century but it was undoubtedly the damages and losses incurred by the United Kingdom during the Second World War that hastened this process and made it irrevocable. With overseas investment down by 25 per cent due to the necessity of paying off the war effort, dollar and gold reserves reduced by almost 50 per cent to just over £450 million, and existing debts of over £3,000 million, it was evident that military and political expansion would of necessity have to be subordinated to the imperatives of economic consolidation and reconstruction at home. The surprise American decision to terminate the lend-lease programme almost immediately after the end of the war made such a policy even more crucial, as did the ambitious social programmes of the newly elected Labour Party. Thus within the first few years of peace, Britain's international retrenchment was fully in progress and she soon found herself being forced to grant independence to India and Pakistan, surrender the Palestine mandate to the United Nations, and pass over the responsibility for protecting Greece and Turkey to the United States.

The increasing need to impose restraints on rapidly depleting resources meant that the United Kingdom could not avoid the reality that international security and European economic and military well-being was dependent not on its own capabilities as much as on that of the Americans—a recognition that was rapidly realized by 1947–9 through the Truman Doctrine, the Marshall Plan, and the North Atlantic Treaty Organization (NATO). Concomitantly, in terms of the new currency of post-war military might—nuclear power—by the end of the decade, while Britain was still developing her weapon, both the United States and the Soviet Union had tested theirs. This not only threatened to underscore the United Kingdom's loss of international standing but also highlighted the relative dearth of its resources, its dependence on the deterrent strength of the United States, and the enormous potential power that the Soviet Union could bring to bear against it.

Nevertheless, the admission of greater reliance on the United States did not in itself imply that Britain had surrendered a role or a perception of itself as a major actor on the world stage. As Foreign Minister Bevin told the House of Commons in the summer of 1947, the government did not agree with the argument that

we have ceased to be a great Power, or the contention that we have ceased to play that role. We regard ourselves as one of the Powers most vital to the peace of the world, and we still have our historic part to play.[1]

Such optimism notwithstanding, the pace of Britain's global retrenchment and her steady relegation to the status of a second tier power was as disconcerting for those at the helm of leadership in Whitehall as it was sudden. It is not surprising that those who had presided over and had long grown used to a global empire with its attendant prestige and status would draw back from policies that hastened and abetted the Empire and Commonwealth's diminution. At the same time, it was to be expected that policies and armaments appearing to offer both the form and substance of power became increasingly attractive to British decision-makers intent upon retaining their former international position. Consequently, by the mid-1950s, nuclear weapons were to become those armaments and nuclear deterrence based on massive retaliation that policy which was chosen to help ensure Britain's international standing, influence, and security in an era in which her traditional power resources were being depleted as well as overtaken by others.

This is not to imply that the decision to proceed with nuclear weapons research supported by the Maud Committee in 1941 and the decision to produce a nuclear weapon made by the Defence Policy Committee in 1947 were in the main functions of the need to uphold Britain's declining international position. Such a motivation was to become more pronounced in the 1950s, but in the 1940s, as Clark and Wheeler have effectively argued, British policy-makers viewed nuclear weapons as necessary accessories to world power status and Britain, which still perceived itself as such a power, could not be without them. The Maud Committee, for example, was explicit that

Even if the war should end before the bombs are ready the effort would not be wasted, except in the unlikely event of complete disarmament, since no nation would care to risk being caught without a weapon of such decisive possibilities.[2]

Britain would therefore not need nuclear weapons in order to reassert herself but would clearly lose out should she not

---

[1] House of Commons, vol. 437, col. 1965, 16 May 1947.
[2] Quoted in M. Gowing, *Britain and Atomic Energy 1939–1945* (London, 1964), 395.

develop and possess them in the post-war world. This consideration was certainly one of the primary motivating factors behind Britain's wartime and immediate post-war nuclear policy. But by the mid-1950s, as economic and political constraints became ever more pressing and the incongruities in British perceptions and aspirations became more visible, this logic naturally developed into a case for supporting and bolstering an independent world role.

The concept of independence as it relates to Britain's nuclear deterrent has always been an ambiguous one. However, it is apparent that her readiness in 1941 to disregard US overtures for joint nuclear research is indication that at the beginning of the nuclear era she saw herself on equal par with the Americans —certainly in terms of technological prowess—and regarded any joint ventures as potentially politically detrimental to her independence and therefore to be avoided if at all possible.

Nevertheless, the changed balance of power that became increasingly apparent towards the end of the war and in the immediate post-war aftermath could not be ignored or minimized for ever. As Gowing and others have demonstrated, already during World War II Britain became dependent on the American programme, her earlier hesitation at joint co-operation readily giving way to an eagerness to benefit from the greater American resources. Ironically, by the time the British had become convinced of the need to combine resources more fully, the Americans—fearful of British commercial ambitions in the post-war world and believing that their project had little need of British know-how—balked at future nuclear contacts with the United Kingdom.

It was not until after a series of complex negotiations between Churchill and Roosevelt that the Quebec Agreement of 1943 laying out the terms of bilateral nuclear co-operation was signed. The agreement set out five major points. These were: (1) that a free interchange of ideas would take place on a completely joint enterprise; (2) that the weapons would not be used against each other; (3) that neither government would give any of the information to other parties; (4) neither country would use atomic weapons without the consent of the other party; and (5) information to be given to the United Kingdom on commercial and industrial uses would be determined by the

President.[3] This agreement was further expanded by the so-called Hyde Park Aide-Mémoire of 1944 which in paragraph 2 affirmed that full consultation between Britain and the United States would continue in the aftermath of the war.[4] Thus by the end of World War II, British scientists and researchers were well ensconced in virtually all of the Manhattan Project's various enterprises and British policy-makers seemed satisfied that their future nuclear capability would be secured through collaboration with the United States.

The shock of the United States' unilateral termination of the nuclear co-operation agreement with the British could only have underscored the actual dependence of Britain on expanding American power. The McMahon Act passed by Congress in 1946 made collaboration on nuclear issues with foreign powers illegal. This laid the basis for the emergence of two issues in British nuclear defence policy—issues that served to both dominate and motivate the pursuit of an independent British nuclear capacity and which remained constant throughout the 1940s and 1950s. The first had to do with fears of American isolation and the second concerned the retention of a degree of control over the exercise of American nuclear power. Both themes reflected Britain's loss of international standing, her recognition of her dependence on American might, and her perception of the importance of nuclear weapons in addressing these considerations.

That the United States would retreat once more into fortress America and leave Britain alone to face the power of the Soviet Union was a factor that remained crucial to British foreign policy-making both prior to and after the formation of the NATO alliance. Already during World War II Britain had begun to consider future Soviet nuclear capabilities and international territorial and political ambitions. By 1946 the Chiefs of Staff Committee (COSC) was basing its threat assessment on the Soviet Union's representing the main enemy to British interests. In a review of atomic energy requirements drawn up in 1948, the minimum British bomb requirement for 1957 was set at 200 bombs. The assumption was that the United States would provide two-thirds of a total of 600 bombs—a total

---

[3] Quoted in M. Gowing, *Britain and Atomic Energy 1939–1945* (London, 1964), 439.
[4] Ibid. 447.

apparently drawn up with the Soviet Union in mind.[5] How much information at this stage had been exchanged between the British and Americans on targeting and related strategic issues is as yet unclear, but what is certain is that Britain was definitely viewing the Soviet Union as a major source of conventional and nuclear danger and American co-operation on the nuclear level as vital in coping with this challenge.

With regard to Soviet nuclear capabilities the Chiefs were explicit that

Between 1952 and 1957, the possibility of attacks by weapons of mass destruction exists, but for a variety of reasons, we think the chances are slight. After 1957, this form of attack is a distinct possibility.[6]

Soviet nuclear weapons coupled with their overwhelming conventional superiority meant that only with nuclear weapons could Britain hope to deter and if necessary wage effective war against a Soviet invasion of Western Europe. This was even more necessary should the United States decide not to involve itself. Commenting on the period prior to the formation of NATO Attlee was adamant that

At that time we had to bear in mind that there was always the possibility of [the United States] withdrawing and becoming isolationist once again. The manufacture of a British atom bomb was therefore at that stage essential to our defence.[7]

Even following the formation of NATO and increasing co-operation on all levels between American and British strategic planners, the United Kingdom still continued to evince doubts about the reliability of extended deterrence. With the Soviet boosted fission test of 1953 and potential for long range missile capabilities by the later 1950s, the level of British confidence in the American willingness to wage nuclear war on behalf of her European allies was not always high. British nuclear weapons therefore continued to be seen as a guarantee of British security, a tool of last resort, should she find herself alone against a Soviet threat. Not surprisingly, despite various assertions of support

[5] L. Freedman, 'British Nuclear Targeting', in D. Ball and J. Richelson (eds.), *Strategic Nuclear Targeting* (Ithaca, 1986), 111.
[6] DEFE 5/6, COS 263 (47), 11 Dec. 1947.
[7] F. Williams, *A Prime Minister Remembers* (London, 1961), 119.

for proposals underwriting general disarmament, declaratory policy essentially contradicted a firm commitment to nuclear power production and nuclear weapons deployment. The dangers expressed by the Chiefs concerning the potential for Soviet cheating and the military and political attractions of nuclear weapons made sure, as one study has indicated, that 'the necessity to cling to the posture of deterrence was deemed to outweigh the specific benefits which international control might have afforded to Britain'.[8]

The other constant theme in British strategic planning derived, in fact, from the inverse of fears of American isolation. That is, there was grave concern in Whitehall that the Americans could draw Britain into a nuclear war as a result of actions by the United States in circumstances deemed peripheral to British interests. British fears that the Americans were considering using nuclear weapons to strengthen their position in Korea caused Attlee to travel to Washington in December 1950 to caution restraint. A similar concern emerged once more when it seemed that Washington would use nuclear weapons to help the French at Dien Bien Phu in 1954. In such an environment British policy-makers throughout the 1940s and 1950s perceived their own nuclear deterrent force as a means of forcing the United States to take notice of Britain and integrate her into their own strategic planning. Thus, according to Chief of Air Staff Sir John Slessor in December 1951,

Recent experience in discussion with [the Americans] on the policy for use of the Atomb bomb is proof of the grave political disadvantage under which we shall continue to suffer until we are in a position, by virtue of our own contribution, to claim as a right our proper share in the control and direction of what may well be the decisive strategy of any future war . . .[9]

Only by having their own independent force could Britain hope to bend American nuclear strategic planning in to line with British interests. The United Kingdom's attempts to gain access to American nuclear know-how, war planning, and targeting strategies were throughout the 1940s and 1950s based

---

[8] I. Clark and N. J. Wheeler, *The British Origins of Nuclear Strategy 1945–1955* (Oxford, 1989), 82.
[9] AIR 8/1802, Note by CAS, 23 Dec. 1951.

on the premiss that it was in American interests to aid the only other country in the world capable of boosting the West's nuclear deterrent. Independent possession would, it was felt, facilitate co-operation, thereby ultimately enhancing British security through both unilateral and bilateral means. It was these two paradoxical concerns—for independence on the one hand and interdependence with the Americans on the other— that were to set the guidelines for British nuclear policy throughout the 1940s and 1950s.

## The Advent of Thermonuclear Weapons: Continuities in Rationales and Implications

The decision to proceed with the production of thermonuclear weapons was in many respects the logical culmination of the earlier rationales which underpinned the production of atomic weapons. Despite some initial fears that the development of thermonuclear weapons would detract from atomic production and deployment, the decision to acquire these weapons followed naturally on from Britain's ongoing atomic production programme.

By the mid-1950s the British development of atomic power was proceeding apace. Thus, the decision taken in 1945 to form an advisory committee on Atomic Energy and a research and experimental station at Harwell was soon followed by the establishment in 1946 of a production organization at Risely to manufacture fissile material from plutonium for military purposes and in 1949 an Atomic Weapons Research Establishment at Aldermaston. Three years after the Defence Policy Committee decided that Britain must produce an atomic weapon, the plutonium-producing Windscale pile went critical. The first civil reactor programme was given the go ahead in 1952 and in 1954 the United Kingdom Atomic Energy Authority—similar in function to its US counterpart—was established. The American decision in 1954 to amend the 1946 McMahon Act so as to allow for the sharing of information on the yield, size, and effects of nuclear weapons, while not obviating the need for Britain to undertake a megaton test programme, indicated that in future further nuclear co-operation between the two countries might be made possible.

According to one calculation, by 1960 there was production at four reactors at Calder Hall and four at Chapel Cross with an annual production of weapons-grade plutonium of approximately 363 kilograms. It has been estimated that by 1960 gross cumulative production of weapons-grade plutonium was 1,139 kg. For the year of Sandy's first defence White Paper annual production stood at 103 kg. with gross cumulative production at 390 kg. Military requirements accounted for the vast majority of Britain's atomic programme. In 1952 a 25 kiloton device similar to an American MK 3 warhead was tested at Monte Bello. The following year saw 10 kt. and 8 kt. tests at Woomera in Australia of a plutonium device of a modified Blue Danube design. A short testing break then ensued until the mid-1950s when thermonuclear devices and experimental plutonium devices began to be tested.[10] It has also been calculated that by 1955 testing and production had resulted in the manufacture of ten Blue Danube nuclear weapons.[11] In short, by the mid-1950s Britain's nuclear programme in general and military production programme in particular were advancing apace, reflecting the serious intent behind both the Labour and Conservative governments' pursuit of nuclear power and nuclear weaponry.

Although in his autobiography Anthony Eden claims that the decision to produce a British thermonuclear weapon was taken in 1952[12]—a contention sustained by Richard Rosecrance in his study of post-war defence policy[13]—Margaret Gowing has written that in 1952 the government's Chief Scientific Adviser had informed the Cabinet that Britain was as yet not technologically ready to manufacture fusion weapons.[14] However, by 1954 Britain's capacity to produce an H-bomb had increased dramatically with experience gleaned from her own nuclear research and clues derived from debris from the Soviet and American test programmes.[15] American attempts to encourage Britain to support an international moratorium on

---

[10] J. Simpson, *The Independent Nuclear State* (London, 1983), Appendices 1 and 4.

[11] Ibid. Appendix 4.

[12] A. Eden, *Full Circle* (London, 1960), 368.

[13] R. N. Rosecrance, *Defence of the Realm: British Strategy in the Nuclear Epoch* (New York, 1968), 165.

[14] M. Gowing, *Independence and Deterrence* (London, 1974), i. 438–9.

[15] Simpson, *The Independent Nuclear State*, 102–3.

nuclear testing were apparently rejected by a special committee on the H-bomb in 1954 with the decision to proceed with thermonuclear weapon development being taken by the Defence Policy Committee in June of that year leading to full Cabinet approval the following month.[16]

The announcement of Britain's decision to produce a thermonuclear weapon was made in the 1955 Defence White Paper. There it was stated that similarly to the United States and the Soviet Union

The United Kingdom also has the ability to produce [thermonuclear] weapons. After fully considering all the implications of this step the Government have thought it their duty to proceed with their development and production.[17]

The development of fusion weapons reinforced the British proclivity towards nuclear deterrence based on massive retaliation. Indeed, according to Andrew Pierre, the evolution of strategic doctrine has supported H-bomb production as the acme of an independent British nuclear deterrent.[18] Yet, as Clark and Wheeler have demonstrated, in the context of the British H-bomb decision process, of more significance than the goal of British independence or the fear of Soviet capabilities was the need to retain a sufficient degree of international standing in order to influence the Americans to follow policies favourable to British interests and to take Britain more fully into account when it came to their strategic planning. For this contention they cite as part evidence a 12 May 1954 statement that 'it would be dangerous if the United States were to retain their present monopoly since we would be denied any right to influence her policy in the use of this weapon'[19] and Lord President of the Council Lord Salisbury's view that Washington would have more respect for Britain if she helped contribute to countering the Soviet Union's thermonuclear capability.[20] Clearly, there was continuity in British strategic thinking when

---

[16] Clark and Wheeler, *The British Origins of Nuclear Strategy*, 214.
[17] *Statement on Defence*, HMSO, Cmd. 9391, 1955, para. 3.
[18] A. Pierre, *Nuclear Politics* (London, 1972), 91.
[19] Quoted in Clark and Wheeler, *The British Origins of Nuclear Strategy*, 214.
[20] Ibid. 214–15.

it came to the perception of the significance of nuclear and thermonuclear weapons primarily as means of reinforcing Britain's international sway—albeit with the less ambitious goal of influencing the United States.

This did not of course mean that the possibilities for independent British deterrence were ignored by British policy-makers or that the implications of thermonuclear weapons for reinforcing peace or for conducting war should it occur were overlooked. Robert Rhodes James has pointed out:

In his discussion with Eisenhower, and reading papers submitted by the Ministry of Defence [Churchill] had come to the conclusion that the development of the hydrogen bomb had changed everything. To [Sir John] Colville he said that 'the difference between the hydrogen bomb and the atomic bomb is greater than that between the atomic bomb and the bow-and-arrow' . . .[21]

A 1954 strategy paper, which was drawn up by the Joint Planning Staff (JPS) so as take account of these differences, underlined the view that deterrence was now easier and more affordable for Britain.[22] Whereas hundreds of kiloton weapons would have been required to deter the enemy, now only a few megaton weapons needed to be procured. What had previously only been an aspiration of the super powers was now within the grasp of a middle ranking power such as the United Kingdom. In addition, it was recognized that with attainable explosive power now 'multiplied a hundred fold'[23] the Soviet leadership would be influenced in the direction of greater caution in foreign and military policies. Indeed, the Cabinet was informed that '[i]t was at least possible that the development of the hydrogen bomb would have the effect of reducing the risk of major war'.[24] Moreover, it was the Cabinet's view in mid-1954 that 'unless we possessed thermo-nuclear weapons, we should lose our influence and standing in world affairs'.[25] This was a perspective that was to remain constant—especially on the right wing of the Conservative Party—throughout the 1950s.

[21] R. Rhodes James, *Anthony Eden* (London, 1986), 382–3.
[22] DEFE 4/70, JP (54) Note 11, discussed at COS 53 (54) 1, 12 May 1954.
[23] DEFE 4/69, COS 34 (54) 1, 26 Mar. 1954.
[24] CAB 128/27, CC 48 (54) 2, 8 July 1954.
[25] Ibid.

Reflective of this tendency was Julian Amery's statement in February 1956 that

It will seem that the hydrogen bomb, when we have it, will make us a world Power again . . . It cancels out the disparity between populations and big areas of territory and smaller ones. It would be just as dangerous for the Soviet Union or the United States to incur thermo-nuclear bombardment as it would be for us.[26]

Two years later, Randolph Churchill was to reiterate this statement with the view that 'we are a major power again'.[27]

However, of equal significance for Britain was the implications of the Soviet acquisition of the H-bomb. Vulnerability to Soviet H-bomb attacks carried with it ramifications for questions of the credibility of the British nuclear threat, American strategic guarantees, the meaning of nuclear superiority, and, at root, national survival.

One of the most significant studies of this period which both directly and indirectly tackled these concerns was the Strath Report on the effects of a thermonuclear attack on Britain presented to the Defence Committee in February 1955.[28] The still classified report claimed that a Soviet attack using only ten H-bombs would leave 12 million dead, 4 million wounded, and many millions pinned to their homes for at least a week. Over half the country's industrial capacity would be destroyed. There would also be a grave dislocation of essential services and wide disruptions in social and economic processes. The study warned that the combined result of these consequences 'would be to set-up a "chain reaction" in the social and economic structure which cannot be precisely measured'.[29]

The difficulties of ensuring national life, let alone conducting military operations, were reinforced in a paper presented by the Director General of Civil Defence, General Kirkland, to the Chiefs of Staff Committee on 24 November 1954.[30] Here it was

---

[26] House of Commons, vol. 549, cols. 1091–2, 28 Feb. 1956.

[27] Quoted in Pierre, *Nuclear Politics*, 96.

[28] The Strath Report remains classified 3(4) but its major findings can be gleaned from a memorandum presented to the Chiefs called 'An Appreciation of the Likely Form and Duration of a Future Major War—With Reference to the Problem of Stockpiling in the United Kingdom', DEFE 5/80, COS (57) 278, 18 Dec. 1957.

[29] Ibid.          [30] DEFE 5/55, COS (54) 359, 22 Nov. 1954.

demonstrated that so great were the potential consequences of a thermonuclear attack on Britain that even an assault consisting of only one H-bomb dropped on each of Britain's five major population centres would present extreme difficulties for Britain's civil defence forces. For, it was shown that on the basis of the optimistic assumptions that half the population had been evacuated and a quarter had taken to shelters, there would still have resulted 820,000 'accessible trapped living casualties'—a figure far beyond the capabilities of Britain's meagre civil defence forces. Moreover, each thermonuclear explosion would result in as many as 100,000 fires stretching in a ring exceeding 12½ miles around the point of explosion (this compared to the worst night of the Blitz in 1941 when only 2,100 fires were started)—again, far beyond Britain's existing or future fire-fighting capabilities. Policy-makers were, no doubt, left to ponder how in this context Britain could serve as a base in any future thermonuclear war.[31]

Consequently, it is clear that during the mid-1950s, British military policy-makers were receiving information that pointed to the increasing sagacity of relying on the hydrogen bomb to deter thermonuclear war and the irrelevance of conventional planning for such conflicts. The documents do not reveal any opposition amongst the Chiefs and service departments with regard to the findings of studies conducted into the effects of thermonuclear weapons; indeed, the Chiefs described the Kirk-land report as 'useful background'.[32]

Yet, despite this general concurrence, by 1955 not only were the broader international political purposes of the British nuclear deterrent and its role within the context of the Anglo-American alliance yet to be resolved, but so too was the related issue of its implications for the British nuclear–conventional force balance. Consequently, the Eden government was to inherit an expanding development programme but no clear

[31] The report on rescue requirements was accompanied by a number of other still classified studies in 1953 and 1954 on the implications of a thermonuclear attack on Britain. These included the 1953 Hall Committee study which analysed the civil economy in the initial phase of global war; the Padmore Committee which reported on the position of the seat of government during such a conflict; and the Maclean Working Party which investigated the position of the armed forces in the initial stages of global war. See DEFE 4/68, COS 17 (54) 1, 17 Feb. 1954.

[32] DEFE 4/74, COS 125 (54) 1, 24 Nov. 1954.

and coherent strategic posture in which to frame these new capabilities.

## The Broader Strategic Debate in Britain: Graduated Deterrence and Massive Retaliation

The need to clarify policy was reinforced by the tendency in the mid-1950s for Britain's nuclear strategy increasingly to become part of the public debate and also subject to the vagaries of party politics.

The origins of British nuclear programmes and strategy, both during the war and in that conflict's immediate aftermath were cloaked in such secrecy that most members of the Labour government knew nothing of their Prime Minister Clement Attlee's decision to manufacture nuclear weapons. However, by the mid-1950s, the government could not hope to keep the subject removed from both public and parliamentary purview. In the House of Commons, Labour Party members of Parliament began pressing the Conservatives for more details on planning and strategy, while press and scholarly interest into the intricacies of nuclear strategy began to expand. The writings of military analysts such as Slessor, Liddell Hart, and Buzzard were finding a growing audience, while American commentaries on the concept of deterrence were increasingly making their way across the Atlantic.

In the realm of the broader 'expert' debate within Britain on the future of British nuclear strategic planning, doubts as to the credibility of American threats of massive retaliation fuelled the anxieties of those who were, in any event, seeking a more measured response to Soviet aggression. Chief amongst these sceptics was Sir Anthony Buzzard, a former head of Naval Intelligence and the leading exponent of what became known as graduated deterrence—an argument whose thrust was taken up by a number of defence intellectuals in the Labour Party. Already during the Radical Review of 1953 Buzzard had criticized the policy of massive countervalue attacks against the Soviet Union on the basis that it would not succeed in restraining the advancing Soviet armies nor would it encourage restraint in Soviet responses. Following the H-bomb test in the United

States and the boosted fission explosion in the Soviet Union, Buzzard expanded his public attacks on the policy of massive retaliation.[33] It was Buzzard's contention that massive retaliation would not be a credible instrument for dealing with smaller Soviet incursions or for more limited wars in other parts of the globe. Moreover, in the mid-1950s, what was of concern to him was that with the onset of mutual vulnerability, American willingness to defend Europe with nuclear weapons would be undermined and that the United States would in future not resort to massive retaliation unless its own homeland was directly threatened.

Consequently, Buzzard called for a unilateral and immediate Western declaration setting out a distinction between strategic and tactical uses of nuclear weapons and a public adherence to the principle of not using more force than was necessary. In the context of such a policy, the threat of massive retaliation would remain omnipresent but smaller wars could, at least at the beginning, be contained at the tactical nuclear level. The option would always remain open for the aggressor to withdraw before escalation to the strategic employment of the weapons—that is against cities—took place. Similarly to Bernard Brodie in the United States, Buzzard demanded that in a future global war Soviet cities be left 'hostages' and used as bargaining levers in bringing about the termination of conflict.[34]

Buzzard was certain that in a period of expanding nuclear capabilities in both the West and the East, the threat of a more limited response to Soviet aggression coupled with the possibility of escalation would be a more credible threat than that of immediate all-out escalation. With credibility enhanced deterrence would naturally be buttressed. Buzzard was confident that a unilateral Western pronouncement on such limitations would in the short term suffice as in the long term it would serve to encourage the Soviets to limit their targeting to purely military objectives. It was the retired Rear-Admiral's belief that, ultimately, a move away from massive retaliation to

[33] See e.g. Sir Anthony Buzzard, 'Massive Retaliation and Graduated Deterrence', *World Politics*, 32, No. 2 (Jan. 1956); Sir Anthony Buzzard, Sir John Slessor, Richard Lowenthal, 'The H-Bomb: Massive Retaliation or Graduated Deterrence—A Discussion', *International Affairs*, 32, No. 2 (Apr. 1956).

[34] A. J. R. Groom, *British Thinking about Nuclear Weapons* (London, 1974), 75–84.

graduated deterrence would facilitate a reduction in tension and that 'experience in the limited use of armaments would also nourish the trust essential for limiting their possession'.[35]

Towards the end of 1955 the Joint Planning Staff made a formal consideration of Buzzard's thesis 'with a view to determining whether the adoption of such a policy would strengthen our aim of preventing war'.[36] In such a consideration the theoretical challenge posed by Buzzard had, of necessity, to be juxtaposed alongside a widespread and entrenched viewpoint that had at its core a solid attachment to the benefits of an undiluted threat of massive nuclear response.

Throughout this period the chief and most explicit proponent of a strategy of massive retaliation remained Sir John Slessor. It was Slessor's view—while Chief of the Air Staff and during his retirement—that atomic weapons had abolished total war and that the primary focus of defence activities should be to bolster the deterrent. It was his influence that underlay the nuclear emphasis of the British 1952 Global Strategy Paper. Slessor was certain that the nuclear emphasis should come at the expense of investment in conventional forces and that with escalation in Europe automatic, all that the British Army on the Rhine (BAOR) would need to do would be to effect a pause on advancing Soviet forces. He remained convinced that it was impossible to limit the use of nuclear weapons. Attempts at control would inevitably give way to processes of escalation, and attempts to attenuate the enormity of the threat would only serve to undermine the stability of peace.[37]

Also suspicious of the limited use of nuclear weapons were Sir Basil Liddell Hart and P. M. S. Blackett. Similarly to Slessor they did not believe that nuclear warfare could be controlled but unlike Slessor they stressed that in an era of growing mutual nuclear vulnerability the nuclear deterrent should be complemented with adequate conventional forces necessary to hold a Soviet invasion.[38] Not surprisingly, this was

---

[35] *World Politics*, op. cit. 230.

[36] DEFE 4/81, JP (55) 147 (Final) discussed at COS 104 (55) 2, 15 Dec. 1955.

[37] For an example of Slessor's view see J. Slessor, *Strategy for the West* (London, 1954) and *The Great Deterrent* (London, 1957).

[38] For an example of Liddell Hart's view see B. Liddell Hart, *Deterrent or Defence* (London, 1960). For Blackett see P. M. S. Blackett, 'Thoughts on British Defence Policy', *New Statesman*, 5 Dec. 1959.

a perspective strongly supported by the Army and Navy which sought to retain hold of their traditional forces, capabilities, and roles in the face of attempts to replace them with nuclear and thermonuclear weapons. However, the effect of economic pressures as already evidenced by NATO's failure to meet the ambitious Lisbon force goals of 1952, meant that this was not a realistic option—at least in terms of providing forces that the services would have regarded as anywhere near sufficient to wage effective conventional war.

In any event, by the mid-1950s, NATO deployment policy was moving towards supplementing the threat of massive nuclear retaliation against the Soviet heartland with the capability for employing tactical nuclear weapons in support of the Supreme Allied Commander in Europe's (SACEUR) land battle. At the December 1954 NATO Council meeting the decision was taken that tactical nuclear weapons could be used in the defence of the central front against superior invading conventional forces. As one writer has put it 'tactical nuclear weapons enabled a forward posture to be maintained without the necessity of raising costly conventional forces'.[39] The object thus continued to be the maintenance of the minimum amount of forces needed to retain the American commitment to Europe and did not in itself necessarily signify that nuclear war could be limited. Indeed, the decision was not intended in any way to signify that the threat of massive nuclear response against the Soviet Union was less likely than before or that escalation to the strategic level was anything but inevitable.

Consequently, it is not surprising that it was the JPS's view that despite Buzzard's desire to move British nuclear strategy towards more controlled and limited nuclear responses, they were still certain that '[t]he threat of massive retaliation was the only effective deterrent to Global War both now and in the future'.[40] To strengthen this point they further concluded that: (1) there would be few benefits to the Western allies in making a unilateral statement promising a limitation in nuclear response; (2) it was extremely difficult to clarify a sharp distinction between strategic and tactical targets for nuclear weapons; and (3) it was not possible to draw a clear dividing line between

[39] Groom, *British Thinking about Nuclear Weapons*, 68.
[40] DEFE 4/81, JP (55) 147 (Final) discussed at COS 104 (55) 2, 15 Dec. 1955.

small and large nuclear weapons. In short, many British policy-makers in the mid-1950s remained unimpressed by attempts to weaken the threat of massive retaliation with promises of graduated response.

For those for whom 'graduated deterrence' represented an unwelcome theoretical intrusion into the ongoing strategic debate, the announcement of the American 'New Look' promised useful ammunition in the cause of massive retaliation. Ironically, however, the British response to the American formulation was both sceptical and critical. British scepticism focused on the problem of both the originality of Dulles's pronouncements and the degree to which they could be taken literally. In the first place, the similarities between the 'New Look' and the 1952 Global Strategy Paper were immediately recognized with the negative American initial reaction to the British document certainly not forgotten. Secondly, as the British embassy in Washington was quick to point out,

The warning of 'retaliation with weapons and at places of our own choosing' is difficult to accept literally . . . Dulles's warning seems to be largely bluff. Perhaps it was made, like the President's mention of 'massive instant retaliation' without much other serious purpose than to persuade doubters amongst the electorate that the Administration are finally showing signs of determination in foreign affairs and can express it in good straight American terms.[41]

In turn, British criticism of this policy derived not as much from fear of escalation in Europe but rather from concern that she would be drawn into a nuclear war by the Americans as a result of an issue of peripheral importance to British interests. These concerns were also manifested in Parliament, the press, and in the general theoretical debate between Slessor and Buzzard over the concept of 'graduated deterrence'.

In any event, already across the Atlantic, Dulles's threat of massive retaliation against a wide range of contingencies had been undermined by his own admissions, by the growing criticisms of the American strategic community during this period—particularly in the writings of Kissinger, Osgood, and Brodie among others—where preferences were expressed for limiting war rather than basing policy on the threat of massive

---

[41] FO 371/109100, AU 1013/5, 28 Jan. 1954.

retaliation,[42] and by the strategic reality of increasing American vulnerability to Soviet thermonuclear attack.[43]

British observers could not but take heed of these reproaches and expressed uncertainties. However, the recognition in Britain that the 'New Look' was something less than new and that it was not without all manner of limitations was accompanied by an awareness that a pattern was being set whereby conventional firepower would ultimately be replaced by the cheaper nuclear variant. With this tendency in mind, the Foreign Office informed the Chiefs in March 1954 that as a result of the increasing availability of 'new' aircraft and 'new' weapons, the American government was coming round to the view 'that they offer a much better return for investment than conventional weapons, and should be substituted for them whenever practicable'.[44] Thus, it was stated that

the trend is unmistakable and we must assume that as time goes by more emphasis still will be laid in US military planning on airpower and modern weapons, both from a tactical and strategic point of view.[45]

It is thus evident that during the mid-1950s the British defence decision-making community was well aware, both from British and American sources, of the strategic and economic virtues of relying on nuclear threats of massive retaliation. While they were cognizant of the arguments that problems of vulnerability led to problems of credibility and that massive retaliation was a strategy of extremely limited applicability, the

[42] For some American commentaries on the need for limiting nuclear responses see P. H. Nitze, 'Atoms, Strategy and Foreign Policy', *Foreign Affairs*, 34, No. 2 (1956), 187–98; R. Osgood, *Limited War* (Chicago, 1957); H. A. Kissinger, *Nuclear Weapons and Foreign Policy* (New York, 1957).

[43] For a 1980s perspective on US vulnerability in the 1950s see R. K. Betts, 'A Nuclear Golden Age? The Balance before Parity', *International Security*, 2, No. 3 (1986/7), 3–32.

[44] DEFE 5/52, COS (54) 127, 20 Apr. 1954.

[45] Ibid. Certainly, this dual emphasis on nuclear weapons and economies was by 1956 reaffirmed in the United States in Eisenhower's so-called 'New New Look' which sought to circumvent the dilemmas posed by growing US vulnerability and escalating service demands for additional nuclear resources by emphasizing the (ambiguous) criteria of 'adequacy' as a means for determining procurement. Nuclear deterrence through the threat of massive retaliation remained central to American security efforts while fiscal restraint was ensured. See S. P. Huntington, *The Common Defence: Strategic Programmes in National Politics* (New York, 1961), 104.

available literature does not suggest that there was major disagreement with the concept that global nuclear war was now more unlikely than ever or that Britain would suffer enormous damage should such a conflict occur. Nor did policy-makers appear to disagree with at least the principle that reliance on nuclear weapons might lead to some (undefined) reductions in conventional forces.

## Economic Imperatives and Service Recalcitrance

In the first decade of British nuclear power, nuclear weapons served an internal bureaucratic function as well as externally directed military and foreign policy objectives. While Clark and Wheeler are correct in arguing that in the period immediately after World War II, the relationship of nuclear weapons to economic savings was not stressed—the ultimate costs of the nuclear development programme were far from clear—by the mid-1950s nuclear weapons were clearly perceived as a useful means of curtailing burgeoning defence spending and reducing manpower requirements.

The need for Eden to define a new balance between an expanding nuclear arsenal and the size of Britain's conventional forces as well as the requirement for expressing a more lucid and coherent stance with regard to the role of Britain's nuclear deterrent was made ever more urgent in the mid-1950s due to increasing pressures on the government to constrain public expenditure. One year prior to Eden's replacement of Churchill as Prime Minister, Chancellor of the Exchequer R. A. Butler had been adamant that

Significant savings in defence expenditure could only be secured by reducing the size of the armed forces and this in turn would involve reductions of our overseas commitments.[46]

It is evident from economic discussions of this period that central to this focus was·the growing recognition of the importance of defence spending, both as a component of domestic expenditure (especially with its heavy requirements on the metal using industry) and as a contribution to overseas spending.

[46] CAB 128/27, CC 14 (54) 7, 3 Mar. 1954.

It was also attractive in a political sense as reductions in defence expenditure did not carry the political odium of further credit restrictions of increases in taxation. In addition, savings in this area, unlike restrictions of imports, would attack the problem of inflation directly.

Of greatest concern was the influence of defence expenditure on the British balance of payments. During 1955, Butler informed the Cabinet Defence Committee that while all government expenditure had to be met from Britain's own resources, external expenditure (of which defence was a major component) imposed an even greater strain as it required that increases in output would have to take the form of an expansion of exports. In referring to military spending, he came to the crux of the matter when he stated

I know that the object . . . is to strengthen our political standing and economic influence in the world. But there is a great danger that we may defeat our own object if we take on more than we can afford. There is no doubt that our economic difficulties this year have been watched with critical eyes abroad.[47]

This was not a reality denied by British military policy-makers. Writing in the mid-1970s, the former Permanent Secretary at the Ministry of Defence, Sir Richard Powell, stated that 'From 1951 on there was a running battle between military requirements as stated by Allied Commands and national Chiefs of Staff and the ability and will of Governments and electorates.'[48] Indeed, the amount of national resources devoted to defence had been going down since 1953. As a percentage of GNP, defence expenditure dropped nearly 3 per cent in five years: from just under 10 per cent of GNP in 1952 to 7 per cent in 1957.[49] David Greenwood in his research on the economics of British defence spending has stressed continuity in terms of the far-reaching implications of economic policy for strategic planning throughout the post-war period and has indicated that even during the major Korean War rearmament programme,

[47] CAB 129/78, CP (55) 184, 29 Nov. 1955.
[48] Sir Richard Powell, 'The Evolution of British Defence Policy', in *Perspectives on British Defence Policy* (Southampton, 1978), 53.
[49] See table in Pierre, *Nuclear Politics*, 343.

economic imperatives made sure that no attempt was made to place the economy on a war footing.[50]

In a paper presented by the Directors of Plans to the Chiefs of Staff Committee in 1954 it was admitted that

Over-expenditure on rearmament leading to a serious economic depression could destroy the will of Western Europe and other countries of the Free World to resist Communism and this [could] present Soviet Russia with a bloodless victory.[51]

The crucial question, of course, was where the reduction would take place. By the mid-1950s recognition that nuclear firepower was far more economical than the conventional variant was coupled with the growing appreciation in British military circles of the strategic implications of thermonuclear warfare—a perspective that set definite pointers for costing exercises, given the view that conventional forces were not only expensive but could probably not be mobilized, deployed, or controlled from a thermonuclear devastated Britain.

In this strategic and economic context, major savings in conventional preparations for global war could be secured with attention being refocused to more likely and immediate contingencies such as the maintenance of security in Britain's colonial possessions. As far as global war was concerned, the Assistant Directors of Plans were adamant that with

mutual annihilation the price of global war, it would seem unnecessary to continue to aim at contributing towards the deterrent by means other than the production of the H-bomb, the provision of up to date methods of delivery, and development of the capability of instant retaliation.[52]

Consequently, during the mid-1950s costing exercises, the Chiefs agreed to the descending planning priorities of (1) the prevention of global nuclear war through reliance on the threat of nuclear and thermonuclear retaliation, (2) Britain's cold war commitments—that is preparations to contain insurgency and deal with limited wars—and only finally, (3) conventional preparations for global nuclear war.

[50] D. Greenwood, 'Defence and National Priorities Since 1945', in J. Baylis, *British Defence Policy in a Changing World* (London, 1977).
[51] DEFE 4/70, JP (54) Note 11 discussed at COS 53 (54) 1, 10 May 1954.
[52] DEFE 7/963, fo. 22, 18 June 1955.

Such a priority list, reflecting as it did the link between an emphasis on British nuclear weapons and savings in defence expenditure had become increasingly visible following the upward spiral of defence spending as a result of the Korean War rearmament programme and the ambitious Lisbon force goals of 1952. The Global Strategy Paper of 1952 had been explicit that the deployment of nuclear weapons in NATO forces would make preparations for a major European war the bottom of a strategic planning priority list with the funding of the deterrent and defence of Britain's colonial and Commonwealth interests receiving precedence.[53] By September of that year the COSC was stressing that if

atomic airpower . . . and adequate forces on the ground in Europe were properly built up and maintained, the likelihood of war would be much diminished and we could in consequence ease our economic position by accepting a smaller and slower build-up of forces, equipment, and reserves for war.[54]

Yet, a number of studies have indicated that in the first decade of British nuclear power the translation of these declaratory statements into a policy which reflected such an altered force posture was anything but automatic. Indeed, a constant theme in discussions on defence matters during the first half of the 1950s was the inability of the armed services to follow through on the logic of their strategic arguments and to cut back on respective orders of battle.[55]

During the 1952 Global Strategy Paper discussions and the 1953 Radical Review negotiations that followed, as well as in the context of the general bargaining associated with the annual defence white papers, the service departments proved tardy in surrendering roles and capabilities deemed less important or even unnecessary in a thermonuclear environment. The unwillingness of the Navy to support a 'short war' concept that would have legitimized major reductions in its battle fleet and the Army's recalcitrance when it came to agreeing to phase out elements of deployed manpower in favour of nuclear weapons

[53] Grove, *From Vanguard to Trident* (London, 1987), 82 n.

[54] CAB 131/12, D (52) 41, 29 Sept. 1952.

[55] See e.g. N. J. Wheeler, 'The Roles Played by the British Chiefs of Staff Committee in the Development of British Nuclear Weapons Planning and Policy-making 1945–55' (Ph.D. Thesis, Dept. of Politics, University of Southampton, 1988).

led to what can been termed—to use Sir John Slessor's phrase when he described the Lisbon force goals—the 'superimposing [of] the new atomic strategy on the old conventional strategy'.[56]

It should, however, briefly be pointed out that the success of the services in retaining hold of their traditional visions and capabilities in the face of the strategic new thinking was at least partly rooted in the organization for decision-making which allowed them to prosecute and follow through on their separate objectives.

In this regard, Laurence Martin has described the decision-making process prior to 1957 as that of 'Defence by Bargaining'. He writes:

The chief failing [was] . . . the typical tendency of committees to decide by compromise rather than reason . . . [and that] the allocation of money year by year seems to have proceeded more on the basis of 'fair shares' than a coherent overall strategic plan.[57]

In turn, Martin Edmonds states that the 1946 White Paper *Central Organization of Defence*[58]—that document which laid the organizational basis for defence decision-making (with slight variations) until January 1957—created a small and weak Ministry of Defence and failed to institute a system which embodied the principles of centralized command. Rather, it established a very diffuse and fragmented higher defence organization and set the ground rules by which the services could

separately and collectively prosecute their particular interests against attempts from the Ministry of Defence at the centre to introduce functional, joint and defence-orientated policy and planning.[59]

Despite attempts to strengthen the power of the Ministry of Defence relative to the large and powerful services (most notably in 1955—an attempt which included the creation of the role of chairman of the COSC), Howard, for one, underlines the weakness of the Ministry of Defence relative to the services

[56] DEFE 4/55, CAS minute 1468, 5 July 1952.

[57] Martin, 'The Market for Strategic Ideas in Britain', *American Political Science Review* 56, No. 1 (1962), 24.

[58] *Central Organization of Defence*, Cmd. 6923, HMSO, 1946.

[59] M. Edmunds (ed.), *The Defence Equation: British Military Systems—Policy Planning and Performance Since 1945* (London, 1986), 61.

in the pre-Sandys period.[60] On beginning his tenure in 1955 one of the major challenges facing Eden was the unwillingness of the services to surrender traditional tasks and methods and the complications this posed for the British adoption of a 'New Look' force posture. How he, and later Macmillan, were to cope with this predicament was to underline the revolutionary import of at least some of Sandys's policy formulations.

As has been indicated in this chapter, by the mid-1950s still left unresolved by British strategic debates were the problems of how to define the degree of independence of Britain's nuclear force in relation to that of the United States and the necessity of avoiding the expensive and strategically redundant approach of imposing a nuclear strategy on a conventional one. It was these areas that were to characterize much of the content of strategic discussions during the mid-1950s.

However, by the mid-1950s what was clear was that British defence policy was increasingly being framed with reference to nuclear weaponry. In this context, nuclear forces served domestic bureaucratic goals, objectives of international political status, as means of influencing American policy and as instruments for deterring Soviet power as well as, if need be, of helping counter its military might. These themes remained both constant and progressively more apparent throughout the first decade of British nuclear power.

Indeed, the growing importance that Britain attached to declaratory promises of nuclear employment and British perceptions of the relationship of nuclear weapons to conventional forces may be clearly noted from an analysis of the role of nuclear weapons in the context of her European and extra-European alliance commitments in the two years prior to 1957, a subject to which the next chapter turns.

[60] M. Howard, *The Central Organization for Defence* (London: Royal United Institute for Defence Studies, 1970).

# 2

## Nuclear Weapons and British Alliance Commitments, 1955–1956

I T has been argued by one writer that 'The paramount considerations guiding British defence policy in 1955 were the desire to create an effective nuclear capability, the belief that in Europe the Soviet threat might be lessening but that elsewhere—and especially in the Middle East—it might increase, and the conviction that the current defence programme was still beyond the nation's resources'.[1] As a world power, Britain was certainly by the summer of 1955 dwarfed in relative strength by both the United States and the Soviet Union, diminished in absolute might as a result of economic and military cutbacks, but nevertheless neither entirely depleted nor dissipated as a powerful actor on the international stage. By the year 1954 of a total of 11⅓ British Army divisions, 10½ were stationed outside the United Kingdom. Four of these were to be found in Germany, two and a half were in the Middle East, two were to be found in Malaya, with troops also in Trieste, Hong Kong, and Kenya. Indeed, with Britain's system of international bases still very much in place and through her support of a variety of military and political agreements, Britain's international position seemed to be in the process of consolidation.

Thus, in May 1955 an armed Germany had been received into the NATO alliance, visibly and materially strengthening the West's defences against potential Soviet attack. The previous year had witnessed the apparent solidification of Britain's position in the Far East, through the signing of the collective defence organization, the South East Asia Treaty Organization

[1] C. J. Bartlett, *The Long Retreat: A Short History of British Defence Policy* (London, 1972), 105.

(SEATO), and in 1955–6 by the Australian and New Zealand agreement to help build up a Commonwealth Reserve based in Malaya and Singapore. In 1955 a similar agreement to SEATO was concluded in the Middle East. There, the so-called Baghdad Pact was signed between Britain and a number of regional powers, while in the South Atlantic, the Simonstown Agreement between London and Pretoria allowed for continued British use of the naval base in times of war. In short, an international alliance infrastructure which manifested itself in both declaratory commitments and actual deployments, reflected the British perception of herself as a world power and her willingness to project force globally if necessary.

Yet, as noted, during this period, the traditional conventional means whereby Britain could or should project or maintain power was increasingly being brought into question by the exigencies of economic constraints and the dangers and opportunities consequent upon the acquisition by Britain, the United States, and the Soviet Union of nuclear and thermonuclear weapons. The issue for Britain was to what extent could the costs of conventional forces be obviated through an increase in dependence on nuclear weapons both as a means of deterrence and as tools of war fighting in the European and extra-European theatres. At the same time, underlying this conundrum, was the appreciation that Soviet nuclear weapons made the deployment and employment of British conventional manpower during a global war highly unrealistic and that dependence on nuclear weapons remained the only practical option available.

The role of nuclear weapons in the context of British strategic planning for her three major alliance networks—NATO, SEATO, and the Baghdad Pact—and their relationship to conventional forces deployed or potentially designated to the respective theatres is therefore the subject of this chapter. The degree to which nuclear weapons and the strategy of massive retaliation became means whereby the United Kingdom sought to bridge the gap between extensive international commitments and declining economic and military resources is the focus of interest as is the extent to which Britain was irrevocably moving towards the 'New Look' strategy explicitly adopted in April 1957.

## Nuclear Weapons and Britain's Extra-European Alliances: The Baghdad Pact and SEATO

A review of the documents associated with British strategic planning in relation to the Baghdad Pact and the South East Asia Treaty Organization during 1955–6 reveals that growing emphasis was placed on strategic and tactical nuclear weapons for deterrence and war fighting purposes. The immediate object was not simply strategic, but also economic, with the requirements of an economically preferred force posture sometimes receiving precedence over questions of strategic credibility.

When Foreign Secretary in the Churchill government, Eden had negotiated an agreement with the Egyptians in October 1954 which provided for the withdrawal of British troops from the Canal Zone to be completed by the summer of 1956. This did not signify total British withdrawal from a region regarded as vital to British international political and military interests as allowance was made in the treaty for a return of British troops should members of the Arab League or Turkey be threatened by outside aggression. In any event, as noted, Britain disposed of a number of divisions in the Middle East and there was still the intention of building up Cyprus as an alternate base by which to maintain her influence in the region.

Political problems in Cyprus, however, coincided with the approaching expiry date—1957—of Britain's defence treaty with Iraq which had allowed for the retention of British bases on Baghdad's territory, and followed not too far on the heels of the collapse of hopes with regard to the establishment of a Middle East Defence Organization with the participation of the United States, France, and the Commonwealth. These setbacks and difficulties only served to reinforce British interest in securing the 'northern tier' of states—specifically Iraq, Pakistan, and Iran—as a buffer against Soviet aggression and as countries in which to base British influence. In this, Britain, while not having Washington's promises of formal commitment, had strong American backing for her own membership and contribution.

In pursuit of its regional security objectives, on 30 March 1955, the United Kingdom acceded to the Turco-Iraqi Pact. By the end of the year Pakistan and Iran had joined and it was Eden's hope 'that the Pact could grow into a NATO for the Middle East'.[2] In a sense, a military infrastructure for the defence of the region was already in place with a UK armoured division distributed in an area between Jordan, Cyprus, and Libya and supply and air bases located in all these countries ready to support a deployment of troops northwards.

However, there was a general appreciation in British defence circles that a conventional defence of the Middle East in global war was a far too difficult and expensive an enterprise. Liddell Hart, for one, did not hesitate to make public his doubts whether it was within the capabilities of Britain and the Arabs to muster sufficient conventional strength along the northern tier in order to contain a Soviet advance.[3] Thus, from the beginning of its membership of the Baghdad Pact, Britain sought to avoid large force commitments through a stress on the centrality of massive retaliation as a means of deterring and, if necessary, defeating a Soviet attack. This followed naturally from her understanding of the defence of the Middle East region during global war which recognized that

The planned use of nuclear weapons has completely altered the picture of Middle East defence and, with full co-operation from the Middle East States together with Commonwealth assistance, we can expect to hold the enemy in this theatre.[4]

Minister of Defence Harold Macmillan had said as much to the House of Commons in March 1955 when he had stated that 'the power of interdiction upon invading columns by nuclear weapons gives a new aspect altogether to strategy, both in the Middle East and the Far East'.[5]

---

[2] A. Eden, *Full Circle* (London, 1960), 220. For a recent study that makes extensive use of primary sources from the Public Records Office see David R. Devereux, 'Between Friend and Foe: The Formulation of British Defence Policy Towards the Middle East 1948–56' (Ph.D. dissertation, King's College, London, 1988).

[3] Liddell Hart, *Deterrent or Defence* (London, 1960), 34–5.

[4] DEFE 4/75, JP (54) 101 (RF) discussed at COS 1 (55) 1, 5 Jan. 1955. This chapter does not seek to imply that reliance on nuclear weapons to defend the Middle East was a strategy originating in the mid-1950s. In any event, since the second half of the 1940s the retention of the Middle East bases was seen as essential for prosecuting nuclear air strikes on the Soviet Union. See for example Clark and Wheeler, *The British Origins of Nuclear Strategy 1945–1955* (Oxford, 1989), 108.

[5] House of Commons, vol. 568, col. 2182, 2 Mar. 1956.

By the mid-1950s, the Chiefs were, in any event, convinced that a major nuclear war in the Middle East was unlikely though the possibility existed that such a conflict could start as a result of a miscalculation. In a global war in which nuclear weapons were used it was believed that the Middle East would be a subsidiary theatre which would not effect the overall result. Nevertheless, it was also admitted that Britain could not ignore the views of her regional allies who saw the value of such agreements not only from the political and economic standpoints but also as important guarantees of their borders.[6]

In talks held in London at the end of 1955 between military representatives of the United States, United Kingdom, and Turkey, it was agreed that in the event of a Soviet attack on the Baghdad Pact area, the object of alliance strategy would be to establish defensive positions covering the passes over the Zagros Mountains and to rely on a strategic nuclear air offensive and a theatre nuclear bombing campaign to weaken the Soviet advance. It was admitted that although the defence plans were based on a nuclear force being available in the theatre at the outbreak of war, a British nuclear capability would not be stationed there until 1959. Nevertheless, it was stated that the Americans were studying the possibility of placing their own theatre nuclear force there until such time as the British nuclear force was ready for deployment.[7] The concept for defence of the region was drawn up in close conjunction with the United States when Middle East defence talks took place in Washington during June and August 1955. It was here that the conventional defence line was quickly identified though the British felt what was still lacking from the Americans was 'further detailed agreement . . . especially on the provision and delivery of nuclear weapons on which our present strategy stands or falls'.[8]

It was the British view that in global war the Russians would be unwilling to undertake a major campaign in the Middle East until they had observed the results of the initial nuclear phase of the war and of their land campaign in Western Europe. However,

---

[6] DEFE 4/87, JP (56) 7 (Revised Final) UK Requirements in the Middle East discussed at COS 55 (56) 1, 31 May 1956.
[7] DEFE 4/80, JP (55) 139 (Final), discussed at COS 93 (55) 3, 15 Nov. 1955.
[8] DEFE 4/82, Annex to JP (56) 8 (Final) discussed at COS 7 (56) 4, 13 Jan. 1956.

at the outbreak of global war, the Russians would be able with their forces already in position south of the Caucasus to make a limited advance into Eastern Turkey, in an attempt to capture the Zagros passes as a start line for subsequent operations.[9] Elsewhere it was maintained that the Soviets would be capable of launching a simultaneous attack on West Turkey and Grecian Thrace with the aim of controlling the Bospheros and the Dardanelles, and on Persia and Iraq from the Caspian ports, the Caucasus, and Turkmenistan with the object of capturing the oil fields and moving up the Levant coast.[10]

It was believed that the military aims of the Soviets would be the reduction of the allied air threat to the Southern USSR; envelopment of the defence of Eastern Turkey; denial of the oil of the Middle East to allied powers; seizure of as much of the Middle East as possible so as to increase the radius of activity for Soviet air power and air defence; securing a warm water port on the Persian Gulf and gaining control of the build-up of allied forces. The Soviets would have at their disposal twenty-four divisions against the Baghdad Pact's total of between five and eight.

British operational planning for the defence of the Middle East in a Global War was based on a period of warning of three weeks. The bulk of the Middle East Air Force (MEAF) would be in North East Iraq by D Day plus 3; two units of Royal Engineers whose object it would be to destroy the Zagros passes would be in position there by D day, while a brigade group and an armoured regiment would arrive at the Pasitak Pass between D day plus 10 and D day plus 45. British military officials in the region were adamant that these troops represented the minimum amount that were acceptable by any military criteria and then only as an interim measure.[11] It was not planned to reinforce the MEAF from the UK during the first six months of global war. Though Commonwealth reinforcements from South Africa and Pakistan might arrive, there were during this period no definite plans for their support with South Africa refusing to commit troops to the Middle East

[9] DEFE 4/80, JP (55) 139 (Final) discussed at COS 93 (55) 3, 15 Nov. 1955.
[10] DEFE 4/82, JP (56) 8 (Final) discussed at COS 7 (56) 4, 13 Jan. 1956.
[11] DEFE 5/70, COS (56) 306, 13 Aug. 1956.

and Pakistan having to balance its potential contribution with its commitment to SEATO.[12]

In order to overcome this unfavourable ratio the Pact would have to

(a)  make the most effective use of the expected Allied nuclear superiority . . .

(b)  fight in a position of our own choice which will provide the greatest natural advantages in defence and which will also give as much time as possible both for the occupation of the position and for the allied nuclear superiority to take effect.

(c)  be prepared to sacrifice the defence of national territory in order that the requirments of (a) and (b) above may best be met.[13]

Against this background, the Chiefs agreed that the strategic air offensive targeted on metropolitan Russia would aim at: (1) eliminating or at least greatly reducing the possibility of reinforcement, support, and resupply for the invading forces; (2) hampering and possibly eliminating centralized control of operations; (3) occupying the efforts of Soviet fighters and long range bomber forces so that only a limited air effort would be available for use by them in the Middle East; (4) reducing the airfields from which operations against the Middle East theatre could be mounted; and (5) causing devastation to the Soviet homeland which would sooner or later adversely influence Soviet operations. The strategic air offensive would be accompanied by attacks with theatre nuclear weapons on concentrations of enemy ground forces and lines of communication within the theatre.[14] Thus, on 19 January 1956, the Chiefs of Staff Committee agreed that the 'main effect of the strategic air offensive would be to isolate the Soviet land forces deployed against the Middle East and reduce the Soviet air threat to the theatre'.[15] Concomitantly, theatre nuclear targets would be (1) airfields; (2) mountain passes; (3) ports and concentrations of shipping in the Caspian and Black Seas which were supplying operations in the Middle East; (4) supply and troop concentrations; (5) centres of communications; and (6) marshalling yards and concentrations of railway stocks.[16]

[12]  DEFE 4/82, Annex to JP (56) 8 (Final), discussed at COS 7 (56) 4, 13 Jan. 1956.
[13]  DEFE 4/81, COS 107 (55) 3 discussion of JP (55) 155 (Final), 30 Dec. 1955.
[14]  Ibid.
[15]  DEFE 4/82, JP (56) 3 (Final) discussed at COS 10 (56) 1, 19 Jan. 1956.
[16]  Ibid. Also see DEFE 6/34, JP (56) 3, 4 Jan. 1956.

At their meeting in Teheran in April 1956, the Military Committee of the Baghdad Pact directed that an interim capabilities plan for the defence of the Baghdad Pact area in 1957 should be drawn up. The British submission reflected the strong nuclear emphasis of British operational planning. It was stated that

The successful delivery of a major proportion of the Allied strategic air effort contemplated in the event of war in 1957, should practically demolish the whole fabric of Soviet industry, and should deprive the Soviets of any considerable control over, or direction of, their Governmental, military or economic resources. Soviet forces in being, and such material resources as were not subjected to nuclear attack, would depend for their future support entirely upon their existing supplies.[17]

It was believed that as a result of this offensive, the Soviets would quickly limit their use of nuclear weapons against Pact forces, while no significant reserve ground units would reach the combat area and the flow of military equipment to the combat area would also be slowed. Furthermore, Soviet air forces which were initially unavailable in the forward areas could then not easily be redeployed there in significant numbers. Soviet submarine sortie rates would be reduced, Soviet command capabilities would be drastically downgraded, and such devastation to the Soviet homeland would occur as to sooner or later undermine the morale of the Russian troops.

The United Kingdom therefore planned to provide for the defence of the Baghdad Pact area four squadrons of Canberras, a reconnaissance squadron and a maritime force. During the early part of 1957, a composite force of Canberra, ground-attack squadrons and maritime reconnaissance aircraft would be made available. On the other hand, although the full resources of the United Kingdom Middle East Land Forces were theoretically available to support operations in the theatre, Baghdad Pact planners were informed that the peacetime deployment of those forces precluded any more than a small proportion of them being able to participate in the land defence of the Pact area. Consequently—and this was the crux of the matter—Britain's contribution to the Pact defence would mainly

[17] DEFE 4/88, JP (56) 113 (Final) discussed at COS 68 (56) 2, 12 July 1956.

be in the realm of strategic and tactical nuclear delivery capabilities.[18]

It is important to recognize that this British nuclear emphasis stemmed as much from economic necessity as from strategic considerations. Indeed, throughout 1955 and 1956, the stress on strategic and theatre nuclear strikes derived strong impetus from the need to avoid spending money on conventional forces. In a February 1956 JPS paper entitled 'The Financial and Other Implications of Measures to Increase the Effectiveness of the Baghdad Pact' it was admitted that

The current availability and location of British forces in the Middle East theatre and the possibilities of reinforcement in conditions of global war are clearly out of line with Baghdad Pact planning as it is now proceeding, and could only be brought even partly into line by changes in our current policies and by expenditure on a scale which could not be accommodated with the current or future levels of the Defence Budget. In short, we have neither the men nor the money in current circumstances to make the Baghdad Pact effective militarily . . .[19]

Consequently, Britain could not assign ground forces specifically for the defence of the Baghdad Pact area and Britain's representatives at the Pact were constantly warned by policy-makers back home to be wary of plans that might involve large force requirements.[20] This gave rise to much consternation amongst Britain's allies in the Pact. As a JPS paper put it in November 1956:

The fact that no estimate was given of the size of the United Kingdom land contribution and also that no indication could be given of the time it would take for the forces to reach the scene of operations, caused much concern . . . It required a lot of talking to persuade the other planners that the United Kingdom was not trying to avoid helping in the land battle.[21]

Yet, although it was recognized that 'it would be a blow to the other Baghdad Pact countries' if Britain refused to commit ground forces, this was a risk that seemed readily accepted.[22] It

---

[18] Ibid.                                    [19] DEFE 5/65, COS (56) 79, 21 Feb. 1956.
[20] See e.g. DEFE 4/84, COS 24 (56) 2, 28 Feb. 1956.
[21] DEFE 4/92, JP (56) 169 (Final) discussed at COS 121 (56) 11, 21 Nov. 1956.
[22] See DEFE 4/86, COS 46 (56) 1 discussion of JP (56) 86 (Final), 3 May 1956.

could not be forgotten that in the thermonuclear age global war was unlikely and military preparations were mainly for political purposes. Britain would thus not be deterred from focusing on the nuclear deterrent and avoiding conventional commitments. Certainly, the JPS was being unequivocal when it admitted that

> The United Kingdom policy when setting up the military organisation of the Pact was that there should be the very minimum of expenditure in men and money consistent with maintaining the impetus of planning.[23]

From this discussion it is possible to derive a number of significant points: (1) between 1955 and 1957 there was a growing emphasis on nuclear firepower as opposed to conventional manpower—at least as far as a total global war was concerned;[24] (2) the economic motivations behind such moves were extremely strong; and (3) there do not appear to have been any major objections from the Chiefs or services to the nuclear emphasis. They seem to have willingly gone along with this shift of focus to nuclear weapons, even though they must have recognized that from Britain's regional allies' point of view, it was a strategy that was less than ideal and permeated with credibility problems. This was so because it made the allies very dependent on British intentions and not British capabilities that were plainly visible on the ground (as conventional forces would be) and it also clearly subordinated Middle Eastern to European concerns in that British responses in the theatre were to be determined by Soviet actions outside it.

Furthermore, the British could only have exacerbated allied fears when in July 1956, the Chiefs rejected any suggestion that the Baghdad planners should determine the numbers and

---

[23] DEFE 4/87, JP (56) 97 (Final) discussed at COS 55 (56) 3, 31 May 1956.

[24] It was recognized that troops would still be needed to garrison Cyprus, Kenya, Iraq, Libya, Jordan, and Aden, DEFE 4/87, COS 55 (56) 1, 31 May 1956; also see DEFE 5/64, COS (56) 4, 4 Jan. 1956 and DEFE 5/64, COS (56) 56, 8 Feb. 1956. The major threat to Britain's position in that region was perceived to be subversion. See DEFE 5/64, COS (56) 20, 13 Jan. 1956. When it came to war that was short of global nuclear strategic war it was stated that 'The most effective deterrent to such a war would be knowledge that the United Kingdom and the United States had combined military plans for immediate action against the aggression and the belief that they would be put into effect.' See DEFE 5/69, COS (56) 232, 15 June 1956. Again, how far advanced joint allied planning was at this stage is unclear.

categories of those targets within the USSR, the destruction of which was essential to Pact operations. The Chiefs maintained that

The United Kingdom was not prepared to allow the medium bomber force to be committed in advance to attack definite targets in another theatre since, on the day, we might want to use it against targets which vitally affected the safety of the United Kingdom.[25]

It seemed that Britain was basing much of its policy on a force, the central and decisive component of which could be redesignated when it was needed most.

Whatever the merits of shifting from a conventional to a nuclear focus, it cannot be denied that the above discussion highlights such a progression in the period leading up to the formal announcement of the British 'New Look' in April 1957. Indeed, the case for policy continuity across the mid-1950s centred on the 1957 Defence White Paper is strengthened. For on the one hand it appears that during the period under study there was an increasing willingness to base foreign and military policies on a recognition that nuclear and thermonuclear weapons could achieve what conventional forces could not; and on the other hand, economies were secured as potential conventional force developments were substituted with promises of nuclear assistance. This was a policy that Britain followed in South East Asia as well.

In the mid-1950s Britain defined her military tasks in the Far East as including: (1) the protection of British lives and interests in that region; (2) the maintenance (in conjunction with Australia and New Zealand) of the security of Malaysia and Singapore; (3) the maintenance of the British position in Hong Kong; and (4) the provision of forces for anti-subversion roles throughout the region.[26] In the light of these many and varied tasks, she remained from the early part of the decade interested in joining a defence alliance that would serve to bolster her regional security interests. Yet, despite various attempts to gain admission, the United Kingdom continued to be excluded from the 1951 Anzus Pact between Australia, New Zealand, and the United States. However, following the end of the Geneva

[25] DEFE 4/88, COS 68 (56) 3 discussion of JP (56) 112 (Final), 12 July 1956.
[26] DEFE 5/72, COS (56) 446, 21 Dec. 1956.

conference of 1954, and the unwillingness of Dulles and the South Vietnamese to support the proposed settlement, Britain succeeded in helping create a regional defensive alliance that would underwrite the agreement and prevent what was regarded as communist aggression in that part of the world. On 6 September 1954, representatives of the USA, UK, France, Pakistan, Thailand, the Phillipines, Australia, and New Zealand signed the South East Asia Treaty Organization Pact.[27]

It was accepted by the Chiefs of Staff Committee that in the context of global war, the Far East would be a subordinate theatre and would not influence the outcome of the war. They were also of the opinion that it was unlikely for the Chinese to embark on a campaign of overt aggression in conditions short of total global war in a period up until 1960.[28] Yet, despite the Commissioner General in South East Asia Sir Robert Scott's opinion that there could not be a limited war with China because Russia would not allow China to be defeated, the Chiefs were sanguine about the prospects of preventing escalation in that theatre. Mountbatten, for one, did not believe that the Russians would open themselves up to devastation for the sake of the Chinese off-shore islands and that at the same time, Britain could not totally disregard the possibility of limited local incursions against SEATO—especially if the communists managed to gain control of Laos or Thailand.[29]

The Chiefs contended that a communist instigated conventional war in the region would most likely break out if China committed an act of aggression against SEATO or Hong Kong, or as a result of conflict between the USA and China over the offshore islands and Formosa, or as a result of UN defensive actions in Korea or elsewhere. Significantly, they were adamant that nuclear weapons could be used without the risk of such a conflict escalating to the strategic level with exchanges of nuclear and thermonuclear weapons taking place between the super powers, China, and Britain. There was therefore concurrence in the COSC that nuclear weapons should be used in limited wars in the Far East. In March 1956, the Chiefs stated

[27] See P. Darby, *British Defence Policy East of Suez 1947–68* (London, 1973), 61–5.
[28] DEFE 4/87 COS 56 (56) 7, discussion of JP (56) 104 (Final), 5 June 1956.
[29] DEFE 4/89, COS 73 (56) 1, discussion of JP (56) 122 (Final), 27 July 1956.

that they '[did] not consider that the use of nuclear weapons in a limited war in the Far East [would] necessarily lead to global war'.[30]

Indeed, central to Britain's conception of the defence of the region in global war was the need to deploy during peacetime the minimum amount of troops and to use nuclear weapons— that is, in the near future American nuclear weapons—to make up for the loss of fire-power. According to the Directors of Plans,

The defence of South East Asia is now an Allied responsibility and any United Kingdom contribution can only be calculated in the light of the overall Allied strategic concept assuming the Allied use of nuclear weapons.[31]

Furthermore, the JPS were adamant that 'the use of nuclear air power must form the basis of our strategy [in the Far East]. Care should be taken, therefore, to avoid undue emphasis being placed on the land campaign.'[32] At the same time, manpower and conventional capabilities would still be needed to carry out cold war counter-insurgency roles. Again, similarly to the Middle East, there was also a tension between British desire to gain regional support for their cold war anti-insurgency goals and the regional countries' interest in securing the deployment of large numbers of British troops in order to guarantee their territorial integrity. Not all conventional forces could be totally withdrawn and Britain was forced to stress that

The forces we must retain . . . will be made up of those required to meet the changing Internal Security commitments together with those additional forces needed to maintain the confidence of our SEATO allies and of local populations.[33]

At the same time, British policy-makers never tired of emphasizing that the threat to resort to massive retaliation could allow for reductions in conventional forces designated for the contingencies of global nuclear war and wars limited to South East Asia itself. Indeed, in the period immediately prior to the Suez crisis and the announcement of the British 'New Look', the

[30] DEFE 4/85, JP (56) 61 (Final) discussed at COS 34 (56) 5, 22 Mar. 1956.
[31] DEFE 4/82, JP (55) Note 25 (Final) discussed at COS 1 (56) 5, 3 Jan. 1956.
[32] DEFE 4/87, JP (56) 104 (Final) discussed at COS 56 (56) 7, 5 June 1956.
[33] DEFE 4/89, JP (56) 122 (Final) discussed at COS 73 (56) 1, 27 July 1956.

Chiefs sought to impress upon the other SEATO members that the potential efficacy of strategic nuclear bombardment against advancing communist forces and homelands made unnecessary the deployment of large numbers of British troops in the region. SEATO attempts to gain a British commitment to such deployments were strongly rejected.

Thus, for example, in a discussion of a draft of a United Kingdom position paper on the SEATO strategic concept for the defence of South East Asia, the JPS stated that they agreed that 'in order to be realistic Allied war aims must be related to military resources that are available . . . and that they should therefore be stated in minimum terms'.[34] Consequently, two months later, the Chiefs were able to maintain that they considered 'that it would be unwise to authorise a statement even for planning purposes, of our force contribution'.[35] British policy-makers were continually concerned that SEATO planners were intent upon exaggerating the threat to their region in order to demand that more British troops be deployed there.[36] Britain's preference to leave threat assessments and commitments ambiguous remained a constant despite the fears expressed by the Vice Chief of the Imperial General Staff, Sir William Oliver, that such a policy would alienate Australia and New Zealand because they could argue that Britain had not fully investigated whether SEATO threats were actually exaggerated[37] and was merely seeking a rationale to reduce her own defence expenditures.

Such concerns did not derail Britain's desire to avoid major conventional force commitments to the region and she remained very circumspect about giving detailed answers to military questions. In 1956 Britain was still informing SEATO member states that the strategic concept for the defence of the treaty area was in the process of being worked out and that until this was agreed upon no realistic assessment of orders of battle could be made. Privately, British policy-makers even expressed concern that a detailed UK statement of their force level in Malaya could be misinterpreted by other SEATO members to

[34] DEFE 4/87, JP (56) 104 (Final) discussed at COS 56 (56) 7, 5 June 1956.
[35] DEFE 5/71, COS (56) 324, 27 Aug. 1956.
[36] DEFE 4/93, JP (56) 159 (Final) discussed at COS 127 (56) 1, 29 Nov. 1956.
[37] DEFE 4/93, COS 127 (56) 1, 29 Nov. 1956.

imply that Britain would be willing to use these forces outside Malaya or that she intended to maintain these forces at present levels.[38] In June 1956, for example, the JPS informed the Chiefs that SEATO should not be allowed to define aims that were 'unduly restrictive' by demanding military action linked to a specific geographical area. This, they maintained, would be inconsistent with the agreed upon basis of British strategy which was the use of nuclear power—implying that this power was to be strategically used and not simply related to regional developments as Britain's SEATO allies would no doubt have preferred. Rather, the point was made that a general statement of this type would naturally include the removal of enemy forces from territories they had occupied.[39]

The United Kingdom was also strongly opposed to any suggestion that there even be a study of the threat to the region in global war—a study that, too, could have reinforced the case for substantial British conventional force deployments.[40] Indeed, throughout the period under study, despite the objections of other SEATO members, the United Kingdom managed to retard the development by that organization of global war plans and thereby prevented Britain from having to bear the costs of providing large amounts of ground forces and conventional capabilities.[41] Similarly to the Baghdad Pact, nuclear weapons helped serve the dual purpose of opening up strategic options while at the same time serving to constrain calls for expensive conventional investments.

## Nuclear Weapons and the European Commitment, 1955–1956

In the light of the British emphasis on nuclear forces in exchange for conventional armies in the Baghdad Pact and

---

[38] DEFE 4/82, JP (56) 5 (Final) discussed at COS 3 (56) 2, 10 Jan. 1956.

[39] DEFE 4/87, JP (56) 104 (Final) discussed at COS 56 (56) 7, 5 June 1956.

[40] Ibid. Also see DEFE 5/72, COS (56) 427, 3 Dec. 1956.

[41] DEFE 5/70, COS (56) 274, 18 July 1956. The Chiefs were informed by the UK SEATO planners that during the SEATO attempt to develop a strategic concept and produce an outline military plan and force requirements at the Third Military Staff Planners' Conference (11–27 June 1956), the UK had encountered much opposition due to its tactics of procrastination. It was stressed that 'suspicion of the sincerity of the UK's intention to fulfil her treaty obligations was evident . . .'.

SEATO regions, it is to be expected that a similar focus took hold in the Western European theatre. A reading of the documents reveals that there were definitely pressures in this direction. The starting point was a move away from the Paris Agreements of 1954.

American interest in integrating Germany both militarily and politically into Western Europe during the mid-1950s had clashed with French concern over the long-term implications of such a step for the intra-European balance of power. By 1954, discussions on the European Defence Community had broken down, but while Dulles intimated that he was prepared to proceed without the French, Britain questioned the viability of measures based upon such evident European disunity. In order to reassure France and thereby facilitate the entry of Germany into the Western European Union, the UK promised to maintain on the Continent the British forces which were then assigned to SACEUR—that is, two armoured and two infantry divisions as well as the 2nd Tactical Air Force, or such other forces as the SACEUR regarded as having an equivalent fighting capacity.[42]

That this ran counter to British strategic thinking as reflected in the nuclear emphasis of the Global Stategy Papers of 1952 and 1954, the promise of the 1954 White Paper to reduce manpower, and the NATO decision to integrate into its plans the use of tactical nuclear weapons is evidenced by the hesitation with which Britain approached this comitment. In discussion in the Cabinet on 10 March 1954, it was accepted that

An assurance that we would maintain the present fighting capacity of the United Kingdom forces on the Continent for the next few years did not commit us to maintain there any specified number of divisions and squadrons, and therefore left open the possibility of some reductions in numbers if in the course of time development of new weapons made it possible to maintain the present fighting capacity of our forces on the Continent with fewer men.[43]

An escape clause was duly inserted into the Paris Agreement (the agreement that had formalized this commitment) which stipulated that in the event of an overseas emergency or too

---

[42] Article VI, Paris Agreements, 23 Oct. 1954 in Appendix 10, *NATO Facts and Figures* (Brussels, 1971).

[43] CAB 128/27, CC 17 (54) 4, 10 Mar. 1954.

great a strain on Britain's external finances, British troops could be withdrawn from the Continent.[44]

In the 1954 UK submission to the NATO Annual Review, Britain, though not yet seeking to renege on its commitment, sought to give SACEUR the impression that a large part of the forces designated for 'broken-backed' warfare in the post-nuclear exchange phase would not be forthcoming. This was attributed to financial limitations (the current defence review had set the UK defence budget for 1955/6, 1956/7, and 1957/8 at £1,640 million) and recognition that a thermonuclear attack would interfere with the mobilization, training, and transportation of divisions designated to reinforce the British Army on the Rhine.

This tendency was further reflected in the JPS attitude to SACEUR's 1954 capability study. Thus, while there was agreement between British and NATO planners that global war would begin with a possibly decisive thermonuclear exchange which could be followed by a broken-backed phase, the Joint Planners stressed that 'in the face of the nuclear attack expected on this country, it is probable that our contribution to a second phase, if it occurs, would be negligible'.[45] Again, while NATO claimed that the role of allied land/air forces would be that of a deterrent and that their main tasks would be (1) surviving initial surprise attack, (2) participating effectively in the battle for air/atomic superiority, and (3) arresting Soviet land forces in Europe, the JPS claimed that it considered (3) difficult to achieve because 'there is no more than a reasonable chance of preventing Soviet land advance in Europe'. Furthermore, it was pointed out that forces necessary for this requirement would involve major financial expenditures and that 'To avoid such an increase in defence costs it would be necessary to take some major steps such as considerably reducing the reserve forces, or even slightly reducing the active forces'.[46] This British perspective was strengthened in 1955 when in the context of the Long Term Defence Programme (LTDP), the

---

[44] Article VI of the Paris Agreements. Also see DEFE 5/53, COS (54) 203, 22 June 1954 and DEFE 4/69, COS 43 (54) 4, 12 Apr. 1954.
[45] DEFE 4/72, Annex A to JP (54) 77 (Final) discussed at COS 96 (54) 3, 8 Sept. 1954.
[46] Ibid.

Chiefs approved a paper on factors influencing the allocation of reserves which stated that from the military perspective it was wasteful to develop forces designed only to operate and fight in the post-nuclear exchange phase. It was believed that 'The introduction of thermo-nuclear weapons has changed the requirements for our contribution to NATO. Their present size and equipment is dictated more by political than military reasons.'[47] Not surprisingly, the progress of the 1955 LTDP (see next chapter) led the Directors of Plans to express concern about the conflict between Britain's NATO commitments and economic savings and planning priorities which were based on the assumption that cuts would be least damaging in global war capabilities. For it was stated that the most important global war forces were 'those committed to remain on the Continent of Europe and those naval and air forces assigned to SACEUR, SACLANT [Supreme Allied Commander Atlantic] and CHANNEL COMMAND'.[48] Political obligations entailed, at the very least, the maintenance of UK NATO forces at their present size and the JPS were apprehensive that

If for political reasons the major Global War forces were regarded as sacrosanct for the present, cuts would have to be applied to our Cold War forces and perhaps even to the Primary Deterrent, thus reversing the order of priorities agreed by the Chiefs of Staff . . .[49]

Yet, it seemed that Britain, when faced with a choice between political promises and economic necessities, preferred to jettison the former. The JPS pointed out to the Chiefs that not only had the UK already lowered her planning goals for all three services below the force goals established in the 1953 Annual Review but that

Financial reasons impelled us to this course and are likely, in the near future, to drive our planning goals lower still. When the time comes to report these further reductions to NATO we, as a Standing Group nation, shall be faced with the predicament whether to continue to extort NATO as a whole to strive towards the original force goals whilst not doing so ourselves.[50]

[47] DEFE 5/59, COS (55) 176, 25 July 1955.
[48] DEFE 4/79, JP (55) Note 18 (Final) discussed at COS 73 (55) 2, 13 Sept. 1955.
[49] Ibid.
[50] DEFE 4/79, JP (55) 91 (Final) discussed at COS 73 (55) 3, 13 Sept. 1955.

In a Cabinet Defence Committee meeting on 27 September 1955, it was agreed that the UK presentation to the 1955 NATO Annual Review should be governed by three considerations: (1) the existing pattern of NATO force needs in relation to what the UK thought would happen in nuclear war; (2) the fact that existing NATO forces, if maintained at their present level, would result in a bill which no European country could afford to pay; and (3) that Britain's position in NATO as a leading world power required her to take the lead in bringing these issues into the open. It was therefore unequivocally stated that as Britain's level of defence expenditure could not continue to rise each year, it would be unwise to conceal from NATO authorities that substantial reductions in the size and possibly the effectiveness of Britain's forces would have to be made.[51] Shortly thereafter, the JPS informed the Chiefs that since British defence expenditure on its NATO forces would not be increased above the present levels necessary to adapt NATO forces to a future nuclear war, the costs of an early warning system, an 'atomic posture and capability' and an efficient air defence system would have to be offset by a reduction in the overall size of BAOR.[52] The Chiefs had no difficulty in agreeing with this analysis. The First Sea Lord, Lord Mountbatten, stated that Britain should inject in to the 1955 Annual Review

the thought that each NATO nation should be encouraged to carry out a reappraisal of its own long term military defence efforts and that these reappraisals should receive their due weight in reshaping NATO strategy.[53]

Thus, by the end of 1955, it appeared that British military policy-makers were well on their way to shifting the focus from conventional to nuclear forces. In such a conception specific preparations for broken-backed warfare would be far less important. Conventional forces could be substantially cut back and major financial savings secured.

Britain's attempt during 1956 to draw up a new political directive to NATO again reflected the Eden administration's continued interest in securing financial savings through a

---

[51] CAB 131/16, DC (55) 40, 27 Sept. 1955.
[52] DEFE 4/81, JP (55) 146 (Final) discussed at COS 97 (55) 1, 25 Nov. 1955.
[53] Ibid.

reduction in global war capabilities. During the summer of that year the Prime Minister wrote to Eisenhower and informed him that it was Britain's view that NATO need not be capable of fighting a major land battle and that, at the most, it should seek to hold the invading Soviet forces until such time as the thermonuclear weapons would work their effects.[54] Concomitantly, the Chiefs and services pushed ahead with the 1956 Policy Review which, similarly to its 1955 predecessor, sought financial savings in Britain's global war capabilities.[55] In turn, NATO was warned of Britain's plans for 'harder hitting' forces.[56] Viewed against this background, the New Political Directive was an attempt to legitimize measures that had been adopted for essentially economic reasons. Eden himself admitted that the 1956 strategic reappraisal was vital because the period of US aid was ending and there was a need to find a way of adding £400 million a year to the credit side of Britain's balance of payments.[57]

A JPS paper on NATO strategy and level of forces—presented to the Chiefs in June 1956—served as the basis for the British proposal for the New Political Directive. The thrust of the document was that NATO should base its defence on thermonuclear weapons, adequate means of delivery, and an effective early warning system. It was stated that

it appears that NATO is attempting to achieve militarily what is economically unattainable under current conditions. In addition, NATO has to meet a carefully planned and steady developing Soviet economic offensive. The need, therefore, is to work out an agreed new strategy which will take account of the means at the disposal of the Alliance and give it the margin of economic strength to meet the new Soviet threat.[58]

Conventional forces would be designated solely for purposes of resisting limited incursions and for identifying aggression.

---

[54] Eden, *Full Circle*, 372–3.     [55] Ibid. 371–2.

[56] DEFE 7/773, Cary to Powell, 10 Feb. 1956.

[57] For an analysis of the specific problem of costs of UK forces in Germany see files DEFE 7/876 and DEFE 7/877; for a discussion of the problem of Germany's unwillingness in 1956 to pay support costs see PREM 11/1343. It should be noted that expenditure in Germany was thoroughly investigated by an Air Ministry committee in the summer of 1955. In May, a Cabinet committee was appointed to examine possible savings in Germany. In 1956, costs were running at £12.2 million for 2nd TAF and £56 million for BAOR.

[58] DEFE 4/88 JP (56) 120 (Final) discussed at COS 63 (56) 2, 29 June 1956.

The size of each national contribution to the total land forces assigned to SACEUR would be determined by political factors: (1) an acceptable ratio between the West German forces and East German forces; (2) an acceptable ratio between the West German forces and those of the UK, USA, and France; and (3) the desirability of other NATO countries making suitable contributions.[59] The obvious implication here was that BAOR could be substantially reduced. At the same time, the size and shape of SACEUR's tactical air force would, too, be dictated by the economic, military, and political factors mentioned above. Studies had been going on throughout 1956 on the implications for 2nd TAF of acquiring a nuclear capability, and early in February 1956 the Chiefs agreed that a single squadron of Canberra/Javelins with an atomic capability would be more effective than the whole of 2nd TAF. (Because of political and vulnerability problems, however, such a reduction would not be possible and five squadrons would ultimately be required.[60]) According to the Air Ministry, the 'New Look' 2nd TAF, even if considerably reduced in size, would meet Britain's obligations under the Paris agreements.[61] When it came to the Navy, the JPS maintained that the size and shape of the maritime forces would be governed by the following considerations: (1) the striking fleet armed with thermonuclear weapons must be retained as part of the primary deterrent; (2) maritime forces other than those needed to support the striking fleet would not be required; (3) maritime headquarters other than those needed in support of the striking fleet would no longer be needed; (4) and the Rhine and Elbe squadrons would be disbanded.[62]

With the object now being to convince other NATO countries of the viability of such a doctrine, Britain increasingly began to voice her disapproval of current NATO strategy with its continued emphasis on conventional capabilities. By her submission to the 1956 Annual Review, SACEUR was made well aware that Britain '[did not] accept either the present NATO strategy as being the most suitable and effective in present circumstances,

[59] Ibid.

[60] DEFE 5/64, COS (56) 48, 3 Feb. 1956.

[61] DEFE 5/68, COS (56) 229, 11 June 1956. The First Canberra squadrons would only be equipped with tactical nuclear weapons by 1960. See DEFE 4/88, COS 63 (56) 1, 29 June 1956.

[62] DEFE 4/88, JP (56) 120 (Final) discussed at COS 63 (56) 2, 29 June 1956.

or the present NATO pattern of defence planning'.[63] On 18 June the British Ambassador in Washington, Sir Roger Makins, informed Dulles about Britain's desire for the NATO Council to issue a new directive to the military authorities to review strategy[64] along the lines of a greater focus on the nuclear deterrent and a minimum of land and sea forces.

On 29 June Dulles informed Ambassador Makins that the US government as well as General Gruenther at SHAPE headquarters felt that the British proposal to call an early ministerial meeting of the NATO Council to set out a new directive to the NATO military authorities to review NATO strategy was 'too spectacular' and would lead public opinion to feel that a major crisis existed.[65] Moreover, in a memorandum presented to the Secretary of State by the State Department it was pointed out that the British proposals would seriously undermine German efforts to develop its conventional military which was believed essential to NATO security, as well as impacting negatively on the orientation of German foreign policy.[66] It was furthermore the State Department's view that such a radical review directed from the political level was not necessary as paragraph 39 of MC 48 allowed for the continuing reappraisal of NATO strategy as it stated that 'The most effective pattern of all NATO forces must, of course, be examined continuously in the light of new problems posed by the advent of atomic weapons'.[67]

Nevertheless, despite American objections that this would endanger the alliance and set off a chain reaction of reductions amongst other NATO partners,[68] Britain remained firm in her demand for such a re-evaluation.[69] On 13 July Makins told Dulles that an article in the *New York Times* of that day indicated

---

[63] DEFE 5/70, COS (56) 282, 24 July 1956.

[64] National Archives (NA), RG 59, 740.5/6-1856, Memorandum by Timmons, 18 June 1956.

[65] *Foreign Relations of the United States (FRUS) 1955–57*, vol. iv, Memorandum of a Conversation Between the Secretary of State and the British Ambassador, Department of State, Washington, 29 June 1956, 84–6.

[66] *FRUS, 1955–57*, vol. iv, Memorandum Prepared in the Department of State, 29 June 1956, 87–8.

[67] Quoted ibid. 87.

[68] See e.g. NA, RG 59, 740.5/8-1456, 14 Aug. 1956.

[69] NA, RG 59, 740.5/7-1556, Memo of conversation between Dulles and Makins, 13 July 1956.

that Admiral Radford was seeking an 800,000 reduction in military forces—thus implying that the Americans appeared intent on translating the logic of their 'New Look' declaratory policy into practice and that Britain could not be expected but to do the same. While the Secretary of State denied that such reductions would take place, he stated that President Eisenhower had agreed to discussions with Britain in August 1956 on the subject of a new strategic concept.

In preparation for this meeting British pressure on the United States continued to build up when Eden wrote a letter to Eisenhower on 18 July explicitly putting forward the rationales and principles of the new strategy. He stressed that with both East and West now possessing thermonuclear weapons the possibility of war had receded but should it come about it 'would be very different from anything we have known hitherto'. As an understanding of such developments deepened among the Western publics there would be an increasing reluctance to accept the social and human sacrifices required to maintain large conventional forces. Concomitantly, Eden pointed out that the Russians had decided to increase their labour force for industrial expansion and reduce their conventional armed forces—a policy which they were exploiting for propaganda purposes to the limit. Against the backdrop of these factors allied strategy would have to alter in the direction of placing greater emphasis on nuclear and thermonuclear weapons. Eden did not shy away from stating the radical formulation that

A 'shield' of conventional forces is still required; but it is no longer our principal military protection. Need it be capable of fighting a major land battle? Its primary military function seems now to be to deal with any local infiltration, to prevent external intimidation and to enable aggression to be identified as such. It may be that it should also be capable of imposing some delay on the progress of a Soviet land invasion until the full impact is felt of the thermo-nuclear retaliation which would be launched against the Soviet Union.[70]

The Prime Minister concluded with a reiteration of his opinion that a review of NATO policy along the lines indicated

---

[70] Eden, *Full Circle*, 372–3.

above was both necessary and urgent and he called on Eisenhower to support such steps.

In a draft of the new strategic concept, the Minister of
Defence, Walter Monckton, immediately got to the root of the
exercise when he stressed that it was vital to give guidance on
the initial phase of global war since this would govern the
length of the period in which it would be necessary to hold a
front on the Continent against invading Soviet forces. He
rejected the UK delegation to NATO's suggestion that this
guidance emphasize that the force be large enough to hold a
Soviet attack until the allied strategic nuclear offensive had
worked its effect because this would still leave it to the military
to decide how big the force should be and no reductions in
conventional forces would ensue. Likewise, he rejected NATO's
contention that the initial phase would last for thirty days and
stated that it would not last for more than 'a few days'. The crux
of the matter was that the military forces maintained by NATO
should be the minimum necessary to: (1) keep confidence in the
military effectiveness of NATO and to prevent external intimidation; (2) to deal with local infiltration and incursion; and (3)
to enable Soviet and satellite aggression to be identified as such.
If the Soviet government did commit an act of aggression,
thermonuclear weapons would be used at once. In a limited
war in Europe—defined as one not involving overt Soviet
participation—conventional forces would be armed with an
atomic capability. Conventional forces could thus be substantially cut.[71]

Yet, despite Makins's earlier pleas to the Americans for a
meeting in August to discuss NATO's strategic concept, the
meeting was soon deferred. In addition, in discussions between
Eisenhower, Dulles, Secretary of Defence Wilson, Admiral
Radford, and General Gruenther in the middle of August,
British demands for a new political directive were once more
rejected as was the British preference for withdrawing significant
numbers of troops from the Continent.[72] By October Dulles
was of the opinion that the British and the NATO Council were
to be informed that 'we find unacceptable any proposal which

---

[71] AIR 8/2065, Monckton to Dickson, 5 Sept. 1956.
[72] *FRUS, 1955–57*, vol. iv, Memorandum of a Conversation, Department of State, 13
Aug. 1956, 93–5 and n. 5 to that document.

implies the adoption of a NATO strategy of total reliance on nuclear retaliation';[73] that aside from a certain degree of streamlining, the US had no intention of withdrawing divisions from Europe; and that it was only right that the European countries assume a fairer share for maintaining the shield—in other words, the exact opposite of what Britain was attempting to secure. That the Europeans had to begin contributing far more to conventional forces was a theme restated by Eisenhower at a meeting with Dulles, Radford, and others in the White House on 2 October. Interestingly, when Radford told the group that the British were simply adopting the 'New Look' which the United States had long adopted, Dulles interjected that it was one thing for the United States to depend on a 'New Look' strategy but another thing altogether for the Europeans who faced both insurrectionary threats and the possibility of conventional invasion to do so.[74]

On 12 October 1956 the State Department handed the British Embassy in Washington a memorandum in which it indicated its reaction to the British draft Political Directive and the difficulties it had with it. Britain, nevertheless, presented the unaltered draft to the North Atlantic Council on 19 October while the United States objected to any attempts to prepare a new NATO force plan by December. However, in mid-November the Council agreed to a Canadian suggestion that the final Directive include both an analysis of Soviet trends and a brief guidance to NATO authorities. This was to be discussed at the ministerial meeting of the North Atlantic Council that was planned to be held in Paris between 11 and 14 December.[75]

A recognition of allied lack of eagerness—including Adenauer's strong objections—for Britain's proposed new policy no doubt underlay the new Minister of Defence Anthony Head's warning to the Cabinet in November 1956 of NATO's lack of enthusiasm for Britain's desire to stress nuclear weapons

[73] *FRUS, 1955–57,* vol. iv, Memorandum from the Secretary of State to the President, 97, 1 Oct. 1956.

[74] Eisenhower Library, Whitman Collection, Eisenhower Diaries—Memo of Conference with the President, 2 Oct. 1956; also see NA, RG 59, Recent UK Defence Developments: A Review for Ambassador Whitney, Chiefs of Mission Meeting, Paris, May 1957, 11–13.

[75] *FRUS, 1955–57,* Editorial Note vol. iv, 1956, 102–3.

at the expense of conventional forces. Consequently, Head asserted that the problem facing Britain was

> how large a reduction should we propose to our allies in the interests of our economic position, bearing in mind that if we go too far we may provoke a general reduction in military contributions to NATO, and indeed endanger the very stability of the alliance, as well as damaging the prospects of the closer relationship with Europe . . .[76]

The Minister of Defence was of the opinion that the minimum order of battle that the UK should retain on the Continent (that is with financial reductions limited to 25 per cent of the approximately £68 million in annual German mark costs) was a corps of two infantry divisions and an armoured brigade group (in addition to the Berlin brigade) while substantial cuts in 2nd TAF would only follow the deployment of Canberras with a nuclear capability.[77]

The Cabinet, however, was adamant that economic pressures were such 'that we should seek to secure a rather greater reduction in the Deutschmark costs, even to the extent of eliminating them entirely'.[78] Nevertheless, it was also recognized that it was wrong to give the United States the impression that Britain was not intending to make a fully effective contribution to NATO. According to the Chancellor of the Exchequer, Harold Macmillan (who wanted to reduce German mark expenses by at least 50 per cent),

> We might overcome the difficulty of reconciling a reduction of this order with our commitment under the Paris Agreements to maintain four Divisions and the Second Tactical Airforce in Europe, if we emphasised that there was a growing tendency, for military reasons, to reduce the size of a standard Division and that we could, therefore, continue to honour our commitment if we maintained four Divisions of reduced size.[79]

[76] CAB 129/84, CP (56) 269, 28 Nov. 1956.

[77] Specifically with regard to air power, the SACEUR, General Gruenther, was informed: 'It is envisaged that 2nd TAF will in due course become a Canberra nuclear strike force . . . there will be no fighters in 2nd TAF'. Provisionally Head, basing his figures on an Air Staff plan, envisaged a reduction in the size of the all-weather force in 2nd TAF from four squadrons of 64 planes to four squadrons of 48 planes towards the end of 1958 and a reduction of the ground-attack aircraft to about nine squadrons of 126 fighters during 1958. AIR 8/2065, 21 Nov. 1956.

[78] CAB 128/30 CM 97 (56) 3, 7 Dec. 1956.

[79] Ibid.

In a discussion between British and American officials at the December Paris NATO Council conference, Macmillan defined the parameters of the discussion by telling his American counterparts that it was ironic that the allies had to bear the great costs of occupation while the Germans, the greatest economic rivals to the UK, had no internal or external debt and no armed forces or defence burdens. From February 1957 the UK would have a critical foreign exchange problem with regard to the BAOR. At the same time, according to Selwyn Lloyd, the UK division of 18,500 men was the largest in the world and with increased firepower these divisions could be reduced in number. He also stated that MC 48 contemplated that everyone should have an atomic capability and it was pointed out that Britain was presently procuring Corporal missiles to that end—a procurement which would in any event require a reduction in troops so as to release the necessary funds.[80]

To these comments Secretary of State Dulles replied that the United States '[did] not wish our capability to be so exclusively dependent on atomic weapons that there is no measure of flexibility'. He continued:

The US felt that no unsound strategic concept should be forced on NATO to meet financial problems. The US could not support the view that he believed the UK had once suggested that NATO should go entirely on a 'trip-wire' basis, nor could the US accept the idea that there was no need for substantial manpower because any attack would set off massive retaliation and in that provide a sufficient deterrent.[81]

Dulles opposed the British position. He maintained that while in about 90 per cent of potential situations the threat of nuclear retaliation could cover the situation there were certain types of situations—particularly with regard to the division of Germany and Berlin—which required the presence of German troops. A 'trip-wire' strategy would, he felt, make such deployments appear unnecessary.[82]

The British, however, refused to budge from the point that the UK would have to reduce manpower in order to make

[80] *FRUS, 1955–57,* vol. iv, Memorandum of a Conversation, Paris, 11 Dec. 1956, 123–133.        [81] Ibid. 125–6.

[82] Ibid.; and NA, RG 59, Department of State, Conference File, Lot 62, D181, CF825; DEFE 4/93, COS 133 (56) 7, 18 Dec. 1956.

savings and to balance costs if its forces were ultimately to be armed with nuclear weapons. Chancellor of the Exchequer Macmillan emphasized that a balance would have to be found between 'the trip-wire and the World War II type of organisation'. His suggestion was to work out first how many men this organization would require and then to figure out how much time it would take to develop plans on this basis. An investigation would have to be made in order to determine what contribution the Germans could make until such time as their final and proper deployment was finalized. Concomitantly, the British Chancellor was adamant that attempts were going to have to be made to solve the foreign exchange problem and to ensure that there was no inequality on this score for countries whose soldiers were stationed abroad. Selwyn Lloyd then reaffirmed the point that from a British point of view the answer had to be found in a total of four British divisions of not more than 10,000 men each (together with a fund to help Britain's financial position) backed up by atomic weapons or with US atomic forces brigaded in their support. The Foreign Minister warned the Americans that the consequences of Britain breaking the WEU treaty (by simply unilaterally withdrawing large amounts of troops) would be severe but Britain's financial situation could leave no alternative. He emphasized the escape clause in the 1954 Paris agreement which spoke of 'equivalent fighting capacity' and he said that 'four reduced divisions might be equivalent fighting capacity if they had an atomic fighting capacity behind them'. For this Britain demanded some atomic capacity from the United States or an arrangement to supply her with atomic weapons in an emergency.

Secretary of Defence Wilson then moved some way towards the British position when he stated that it was necessary to get away from talking about numbers of divisions and that smaller divisions supported by special corps could be the solution. Thus while Admiral Radford (with the concurrence of Air Marshall Dickson) agreed that the new Political Directive did not reduce requirements, and while Dulles emphasized that the Germans had been promised that there would be no troop withdrawals, it was clear that the Americans realized that the British were intent upon force reductions. Dulles himself admitted that the United States was planning to reduce the number of men in her divisions and he saw no reason why the United Kingdom could not do the same and even more quickly. As Bluth points out, 'The outcome of the process of the review of strategic doctrine and force requirements in NATO as embodied in the Political Directive adopted by the NATO Council in December 1956 went broadly in the same direction as British thinking, resulting in a reduction of the 1952 Lisbon Force requirements and a greater emphasis on nuclear forces.'[83]

Thus, the trends present in 1955 were being reaffirmed and reinforced in 1956. British military policy-makers appeared intent upon convincing NATO of the irrelevance of extensive conventional force preparations in the context of a thermonuclear war. The focus on nuclear weapons at the expense of conventional forces noted in the SEATO and Baghdad Pact arenas was being replicated in NATO—not a surprising development since the credibility of nuclear response seemed strongest when related to contingencies in this theatre.

In the context of British alliance relations in the period immediately proceeding the 1957 Defence White Paper, the role of nuclear weapons as instruments for containing the United Kingdom's decline in power and world status continued to increase. There was certainly expressed a continued unanimity in defence policy-making circles that fission and fusion weapons were indispensable components of Britain's strategic posture in Europe, the Middle East, and the Far East.

Unfortunately for Britain, the willingness of her policy-makers to place increasing reliance on nuclear weapons and downgrade conventional forces coincided with Washington's continued retreat from a commitment to a pristine and unqualified version of this strategy and gave rise to growing American misgivings about Britain's preferred strategic course. Continued economic pressures, however, resulted in the United Kingdom preferring to ignore negative allied reaction in the European

[83] Christoph Bluth, 'Nuclear Weapons and British–German Relations', in Robert O'Neill and Beatrice Heuser (eds.), *Securing Peace in Europe, 1945–1962: Thoughts for the 1990s* (forthcoming). In April 1957 NATO strategic doctrine as reflected in MC 14/1 was replaced by MC 14/2, while MC 48/2 provided for the drawing up of new minimum force requirements. This process culminated in 1958 in MC 70 which included reduced NATO force goals. Force goals were reduced from 52 to 30 divisions —a reduction to be compensated for by the deployment of nuclear weapons.

and extra-European theatres as she pursued military and political rationales for conventional force cutbacks in Germany and avoided major future conventional force deployments in the Baghdad Pact and SEATO theatres.

It is important to recognize that in the mid-1950s Britain did not possess substantial amounts of nuclear weapons and its long range delivery force was just beginning to be deployed. That there would be a 'credibility gap' between the time troops were withdrawn and nuclear weapons were in place in Europe seemed a problem that British policy-makers were ready to tolerate. Likewise, British officials were not overly perturbed by the credibility gap in the extra-European theatres where there were not many British forces in place and presently few nuclear delivery capabilities and minimal nuclear ordnance to be readily deployed. The omniscience of economic considerations helped make a degree of strategic inconsistency bearable, as did, of course, the general unlikelihood of major war, at least in the immediate future. Indeed, an analysis of the documents associated with Britain's various theatre strategies during this period indicates that discussions of the strategic virtues of a policy of massive retaliation were usually accompanied and often subordinated to reflections on the economic merits of reliance on nuclear weapons and the fiscal dangers of over-extended conventional commitments.

A recognition of the problems of overextended conventional commitments was not, however, accompanied by a readiness to as yet deal with what might have been overextended political commitments. Indeed, as noted, the mid-1950s was a period characterized by a British attempt to join a number of regional alliances so as to consolidate her deteriorating regional position. During this period Britain seemed to follow a grand strategy whereby reliance on the conventional forces of her allies would serve to bolster local British security interests while reliance on her own nuclear weapons would serve both as the symbol of Britain's major contribution to the various pacts and the basis of an economic form of deterrence and war fighting strategy. In this manner hard political choices concerning the nature and scope of Britain's world role could be postponed.

Clearly, it seems that in the period leading up to the announcement of the British 'New Look' in April 1957, there was an irrevocable movement towards a declaratory stress on massive retaliation and changes in force posture based primarily upon cutbacks in conventional forces. It also appears from the above discussion that there was little internal opposition to such a policy. Yet, was this really the case? Similarly to the United States, the British 'New Look' was to serve goals not only in the realm of foreign policy but also on the level of bureaucratic politics—specifically as a means to cap service demands for increased conventional forces which they regarded as necessary to fulfil Britain's extensive commitments. Against such a back-drop it would indeed be surprising if there were little opposition to a strategy whose logic led to the exact opposite conclusion in terms of the amount of conventional forces needed in the thermonuclear era.

# 3

## The Services and War Planning in the Thermonuclear Era, 1955–1956

NUCLEAR and thermonuclear weapons posed serious doctrinal challenges to Britain's Navy, Army, and Air Force and forced these service departments to develop new rationales for their preferred force levels and capabilities. Reviews of both orders of battle and contingency war planning had, of course, been under way for some time, but by the mid-1950s the demand for radical strategic reorientation was ever more pressing as a result of the Eden government's strong desire to cut defence spending while at the same time integrating nuclear and thermonuclear weapons into a coherent military posture.

During the period immediately proceeding the announcement of the British 'New Look', Army and Navy resistance to economic pressures that necessitated procurement and deployment restraint and strategic rationales that legitimized an emphasis on nuclear weapons at the expense of conventional forces, constituted much of the substance of the long-term plannng debates. On one level, the Chiefs of Staff Committee were clearly in agreement over the descending war planning priorities which they described as: (1) the prevention of global nuclear war through reliance on the threat of thermonuclear retaliation; (2) containment of communism (i.e. Britain's cold war commitments); (3) the strengthening of Britain's allies; and (4) only finally, conventional preparations for global nuclear war.[1] However, when it came to translating these prescriptions into actual procurement and deployment decisions, the services balked and the move to the British 'New Look' slowed—the impression of progress towards this end gained from British policy in alliance frameworks notwithstanding.

---

[1] DEFE 4/70, COS 53 (54) 1 discussion of JP (54) Note 11, 12 May 1954.

While the RAF, the sole custodians of Britain's expanding nuclear delivery capability, would undeniably benefit from an emphasis on nuclear power and a strategy that had as its centrepiece a concept of global war limited in the main to a nuclear exchange at the outset of conflict, the role of the Royal Navy and the Army would increasingly be limited to the functions of supply and civil defence. Not surprisingly, this was a strategic future that was not looked kindly upon by these two services, who sought instead to rebut the government's and RAF's preferred short war concept. Rather, they preferred to emphasize the possibility of conventional operations continuing in a post thermonuclear exchange phase as well as upgrading their own role in the delivery of nuclear ordnance. Concomitantly, these two services spent much of the period immediately leading up to the 1957 White Paper challenging the government's attempts to generalize the consequences of its new strategic conceptions so as to include reductions in forces designated for limited and cold war contingencies as well. Service objections here, too, had the consequence of slowing down and complicating attempts by the Eden administration to adopt a 'New Look' force posture.

This chapter seeks to outline Army and Navy perceptions of their roles and required capabilities in the thermonuclear era as they expressed themselves during the Eden administration. The Royal Navy's attachment to both broken-backed warfare and a world-wide cold war role as well as its nuclear ambitions constitutes the subject of the first part of this chapter, while the Army's view of its functions in Europe during wartime, its favoured order of battle, and its attitude to national service in the thermonuclear era constitutes the second part. At the core of these discussions is the Navy and Army's stance on the 'long war–short war' dichotomy and the difficulties of the Ministry of Defence in imposing economic constraints and strategic coherence on disparate strategic visions.

## Naval Planning and Programming in the Thermonuclear Era

According to William Crowe the appearance of thermonuclear weapons 'threatened the Navy's most cherished concepts, threw its strategical thinking into disarray, and threatened its very survival'.[2] These dangers for the Navy could be noted in the 1955 White Paper on Defence which officially announced the British decision to build the H-bomb and at the same time threatened to 'eliminate those parts of our force which have become or are becoming obsolete in modern conditions'.[3] While it was admitted that there was no guarantee that the initial stage of global war would be decisive, no mention was made of the Royal Navy's conviction of the possibility of conventional operations continuing in the post thermonuclear exchange phase—so-called broken-backed warfare.

The concept of broken-backed warfare had received its most explicit formulation during the 1952 negotiations on the Global Strategy Paper when First Sea Lord Rhoderick Mcgrigor had based naval acceptance of an increased emphasis on nuclear weapons on the COSC acceptance of the possibility of conventional activities in the post-thermonuclear exchange phase. The Navy was not surprisingly concerned with the RAF's commandeering of the delivery systems and feared that a focus solely on nuclear exchanges would make the fleet obsolescent and a naval contribution to global war irrelevant. Indeed, the Navy would not have supported the paper had not a broken-backed phase been recognized within the document. As a result of Mcgrigor's pressure the paper finally concluded that a

future war would begin with a short period of great intensity which would be followed, if a decision had not been reached in the first period, by an indefinite period of 'broken-backed' hostilities during which both sides would seek to recuperate from the wounds they had sustained and to recover strength for a further intensive effort.[4]

When it came to naval forces the Global Strategy Paper said that it would be the Navy's objective during global war to keep open vital sea-lanes against enemy submarines, mines, surface combatants, and air attacks. The COSC also agreed that nuclear weapons would have less effect at sea than anywhere

[2] W. J. Crowe, 'The Policy Roots of the Royal Navy 1946–63' (Ph.D. thesis, Princeton University, 1965), 149.

[3] *Statement on Defence, 1955*, Cmd. 9391, HMSO, para. 29.

[4] E. Grove, *From Vanguard to Trident* (London, 1987), 84.

else and war at sea could therefore continue for some time after the nuclear exchange.[5]

The Navy's ability to complement its success at inserting long-war scenarios into the Global Strategy Paper with an upgrading of its order of battle, was compromised by its concomitant agreement to focus most energies on the first phase of global war and the opposition by the other Chiefs of Staff to broken-backed warfare. Indeed, the Navy had been forced to agree to reductions in its planned programme of new frigates by 40 per cent and aircraft by 25 per cent. The Radical Review of 1953 further challenged the Navy's preferred long-war strategy when the civilian leadership in the Defence Committee underlined their support of plans geared towards a short conflict and the necessity of subordinating all plans for global war to the first nuclear phase of such a struggle.[6]

Although remaining firm, the Admiralty appeared by 1954 to have broadened its position into an acceptance of the possibility of nuclear weapons being used throughout the duration of global war.[7] This did not mean that from the Navy's point of view preparations for broken-backed warfare were not required and, indeed, the 1954 White Paper was explicit that a broken-backed phase might occur 'during which the opposing sides would seek to recover their strength, carrying on the struggle in the meantime as best they might'.[8] Yet, clearly, by the beginning of 1955, opposition within wider military and political circles to such a long-war strategy was such that reference to broken-backed warfare was removed from that year's White Paper. The question therefore becomes whether during the Eden administration the Navy began to moderate its position on the long-war conception such that it was willingly moving towards the 'New Look' policies announced at the beginning of 1957.

By the summer of 1955, the new Minister of Defence, Selwyn Lloyd, was convinced that all-round cuts in defence expenditure would have to be made. The upward spiral of defence spending was certainly most unsettling and its potential for going above £1,900 million was something Lloyd desperately wished to

[5] CAB 131/12 Report of the Committee on the Defence Programme, 24 Sept. 1952.
[6] I. Clark and N. J. Wheeler, *The British Origins of Nuclear Strategy 1945–1955* (Oxford, 1989), 184.
[7] Ibid. 203.          [8] *Statement Relating To Defence*, Cmd. 9075, 1954, 5.

avoid.[9] Consequently, at a meeting between the Minister and the service heads on 4 May, it was agreed that the Ministry of Defence would arrange for its officials to undertake a review of the defence programme and its estimated cost over the next five to seven years. It was stressed that all means should be adopted in order to ensure 'fruitful economies' and major savings in expenditure and manpower should be secured.[10] The financial objective would be set by the Chancellor of the Exchequer who had earlier insisted that £1,525 million serve as the upper limit for defence spending in 1955[11] and that spending in later years should not greatly exceed this total.[12]

From the beginning of the exercise, Lloyd recognized the need to reorientate financial allocations to the various services and to base this reorientation on a set of assumptions that reflected the centrality of the nuclear deterrent and the need to reduce conventional forces and programmes. In a meeting between the Minister and the services on 12 July,[13] Lloyd stressed that reductions in costs would have to be made and that future programming would have to reflect the descending priorities of: (1) the 'primary' deterrent which he defined as comprising the medium bomber force and its weaponry, the ballistic rocket and 'such nuclear potential as the Navy possessed'; (2) preparations for cold war which the Minister defined as sufficient forces to meet Britain's overseas commitments, the air defence of the UK, and the minimum civil defence programme necessary to sustain morale; and finally (3)—reflecting the view that global nuclear war was unlikely and the conduct of conventional operations in the post-thermonuclear exchange phase impossible—the Minister stated that a rigorous curtailment under the heading of preparations for global war must take place.[14] The Navy and the Army's roles and capabilities would come under attack from two comple-

[9]  The focus of the programme was on the financial year 1958/9.
[10] DEFE 7/963, Extract from SM 4 (55), 4 May 1955.
[11] CAB 128/27, CC 73 (54) 1, 5 Nov. 1954.
[12] DEFE 7/963, Memo from Ministry of Defence to the Chiefs of Staff, 11 May 1955.
[13] DEFE 7/963, Misc/m (55) 69, 12 July 1955.
[14] During this period forces regarded as primarily designated for global war included BAOR, 2nd TAF, fighter defence for the UK, the Auxiliary Air Force, the bulk of the reserve fleet, submarines, anti-submarine forces, minelayers, and minesweepers.

mentary sources; from the proposed overall reductions of defence expenditure and from the increase in the RAF's allocation. The Minister of Defence was clearly interested in creating a firmer match between, on the one hand, an evolving declaratory posture that placed growing emphasis on nuclear deterrence and, on the other hand, force structure.

On 17 August, Selwyn Lloyd issued a directive on the LTDP to the services. In it he demanded that the fleet would have to be reduced in size and he called for an examination of the Navy 'with a view to deciding what vessels are necessary for cold and limited war roles and what vessels are retained in commission primarily for the global nuclear war'.[15] He was adamant that the navy could not make a contribution to the deterrent and that naval conventional global war capabilities such as mine-sweepers, coastal forces, and submarines would have to be reduced, the reserve fleet (the basis of a broken-backed war capability as it was this fleet that would be mobilized for the second stage of global war) radically cut down, that a new medium carrier which was being built should be scrapped, and economies found in the stockpiling of reserves, afloat support, the administrative base and the seaward defence of European ports.

The 1955 LTDP had the effect of spurring the Navy to set up its own long-term planning committee. To a degree, the 'Way Ahead' committee (formed in June 1955 with the object of an 'Enquiry into the Structure and Supporting Organisation of the Naval Service') seemed to go along with the Ministry of Defence's strategic conceptions. Grove maintains that as a result of these investigations, the Navy supported cutbacks in the reserve fleet. He states that 'The general emphasis was on maintaining the front-line fleet as cheaply and efficiently as possible, at the price of mobilization potential.'[16] This was a major shift from the 1940s when reserve ships had been maintained at the expense of a non-existent home fleet. Yet, as Grove himself points out, this was only accepted in the context of 'the prevailing line of overriding priority for cold war peacetime commitments',[17] a point which, in the light of the recently released documentation, needs to be reaffirmed. For, it appears

[15] DEFE 7/964, Selwyn Lloyd to the Services, 17 Aug. 1955.
[16] Grove, *Vanguard to Trident,* 175.                    [17] Ibid.

that the Navy never really accepted the totality of the Minister's strategic vision, his budget projections, or his list of war preparation priorities.

Indeed, already in early June 1955, in answer to a question of whether it was agreed that the importance of the nuclear deterrent made the Navy's preparations for global war a third priority, the First Sea Lord, Lord Mountbatten, resorted to a reaffirmation of the existence of a broken-backed phase of global war. He stressed that

The Navy would then have a major part to play, against powerful Russian opposition, in the period of resuscitation which would follow such [thermonuclear] exchanges and during which our power and speed of recovery might affect the final outcome.[18]

The Navy, of course, could argue that they were being consistent with the Chiefs' conception of global war as expressed since the Global Strategy Paper of 1952 and the most recent White Paper which had cautioned that 'some provision, though on a lower priority must . . . be made for continuing operations after the initial phase'.[19] Mountbatten was not being out of step when he claimed that priorities

could not be applied so absolutely as to make it necessary to eliminate entirely a lower priority category before any cuts at all were made in the higher categories; the need for balance must be kept in mind.[20]

The Navy's plans therefore required covering forces to protect shipping from Russian fleets and to guard the Baltic and Black Sea exits; it would need anti-submarine forces to attack enemy submarines between Greenland and Scotland and it would need to have ships to protect convoys soon after the outbreak of war. Money would continue to be spent on forces designated primarily for global war such as submarines, minesweepers, and minehunters (the latter two of which the Navy planned to order 70 beginning in 1957/8); and on forces which could be used in varied circumstances including global war such as a new medium carrier (to be laid down in 1958/9)[21] and guided

---

[18] DEFE 7/963, Misc/m (55) 69, 12 July 1955.
[19] CAB 129/73, CC (55) 29, 4 Feb. 1955.
[20] DEFE 7/963, Misc/m (55) 69, 12 July 1955.
[21] Discussions on the future of heavy carriers had been going on throughout the mid-

weapons cruisers (to be started at the rate of one a year up to a total of 12).

In addition, the Navy made it clear that it regarded one of the main implications of the advent of thermonuclear weapons to be the increased cost of programmes. This derived from the need to invest more in logistic support as the UK was now threatened as a supply base, and the necessity of improving mobilization practices, dispersing HQs, and upgrading the readiness of the reserve fleet. Finally, the Navy also went on to reject major reductions in her manpower allotment. While naval manpower was in the process of coming down from 132,000 to 120,000, the Navy warned that this would give rise to problems due to the large size of ships coming into service and the importance of maintaining strong Home and Mediterranean fleets as well as ships in the Far East, the East Indies, the South Atlantic, and in the American and the East Indies stations.[22] Thus, it was one thing to agree to statements in the White Paper that indicated that conventional preparations for global war were being downgraded, but another thing altogether to carry out reductions in force allocations in line with such a statement. It was clear that the Navy's conception of its 'organizational essence' was not changing as fast as its declaratory statements were implying.

Not surprisingly, by mid-September, the Navy had reported problems in complying with Selwyn Lloyd's directive. While the First Lord of the Admiralty, J. P. L. Thomas, admitted that the Minister's August directive was a 'useful guide', it was apparent that the Navy was not ready to envisage cutbacks of the magnitude preferred by Selwyn Lloyd. Thomas was adamant that although the Navy could go a 'long way' to meeting the Minister's financial goals, the implications for Britain's NATO contribution would be most damaging.[23] For, in this latter theatre, Britain's contribution in ships would have to be reduced from 539 to about 357.[24] It was stated that the implications of

1950s with the Navy successfully defending the cold, limited, global war relevance of such a ship. See DEFE 13/66, extract from D (55) 3, fo. 63, 15 Mar. 1955 on the Defence Committee's agreement on the need to build heavy carriers.

[22] DEFE 7/963, fo. 41a, 14 July 1955.
[23] DEFE 7/964, Misc/m (55) 91, 14 Sept. 1955.
[24] DEFE 7/964, Misc/P (55) 45, 29 Sept. 1955.

such a step could be gleaned from the fact that the UK's naval declaration to NATO represented half the number of ships committed by the alliance as a whole, excluding the United States. The Navy expressed doubts as to the ability of the alliance to absorb such a blow; it also questioned the wisdom of relying on the American Navy for the defence of Britain in a global war (a situation that was made more likely if the Minister's proposals were adopted) as the US Navy might well have different priorities from that of Britain. It was the Admiralty's view that 'It will be for Her Majesty's Government to decide whether the vigour of the alliance would be too seriously threatened by such a reduction in our naval contribution.'[25] In addition, from the Navy's perspective, the implications of the Minister's proposed cuts for naval global war capabilities were equalled in severity by the implications for Britain's cold war capabilities and thus her world standing. Indeed, these arguments were often brought in at the same time as the Navy sought to defend its broken-backed war commitments—the arguments of the one instance serving to buttress her case in the other. Thus, at the end of September, the Admiralty pointed out that while it could reduce its budget for 1956/7 to £342 million (plus £12 million for pay inducements) and a manpower ceiling of 113,000 by 31 March 1958, the Minister's proposals would leave the Navy in a position

insufficient to sustain [Britain's] interests world-wide . . . Its training and operations could only be organised by concentrating [the fleet] at home and in the Mediterranean and withdrawing from other foreign stations . . . we should have to reconcile ourselves to witnessing the end of our history as a world-wide naval power with all that this would entail in loss of influence.[26]

In November, Thomas told Selwyn Lloyd that with a budget of £347 million for 1958/9 the Far Eastern station would have to be abandoned and the planned fleet reduced to two fleet carriers, one light fleet carrier, three or four cruisers plus 130 small ships. This, according to Thomas, would be the end of the world-wide Navy. He was unequivocal that

I should regard this as a catastrophe, not only as First Sea Lord but also in my capacity as a member of the Government, and all the more

[25] DEFE 7/964, Misc/P (55) 45, 29 Sept. 1955.    [26] Ibid.

so because I believe that even in Europe our influence will dwindle once we cease to show ourselves bent on maintaining our world-wide interests.[27]

By the end of the year strong naval resistance to the Minister's ambitious cost-cutting proposals forced Lloyd to move at least some of the way towards the Admiralty's financial position though not necessarily to an endorsement of its long-war preference. Thus, the Minister promised the Navy £370 million for 1958/9—a figure which, according to Selwyn Lloyd, was the minimum necessary in order to build a 'modern navy for the 1960s which could carry out cold and limited war functions though not necessarily global war ones'.[28] However, the Navy was not at this stage ruling out a global war role. Indeed, in October it had only gone as far as to state that with a £363 million budget for 1958/9 'the fleet in the long term would not approach the size that would be needed to enable us to play a full part in global war'.[29] This was a far cry from a total rejection of global war capabilities, for a corollary to 'full part' was 'some part'. Furthermore, if Selwyn Lloyd was implying that the fact that the number of ships to be allocated to NATO was going to be reduced was evidence in itself that the Navy was surrendering interest in a global war capability, he was being misleading or mistaken. For, Navy ideas regarding its role in global war stressed a long 'resuscitation' phase and were not dependent only on forces in being in Europe. This perspective was carried forward by the Navy into the second year of the Eden government.

While the 1956 White Paper appeared to reaffirm a war preparation priority list that placed a strengthening of the deterrent as the most important objective,[30] similarly to 1955, the Navy continued to attempt to prevent the implications of such an ordering from undermining its favoured roles and capabilities. Thus, at the beginning of 1956, an assistant secretary

[27] DEFE 7/965, Thomas to Selwyn Lloyd, 25 Nov. 1955; also see DEFE 7/965, Misc/m (55) 122, 9 Nov. 1955; DEFE 7/965, Powell to Selwyn Lloyd, 25 Nov. 1955.

[28] The Minister later demonstrated that this budget would mean an active fleet in 1958/9 of 16 cruisers and above (down from 18 in 1955) with a reserve fleet of 9 cruisers and above and 83 destroyers (down from 13 and 96). DEFE 7/965, DC (55) draft, undated; also see DEFE 7/965, Admiralty to Selwyn Lloyd, 25 Nov. 1955.

[29] DEFE 7/964, Admiralty to Selwyn Lloyd, 11 Oct. 1955.

[30] See *Statement on Defence, 1956,* Cmd. 9691, HMSO, paras. 4–8.

in the Admiralty, J. M. Mackay, was adamant that it was difficult

> ... to maintain the distinction between a navy fitted and organised for cold and limited war and one fitted and organised for global war. Our view has always been that the flexibility of ships does ensure if you have a navy or any kind it will have an all-round function. We should of course like many more ships for global war . . .[31]

Consequently, while the 1956 White Paper presented a seemingly uniform strategic vision, this was not the case. Though, on the one hand, it reaffirmed the oft-stated war preparation priorities, it also provided the leeway by which the services could prepare for global war and retain a large manpower and extensive capabilities. It was stated under the Navy section that the fleet would 'continue to make a substantial contribution to the naval strength of the Commonwealth, N.A.T.O and S.E.A.T.O in meeting the needs of global war'.[32] In such a context it is not surprising that Monckton was forced to report that despite all the cost-cutting of 1955, defence expenditure would in 1956/7 rise above that of 1955/6 (that is from £1,494.2 million to £1,498 million).[33]

This was a view reaffirmed by Monckton in March 1956 when he complained that

> The Navy and Army are still assuming that they must plan for continued global war operations after some months, cf. the War Office study of the Middle East Base and the Naval enquiry about minelaying at D+12 months. Present planning for the defence of southern Europe is also revealing; the assumptions are that once the hydrogen bombs have been dropped the war will get back on to more or less conventional lines, and that . . . naval operations in the Mediterranean will be practicable . . . [t]his is not only nonsense, it is nonsense we cannot possibly pay for.[34]

For Monckton, the major assumption to be made about global war was that the UK would deliver a nuclear counter-offensive and attempt to survive the Soviet nuclear assault as

---

[31] DEFE 7/771, Mackay to Carey, 11 Jan. 1956.

[32] *Statement on Defence, 1956*, para. 23.

[33] DEFE 7/771, 11 Jan. 1956. One of the main problems in reaching the 1956/7 figures was underspending by the RAF.

[34] DEFE 7/966, fo. 34, 8 Mar. 1956.

best she could. Moreover, he was adamant that 'If there is a broken-backed phase the US will have to fight it for us . . . There is no object in deceiving ourselves . . .'[35]

Clearly, despite the work of the 1955 LTDP, there was still room for major reductions in service capabilities. In the summer of 1956 Eden oversaw the establishment of a Policy Review Committee to oversee such reductions.[36] What is of interest to note is that from the start, the Policy Review Committee, for the purposes of coherent planning and effective cost-cutting, re-affirmed the war preparation priorities of the 1955 LTDP. This was the thrust of a still classified paper called 'The Future of the UK in World Affairs' produced without the knowledge of the Chiefs at the instigation of the Cabinet Secretary, Sir Norman Brook. The paper pointed to the need to secure savings especially in Europe where a stronger emphasis on nuclear deterrence could serve as the rationale for substantial reductions in conventional forces.[37] Against this background, Monckton informed the Chiefs that each service should investigate the result of a decision that any planning based on the premise that the UK would serve as an operational base following the onset of thermonuclear war should be discarded.[38] On 3 August, Monckton wrote to the service ministers and told them that the new defence budget projections 'naturally imply sweeping changes in plans for the forces'.[39] Studies would include an anlysis of an adjustment of the Navy's size to the minimum necessary for situations short of global war.[40]

The essence of the ensuing debate differed little—if at all— from the 1955 LTDP discussions. Priorities were first distorted, then global warfare capabilities legitimized (with attempts to retain all manner of cold/limited war capabilities held on to) and the progress towards economies made painfully slow. Thus, at the beginning of June the Chiefs stated that priorities

[35] Ibid.
[36] According to RAF Historian T. C. G. James (Interview, 15 Dec. 1987) the Policy Review Committee consisted of Eden, Selwyn Lloyd, Monckton, and Lord Salisbury. Butler attended most of its meetings, as did the service ministers and the Chiefs of Staff.
[37] This information comes from T. C. G. James (Interview, 15 Dec. 1987).
[38] DEFE 4/87, COS 58 (56) 7, 12 July 1956.
[39] AIR 19/855, Monckton to Birch, 3 Aug. 1956.
[40] CAB 130/120, GEN 548/1st meeting, 9 Aug. 1956. For an outline of the specific studies carried out during the 1956 Policy Review see A. Eden, *Full Circle* (London, 1960), 371–2; and DEFE 5/69, COS 8 (56) 234, 14 June 1956.

could neither be absolute or mutually exclusive. Moreover, they doubted whether large savings could be realized in the fields of cold and limited war capabilities.[41]

The Navy, again, readily took up this refrain. Despite having at the end of 1955 agreed that global war was unlikely until the Soviets could deliver an effective nuclear attack on the USA,[42] the Navy refused to accept that all plans for such a contingency be aborted. While in July it was prepared to make cuts which included the Rhine and Elbe flotillas, 75 ships in the reserve fleet, a quarter of submarines in home waters and some mine-sweeping and coastal forces, it stressed that it could not lose the ability to expand to the minimum measures needed to control Britain's sea communications in global war. It emphasized that the Navy's preparations for global war had suffered from successive economy drives and that 'the aim of the [policy review] had therefore to a large extent been anticipated as far as the Navy is concerned'.[43] Indeed, the Navy was of the opinion that there would have to be additions to the operational fleet (including a new commando carrier, four destroyers, and three frigates) if Britain was to meet her cold and limited war commitments.

Naval concerns were given their most explicit form in a letter from the First Lord, Lord Hailsham, to Monckton on 10 October. Hailsham explicitly rejected the assumption that only the deterrent should be relied upon when it came to global war. In referring to Monckton's 3 August directive Hailsham stated,

To begin with, we were asked to assume that, apart from the deterrent, no preparations should be made for war with Russia, either

[41] DEFE 5/68, COS (56) 219, 7 June 1956; also see DEFE 5/69, COS (56) 235, 16 June 1956.

[42] DEFE 6/34, The Nature, Course and Duration of Global War, 9 Jan. 1956. The Admiralty's study was planned around the year of 1970. Seven war games took place, one of which was attended by Monckton and the Chiefs of Staff. The Minister was so impressed that he ordered that the Navy's strategic studies be reconstituted on an inter-service basis. See DEFE 4/82, COS 1 (56) 8, 3 Jan. 1956 and DEFE 4/82, COS 9 (56) 5, 17 Jan. 1956). Studies were also conducted into the role of central government in global war (see DEFE 6/35, JP (56) 92 (A) T of (C Section), 2 May 1956). A study was also undertaken by the JPS into the instructions to be given to commanders abroad on the action they should take in the event of contact with the central government being cut off during a global nuclear war for a period of up to six months (see DEFE 4/86, COS (56) 131, 1 May 1956). The contents of these studies are still classified.

[43] DEFE 5/70, COS (56) 280, 25 July 1956.

now or in the future . . . this is not an assumption to which I could as at present advised make myself a party . . . I do not believe that it can be right that no provision should be made by the Navy against the contingency of a war with this Power. For the present, however, I need only say that it is an assumption which neither the Chiefs of Staff nor Her Majesty's Government have accepted as a basis for planning. What they have agreed is the very different proposition that for the present, preparations for global war other than for the deterrent should take the lowest place in the order of priority.[44]

Indeed, throughout the period of discussions on the New Political Directive, the Navy sought to question the validity of the deterrent in the context of thermonuclear parity. According to the Navy,

It is lack of money, and more particularly of manpower that forces us to review and change our existing policy. It is not primarily the diminishing probability of global war that has forced the change on us. Global War as a probability has diminished precisely because of this effort we have put into defence.[45]

On 29 June 1956, Mountbatten circulated a draft of a meeting held within the Admiralty in which it was stated that it was common knowledge that

the new concept originated from political and economic, rather than from strategical considerations. Indeed, no serious student of strategy would advocate a policy which, in any forseeable world conditions, made no provision to meet a threat of 400 Soviet submarines, 18 Soviet Cruisers and 1,200 Soviet Naval aircraft.[46]

These protestations did not go unnoticed by the Air Ministry. According to R. C. Kent, an assistant secretary at the Ministry, the Army and Navy seemed to believe that cuts in their own programmes were due to excessive expenditure on the deterrent; in fact, only 10 per cent of all defence expenditure went towards the deterrent.[47] Moreover, he stressed that if there was going to be a serious attempt to reappraise British defence policy, then there was 'no reason in logic why sweeping reductions should not be made in the Navy'. Kent rejected the Navy's assertion

---

[44] AIR 19/855, Hailsham to Monckton, 10 Oct. 1956.
[45] AIR 8/2064, Policy Review—Long Term Defence Policy, undated.
[46] AIR 8/2064, Mountbatten to Stirling, 29 June 1956.
[47] AIR 19/855, Note by R. C. Kent, 17 Oct. 1956.

that priorities as established by the Chiefs allowed for the provision of global warfare capabilities. He stated that only excessive preoccupation with global war could justify the inclusion of 26 submarines in the fleet (and 39 under the £380 million plan), the proposed construction of sophisticated vessels such as guided weapons cruisers and the retention of as many as 27 minesweepers in the active fleet planned for 1965/6 (backed by 169 in the operational reserve).

Thus, Mountbatten's paper on the Soviet submarine threat was strongly criticized by the Air Ministry because they felt it reflected

a concerted effort [by the Admiralty] to oppose any suggestion that the United Kingdom should accept a strategy based on the deterrent which allows for no more than the initial nuclear exchange of a future global war.[48]

Not surprisingly, it was the Air Ministry's view that the Admiralty (and War Office) were intent upon paying only 'lipservice to the deterrent'.[49]

This 'lipservice' did not, however, stop the Navy attempting to prevent the RAF from becoming the sole repository of the nuclear weapons and the delivery vehicles. Certainly, the Navy had long recognized that the growing popularity amongst British defence policy-makers of nuclear weapons meant that it would be imprudent to base its stance solely on conventional forces. Indeed, in the late 1940s and early 1950s the Admiralty had shown a growing interest in a naval role in the first phase of global war. In 1948/9 studies had been undertaken into the possibility of deploying a carrier-borne atomic bomber fleet with the object of attacking those Soviet bases not readily accessible by bombers based in the UK or Middle East, especially the Soviet naval bases in the Murmansk/Archangel region of the USSR.[50] The naval demand for such a role carried on into the next decade and, as Clark and Wheeler point out, it began to mirror the B29-carrier debate in the United States,[51] with RAF–naval rivalry over possession of nuclear strike capabilities at times becoming quite intense.

---

[48] AIR 8/2061, The Role of the Russian Submarine Fleet, 2 Jan. 1957.
[49] AIR 8/2064, Earle to Dickson, 3 July 1956.
[50] DEFE 6/5, JP (48) 7 (Final), 11 Mar. 1948.
[51] Clark and Wheeler, *The British Origins of Nuclear Strategy*, 183.

This discourse, could not, of course be isolated from the general strategic debate with regard to the merits of a strategy of graduated deterrence over that of massive retaliation. Rear Admiral Sir Anthony Buzzard's preference for the smaller allied powers to develop tactical nuclear weapons and for the Western powers to differentiate clearly between strategic and tactical nuclear weapons with the ultimate objective of an East–West declaration promising not to initiate strategic nuclear attacks,[52] served to reinforce the Navy's case for developing smaller yield nuclear weapons (which their aircraft could carry) and to base planning on attacking military rather than civilian targets in the Soviet Union.

In the early 1950s, the Navy began demanding the development of an aircraft which could use tactical nuclear weapons to attack both land-based targets and the threatening new Soviet Sverdlov cruisers—a demand that resulted in the development of the NA 39 (The Buccaneer) in 1952.[53] The Scimitar and Sea Vixen fighters under development during the early 1950s were also capable of carrying Red Beard fission weapons. During the 1953 Radical review, however, the then Minister of Supply, Duncan Sandys, attacked the naval attempt to secure for itself a nuclear role by claiming that the Navy would then be duplicating RAF efforts and there was, in any event, no money for such a capability.[54] Sandys may well have succeeded in terminating the NA 39 project had he not fallen ill. Whatever the case, the following year saw the Navy continuing to argue for the relative invulnerability of aircraft carriers as opposed to airfields. Their warning that 'A "Pearl Harbour" against allied bomber airfields may well leave the carriers as the only British surviving source of nuclear attack'[55] did not impress the Swinton Committee (set up by Churchill to review defence spending) which did not reject the RAF's preferred V-bomber total of 240 and called for the restriction of the Navy's carrier fleet to trade protection.

However, at the beginning of 1955 the Defence Committee agreed to reject calls for savings to be made by reducing the fleet air arm and treating the Navy's heavy carriers as light

---

[52] DEFE 4/81, COS 104 (55) 2 discussion of JP (55) 147 (Final), 15 Dec. 1955.
[53] Grove, *Vanguard To Trident*, 98.
[54] ADM 1/24695 RDP/M (53) 8, 10 Nov. 1953.
[55] ADM 205/97, Admiralty on DR (54) 4th mtg, 14 Aug. 1954.

carriers. It was pointed out that Britain was committed to NATO to produce two heavy carriers for the Atlantic Striking Fleet and had already been asked for a third such ship. Moreover, the elimination of Britain's heavy carriers from the Striking Fleet and their limitation to a trade protection role would reduce the United Kingdom's influence on overall NATO naval strategy and prevent her from exercising leverage on the employment of the strike fleet. It was also of concern that if there were no heavy British carriers on the European side of the Atlantic, there would be no means of operating in waters subject to heavy enemy air attack and outside the range of shore-based air cover until the United States carriers arrived.[56] Thus, by the time of the 1955 LTDP the Navy was stating adamantly that

A powerful striking force equipped with aircraft carrying nuclear weapons will be needed to play our part with our Allies in gaining command of the sea from the outset by destroying the enemy fleet, his mercantile shipping and his bases. If the UK becomes a major target for nuclear bombardment the carriers will be increasingly important because of their mobility.[57]

Indeed, Mountbatten remained unwilling to give up a carrier-borne nuclear strike capability even though he admitted towards the end of 1955 that because the NA 39 was too small to carry radar, a tactical nuclear attack on the Soviet Sverdlov cruisers would have to be made at very close range and would virtually be suicidal.[58]

The Policy Review of 1956 took up the assault with a call for an examination of the need for projects which were liable to 'give rise to heavy costs in the future—e.g. the NA. 39 . . .'.[59] The·Minister of Supply, Reginald Maudling, was to conclude that the development and production of naval aircraft was an uneconomical proposition and the NA 39, for one, should be dropped.[60] The Navy, however, remained true to its long-held position that the role of and the need for the striking fleet would remain unaltered under the new concept being pushed by the

[56] CAB 131/15, D (55) 1 Defence Policy: Heavy Aircraft Carriers, 7 Jan. 1955.
[57] DEFE 7/963, PD REF 49/119/1, 7 June 1955.
[58] DEFE 7/965, Misc/m (55) 128—undated.
[59] AIR 19/855, PUS, NOL 6253, 15 June 1956.
[60] AIR 19/855, Broadbent to Birch, 11 Sept. 1956.

British in the NATO Council,[61] It went on to reject suggestions that the US be asked to supply Britain with an aircraft of the NA 39 type, by pointing out that the American aircraft were too big for British carriers.[62] Elsewhere, the First Lord, Lord Hailsham, buttressed his case by stating that 'It is hardly necessary to point out that the Fleet Air Arm alone possesses the strategical and tactical mobility required for limited wars.'[63]

During the mid-1950s not only did the Navy continue to evince interest in delivering a nuclear strike with its own carrier-borne bomber force, but it also matched the RAF's desire to acquire a nuclear force[64] with its own interest in such weapons—in this case, nuclear missiles deployed on nuclear powered submarines. The Navy had, of course, observed the evolving American nuclear submarine programme and the commissioning by the USA of the nuclear powered submarine *Nautilus* in 1954. As Grove points out, this helped to spur the Royal Navy on to organize research and development on the system and to increase their representation at the Harwell nuclear research laboratory.[65]

Not all of the Admiralty was equally convinced with regard to the virtues of a nuclear submarine and missile programme, viewing it as a threat both to the Navy's budget and a drain on its skilled manpower.[66] Mountbatten, however, who became First Sea Lord in April 1955, was certain of the strategic benefits of such an investment and its merits as a means whereby the Navy, too, could secure a role in the delivery of Britain's nuclear deterrent. During his visit to the United States towards the end of 1955, his desire to visit the *Nautilus* was blocked by Admiral Hyman Rickover, chief of the US Naval nuclear programme, who, with backing from the Congressional Joint Committee on Atomic Energy, was opposed to providing the British with access to nuclear know-how.[67] Mountbatten, however, was able to secure the support of US Chief of Naval

[61] AIR 8/2064, VCIGS to Stirling, 'Long Term Defence Review, Nato strategy and level of forces', 3 July 1956.

[62] AIR 19/855, Misc/m (56) 129, Meeting of Ministry of Defence on Research and Development, 27 Sept. 1956.

[63] AIR 19/855 Hailsham to Monckton, 10 Oct. 1956.

[64] See Ch. 6.                                [65] Grove, *Vanguard to Trident*, 230.

[66] A. Pierre, *Nuclear Politics* (London, 1972), 200.

[67] P. Ziegler, *Mountbatten* (London, 1985), 58.

Operations Admiral Arleigh Burke who in 1955 informed him that the US was trying to develop a solid-fuelled rocket which could be fired from a submarine. Burke was having his own problems with the United States Air Force who were proving recalcitrant about helping the US Navy build such a system and Mountbatten was able to convince him to allow a Royal Navy officer with missile experience to be attached to the American Navy's IRBM programme.[68]

By 1956 the American Defence Department was supporting the British request for information on nuclear propulsion and in June 1956 an agreement was signed giving the United Kingdom information on ship propulsion. In August of that year, Admiral Rickover visited London where he was apparently 'won over' by Mountbatten[69] and the US–UK nuclear submarine–missile link strengthened. Thus while during this period the Air Ministry continued to voice concerns that the Navy was intent on opposing the idea of an independent deterrent,[70] the Navy's views and actions with regard both to the carrier-borne deterrent and research into a nuclear-missile submarine force indicated that it was in fact more concerned with preventing the RAF becoming the sole repository of Britain's nuclear arsenal.

### The Army, Nuclear Weapons, and Conventional Forces

Throughout 1955–6 the Army remained very keen about integrating nuclear weapons into their strategic planning but continued to be very circumspect when it came to agreeing that such weapons allowed for reductions in their conventional order of battle or that there should be no planning for broken-backed warfare. Thus, while on one level the United Kingdom sought to reject American attempts to distinguish between limited and global war in Europe, on another level British policy-makers intent upon securing reductions in conventional forces had to convince Army bureaucrats that nuclear fire-power could now substitute for their traditionally large manpower requirements.

When in 1954 NATO had decided to integrate tactical nuclear weapons into its strategic plans, British defence policy-makers

---

[68] See statement by Mountbatten, quoted in Grove, *Vanguard to Trident*, 234.
[69] Ibid. 230.
[70] AIR 8/2044, Earle to Dickson, Air Ministry File no. 11/18, 30 Sept. 1955.

rapidly agreed it to be unacceptable for Britain to remain entirely dependent on a US tactical nuclear capability and that the United Kingdom would have to make its own contribution.[71] In fact, BAOR went on to adopt an atomic strategy even before it had the missiles or the warheads for the implementation of such plans. The Honest John and Corporal missiles were not deployed in Europe until the late 1950s and the British did not receive warheads of their own for these systems until 1960.

In early 1955 the Army appeared to have gone along with the idea of reducing global war preparations when it agreed that only the two TA divisions assigned to NATO would be equipped with supplies for global war. The other nine divisions would be assigned to civil defence duties only. However, Chief of the Imperial General Staff Sir Gerald Templer remained convinced that war would continue up to some months after the initial nuclear exchange and conventional forces would be required.[72] Indeed during the 1955 LTDP discussions the Army presented its tasks as including not only counter-insurgency and civil defence but also operations during global war.[73] Similarly to the Navy, the War Office was of the opinion that the advent of thermonuclear and tactical nuclear weapons led to an increase in costs rather than savings. Indeed, in the near future only a slight decline in total manpower was expected (from 400,000 in April 1956 to 380,000 by 1963) as changes in tactics and organization would put a premium on redundancy.[74]

Thus as the 1955 costing exercise progressed, the War Office continued to point to the dangerous strategic implications that would follow from the implementation of Selwyn Lloyd's LTDP guidelines.[75] It was strongly against any reductions in its forces in Germany and stressed the political implications of such a step (although, most probably, also taking note of Selwyn Lloyd's statement that the Army should be prepared to 'give a good account of itself in global war').[76] The Army believed that

[71] DEFE 6/26, JP (54) 77 (Final), 3 Sept. 1954.
[72] J. Cloake, *Templer, Tiger of Malaya: The Life of Field Marshall Sir Gerald Templer* (London, 1985), 335.
[73] DEFE 7/963, fo. 12—undated.
[74] DEFE 7/963, The Long Term Defence Programme, Paper by the War Office, 6 June 1955.
[75] DEFE 7/964, Misc/P (55) 46, 29 Sept. 1955.
[76] DEFE 7/964, LTDP: Memo by Minister of Defence, 17 Aug. 1955.

the war reserves situation should be improved rather than cut down and the level of reserves already allocated was inadequate for anything except the very beginning of a global war.[77]

The Army's position received a degree of support as a result of the Ministry of Defence's ambiguous position with regard to the issue of 'secondary deterrents'. According to Minister of Defence Selwyn Lloyd in August 1955, while the Russians would be deterred primarily by the fear of nuclear retaliation they would also be deterred by conventional forces designated to thwart their nuclear and conventional attacks such as forces aimed at maintaining sea communications and '[t]he forces taking the first onslaught in Germany'.[78] By admitting the problem of secondary deterrents—that is, that there were conventional forces that reinforced the deterrent effects of the 'primary' nuclear deterrent—Selwyn Lloyd was providing the services with a rationale to demand conventional forces whose task it would be to aid the primary deterrent but which also had far-reaching implications for issues of manpower and cost. Why the Minister of Defence did so stemmed possibly from his own doubts as to the wisdom of reducing all conventional preparations for global war, and probably also the recognition that the services would mount a strong defence of their preferred roles and capabilities, and consequently, it would be best to moderate Ministry of Defence demands from the outset.

Whatever the case, by 1956 Templer was moving away from protecting his preferred force posture to attacking the very basis of a strategy that relied on nuclear weapons and allowed for the reduction of conventional forces. In the context of discussions on the New Political Directive he complained that

the Chiefs of Staff were being pushed into a dangerous position by being forced for economic reasons into the hurried acceptance of a concept which they were not sure about.[79]

He went on to state that

It was quite possible, however, that some form of aggression by proxy might take place, such as an attempted East German occupation of Berlin. In such circumstances he did not think that any Ministers

[77] DEFE 7/965, Hobbes to Powell, 9 Nov. 1955.
[78] DEFE 7/964, Selwyn Lloyd to services, 17 Aug. 1955.
[79] DEFE 4/88, COS 63 (56) 2, 29 June 1956.

would take the decision to embark on thermonuclear warfare. We now therefore had to consider for the first time the possibility of limited war in Europe in which we should need conventional forces from all three services.[80]

Certainly, the Army had indicated that the issue for them was not only one of deterrence, but also one of war fighting. In February it had stated that if there were further cuts plans for global war would be influenced. This was so because the removal of a British division from the Rhine would reduce the fighting power of the Northern Army group by about 13 per cent and because the designated German contribution would not be ready for a number of years. It was therefore the War Office's contention that the ability of NATO forces to impose sufficient delay on advancing Warsaw Pact forces in front of the Rhine would then be extremely difficult with the consequent delay of the implementation of SACEUR's forward strategy.[81]

That there was little acceptance for a move away from conventional planning for global war was further indicated in a note from a deputy secretary in the Ministry of Defence, R. C. Chilver, to Minister of Defence Monckton in February 1956. Chilver was adamant that there were a number of signs 'in the past few months that some elements at least of the Service Departments do not realize what the Strath report implies'[82]— that is the study of the effects of a thermonuclear attack on Britain.[83] He then proceeded to give examples of service preparations for global war which included: (1) the War Office had proposed to the Chiefs that plans should be made for the development of a new main base in the Middle East for use in global war; and (2) the Principal Administrative Officers Committee were considering plans for maintaining and constructing a reserve of landing ships for use in North West Europe in global war; Chilver went on to state:

My point is that if the Service Departments are putting forward proposals—and these are merely things that happen to have figured in Chiefs of Staff papers in the last month or two—that would be of very doubtful value even if we had taken the steps needed to secure the bare survival of this country through the initial phase of global war.

[80] Ibid.       [81] DEFE 5/65, COS (56) 74, 14 Feb. 1956.
[82] DEFE 7/966, Chilver to Monckton, 24 Feb. 1956.       [83] See Ch. 1.

One is bound to suspect that their present programmes may contain a good deal that is of lower priority than those survival measures.[84]

Minister of Defence Monckton was also quick to recognize that service non-acceptance of these principles was only part of the problem; the other part had to do with the absence of any agreed upon definition of limited war and the resulting open ended demands for limited war capabilities. Monckton therefore made the assumption that: (1) in any limited war (other than certain anti-subversion scenarios) the UK could count on allied help; (2) if a limited war started in areas in which the UK had peacetime obligation (e.g. Malaya or in the Middle East) the UK should have enough forces and reinforcements to hold the ground until allied help arrived; and (3) war in other areas (Korea, Indochina, or Greece) must not be planned for.[85] Yet, during the Policy Review discussions the Army took note of a JPS report on the nature, scope, and duration of limited war presented to the Chiefs of Staff in June 1956 in which it was stated that since the use of tactical nuclear weapons in limited war could only be made by the government of the day, it was essential for Britain to retain the ability to fight limited wars either with nuclear weapons or with conventional weapons alone.[86] Thus, as 1956 progressed, the Army seemed very ambivalent with regard to concepts which replaced conventional with nuclear power or with strategies that placed much emphasis on American assistance. Ministry of Defence success in converting the War Office to such a position seemed far off.

In essence, the Ministry of Defence need not have sought to convince the Army of the virtues of its strategic conception; rather, it could have directly attempted to undercut their

---

[84] DEFE 7/966, Chilver to Monckton, 24 Feb. 1956. The influence of these problems on expanding the budget can clearly be seen in this example. Chilver was demanding a large allocation (£70 million) for civil defence expenditure despite the general policy recommended by the Home Defence Committee which stated that the amount of spending on civil defence 'must be influenced by the extent to which it is government policy to prepare for global war' (DEFE 7/966, fo. 28, Annex to JP (55) 165D). Chilver knew that the government was officially intent on reducing global war expenditure but he found himself forced to state that 'So long as the service departments are proposing to spend money on such preparations . . . the civil expenditure without which they will be useless must be kept in step' (DEFE 7/966, Chilver to Monckton, 12 Feb. 1956).

[85] Ibid.

[86] DEFE 4/88, JP (56) 115 (Final) discussed at COS 63 (56) 3, 29 June 1956; also see DEFE 4/87, COS 54 (56) 4, 29 May 1956 and DEFE 6/36, JP (56) 115, 8 June 1956.

position by terminating the national service programme and thereby undermining the Army's large manpower base. The crucial questions then become (1) whether the government was succeeding in terminating the programme in the period prior to the announcement of the British 'New Look'; (2) whether arguments for ending national service were related to strategic conceptions that downplayed conventional forces in the thermonuclear age; and (3) what strategic rationales those opposing the termination of the programme were basing their arguments upon.

The 1955 White Paper stated that the government had naturally considered whether the thermonuclear revolution had influenced the problem of manpower but had concluded that the need to station forces in various parts of the world and the policy of building up the strategic reserve meant that a manpower reduction could not take place.[87] But in fact it was not strategic as much as political considerations that led Macmillan in January 1955 to state that he now doubted the wisdom of the government at the present juncture proposing a reduction in national service 'even if it were not militarily impracticable'.[88] He felt then that any reduction would lead to Labour Party counter-proposals for an even greater reduction in forces which would endanger British national security.[89]

In Parliament the government continued to refuse to admit that it was considering a reduction in the period of national service and a Labour Party motion in July 1955 to reduce conscription to 12 months was duly rejected. It was the Conservative's position that a diminution in the strength and efficiency of the active forces could only be accepted if the size of Britain's commitments 'justified such a step'.[90] The Minister of Defence, Selwyn Lloyd, was unequivocal when he told the House of Commons that

To reduce the period of National Service now would affect our power to play our part in the world. It would discourage our Allies and

---

[87] *Statement on Defence, 1956,* paras. 67–9.
[88] DEFE 13/53, Extract from SM/M (55) 1, 26 Jan. 1955.
[89] CAB 131/15, DC 2 (55) 2, 27 Jan. 1955.
[90] DEFE 13/53, fo. 82, 25 July 1955, and DEFE 13/53, Parker to Selwyn Lloyd, 21 July 1955.

would encourage our enemies, and so far from reducing world tension, it might increase it.[91]

It was, nevertheless, Lloyd's private view that some form of reduction would have to take place because, as a result of the nature of thermonuclear war, 'the earlier conception of national service as a means of building up a large pool of trained reservists is out of date'.[92] Yet, the rationale for this position seems to have been added only as an afterthought and the prime considerations continued to be economic and political. Indeed, Prime Minister Anthony Eden appeared more interested in balancing the need to avoid entering into a round of counter-proposals with the Labour Party over the future of national service with the attempt to secure economic and political advantages of reducing conscription than he was with balancing the reduction of conventional forces with an increase in nuclear fire-power.

However, with the 1955 election out of the way, the issue of Labour Party pressure presented less of an immediate obstacle. Consequently, on 2 August 1955, the services were informed that economic objectives and the goals of the LTDP made it imperative that service manpower be cut from approximately 835,000 in 1955 to 700,000 by April 1958. The Navy would be allocated 110,000–115,000, the RAF 235,000–240,000 and the Army 345,000–355,000.[93] The complete termination of national service therefore did not at this stage seem possible. Consequently, on 22 September 1955, the Cabinet approved a motion that the reduction to a manpower level of 700,000 by the end of March 1958 be achieved by maintaining the period of national service at two years and allowing the age of call-up to rise.[94]

Not surprisingly, the 1956 Defence White Paper paid much attention to the issue of increasing the regular component of the armed forces, but no mention was made of the possibility of terminating the programme.[95] In Parliament, the government

[91] House of Commons, vol. 540, col. 1101, 28 Apr. 1955.

[92] CAB 129/77, CP (55) 125, 19 Sept. 1955.

[93] DEFE 7/963, 2 Aug. 1955.

[94] DEFE 7/771, fo. 1, Speech by Eden at Bournemouth, 8 Oct. 1955.

[95] CAB 129/79, CP (56) 30, 8 Feb. 1956. The White Paper stated that two things were needed to improve the regular structure of the armed forces: (1) an increase in the number of recruits and (2) as many recruits as possible signing on for long

continued to deny that it was intent upon reducing armed forces manpower below the 700,000 level. For example, on 8 February,[96] 30 May,[97] 6 June, [98] and 13 July,[99] the Minister of Defence, Walter Monckton, rejected Labour Party demands for a termination of the national service scheme. In May 1956, Monckton told the House of Commons that the government was not considering reducing the period of national service beyond the reductions announced in 1955.

The terms of the debate changed little in 1956 when the problem of national service fell under the scrutiny of the Policy Review Committee. Once again, political and economic motives clashed with a strategic conception that had little to do with relating conventional force levels to thermonuclear warfare. Within the context of the Policy Review, much attention was given to the possibility of reducing the period of national service and ultimately returning to an all-regular force. At a meeting between Monckton and the Chiefs at the beginning of June, the Minister of Defence emphasized the link between reducing manpower and securing economic savings. It was estimated that over the next 10−15 years the average cost per annum for each soldier would be approximately £3,000. With the annual defence budget set at £1,400 million, a manpower limit of 460,000 could be set.[100]

Eden remained firm and continued to maintain that the national service programme should end as soon as possible— arguing primarily not on the basis of the exigencies of thermo-nuclear warfare but because 'he did not believe that the nation [would] continue to accept, after 1958, National Service as it now [was] unless the international situation deteriorate[d]'. It was the Prime Minister's view that Britain would have to try and meet her commitments with less than 500,000 men and a

---

engagements. An initial engagement of three to five years was too short and it was hoped that men would be encouraged to accept initial engagements of six, nine, or twelve years. It was stressed that regular recruitment which had very largely been of men on short-term engagements had fallen from its post-war peak of 100,000 in 1952−3 to about 62,000 in 1955−6.

[96] House of Commons, vol. 548, cols. 1668−70, 8 Feb. 1956.
[97] House of Commons, vol. 553, cols. 224−6, 30 May 1956.
[98] House of Commons, vol. 553, cols. 1064−5, 6 June 1956.
[99] House of Commons, vol. 556, cols. 1209−11, 18 July 1956.
[100] DEFE 5/68, COS (56) 219, 7 June 1956.

greater effort would have to be made to get the number of regulars above 300,000.[101]

Monckton, in turn, was to argue that, following Germany's mid-1956 decision to reduce its national service to one year, it was difficult to see how it would be politically possible domestically for Britain to continue with two years of national service.[102] The government would be under great pressure from the Labour Party to follow the German lead. It is important to note that only once having clarified this aspect of the problem was it agreed that 'so far as the Rhine army is concerned, if our troops only need to be policemen, they can be less well trained'. This latter argument was clearly a secondary concern—if not a rationalization in the context of the discussion.

Similarly to 1955, the services and the Chiefs of Staff bitterly opposed attempts to deprive them of forces, and as 1957 approached their opposition strengthened. The extent to which they were prepared to consider further reductions was sometimes only a function of their perception of the government's willingness either to reduce commitments, or more importantly, increase pay and benefits to regular personnel. Here possible reductions in the national service scheme served as a bait for improved regular employment conditions. Yet, even following the 1956 White Paper on Pay and Pensions which promised an increase of £67 million[103] in emoluments, the Chiefs warned that if national service was abolished the services could not meet Britain's present commitments.[104]

Later, the Secretary of State for War, Anthony Head, warned that any decision to terminate national service would have to be accompanied by a public declaration that the international situation might make it necessary to defer the termination of the programme. Measures would therefore have to be taken to allow for the possibility of increasing the national service intake should that be necessary. Attention focused more on the possibility of limiting the national service intake through a selective scheme than on terminating it completely. Monckton was forced to agree that

[101] DEFE 7/808, Eden to Monckton, 7 July 1956.
[102] DEFE 7/808, Powell to Monckton, 1 Oct. 1956.
[103] House of Commons, vol. 549, col. 1021, 28 Feb. 1956.
[104] DEFE 5/68, COS (56) 219, 7 June 1956.

In view of the need to consult N.A.T.O and the difficult implications of a decision to end national service, it was unlikely that anything definite could be said during the debates on the Defence Estimates next spring, although there would be pressure for a statement of government policy.[105]

Service objections towards the termination of national service were also reinforced at this time by discrepancies that were becoming apparent between a study on long-term Army manpower requirements in the event that national service was discontinued and figures presented by the Central Statistics Office on the size of an all-regular force which might be recruited following the abolition of conscription. According to Sir Gerald Templer's official biographer, the commission came up with an Army figure of 200,000 (excluding Ghurkas and locally enlisted personnel) and following pressure by Head, reduced this to 185,000. The gap between this figure and the Central Statistics Office maximum projection of Army recruitment of 165,000 could not be breached and deadlock remained until Head was replaced by Sandys in 1957.[106] It was, no doubt, these difficulties that led it to be stated in an internal memorandum within the Ministry of Defence that although national service would ultimately be terminated, 'It is clear that Ministers cannot be advised that it is safe now to take a decision not to renew the present call-up legislation after it expires on 31 December 1958.'[107] While at the same time it was also admitted that the termination of conscription would not necessarily be disastrous, Anthony Head's 20 December directive made no mention of the possibility of discontinuing the national service programme. Once again, it is possible to note the service tendency to agree on broad statements, but their failure to translate these into actual procurement and deployment decisions.

Thus, discussions on the national service programme in 1955–6 indicated that a strategic conception which emphasized nuclear weapons at the expense of conventional forces was in large measure being subordinated by the government's economic

[105] DEFE 7/808, Future of National Service, 4 Oct. 1956.
[106] Cloake, *Templer: Tiger of Malaya,* 358–9; also see DEFE 7/808, Wilson to Newling, 29 Nov. 1956.
[107] DEFE 7/808, memo to Powell, 30 Nov. 1956.

and political objectives, and being marginalized by the services in favour of a posture of multiple capabilities. Debates as to the size and roles of Britain's services in the thermonuclear era also indicated that the services were less than willing to alter their strategic conceptions to take account of new considerations. British statements in international forums had yet to be matched by actions on the level of decision-making.

With regard to the issues of war preparation priorities, economic savings, and varying service conceptions, it would have been possible—to paraphrase Warner Schilling[108]—for a policy-maker to have gone to sleep in mid-1955, risen in mid-1956, and resumed the debate without much sense of loss or disorientation. The slow progress towards economic reductions that occurred during 1955 was mirrored in the 1956 discussions. The problems encountered in imposing strategic conceptions on disparate service inclinations during the 1955 LTDP was repeated during the 1956 Policy Review. The frustrations expressed by the Minister of Defence and his associates in 1955 were restated with added vigour during 1956. The arguments put forward by the Navy in 1955 for broken-backed forces resurfaced in the 1956 discussions, as did the Army's demands for global war forces.

Consequently, in 1955–6—similarly to the case of the growing emphasis on nuclear weapons in the context of alliance commitments—when it came to specific British force programming exercises there was reflected a definite sense of policy continuity. In this case, however, it was not a continuity that seemed to be consistently progressing without obstacles or serious reservations towards the type of policies announced in the Sandys White Paper of 1957—at least not at the speed that would have made their expression inevitable in the first few months of 1957. In the years 1955–6 it did not appear that the superimposition of a conventional strategy on a nuclear one in the form of the retention of large forces for purposes of participation in some form of 'broken-backed' phase during global war was on the verge of being immediately discarded.

---

[108] W. R. Schilling, 'US Strategic Nuclear Concepts in the 1970s', *International Security*, 6, No. 2 (1981), 48–79.

Nowhere is this clearer than in connection with the question of national service. While the 1957 decision to terminate conscription was the culmination of a trend in thinking that had been present prior to 1957, this was not the only trend, nor necessarily the dominant one amongst the services. Service pressures to maintain at least some form of national service— the very basis of a posture of multiple capabilities—were undeniably strong. In the context of differences between declaratory and action/procurement policies, it was easier for the service departments to agree to the principle of termination than on an actual date for such a policy to commence. The problem was exacerbated because arguments to end the draft were framed mainly in political and economic terms. Thus, when the services sought to justify the retention of the programme on the basis of a strategic conception that paid little regard to the implications of thermonuclear weapons for conventional forces, in many cases this tended to go unchallenged. Furthermore, the nature of the decision-making process enabled the services to resist even the economic and political arguments put forward against continuing conscription. Thus, the continuity of policy in 1955–6 is underlined and, as shall be noted, the break between the years 1955–6 on the one hand, and 1957 on the other, is further exposed.

Of course, it can be argued that the period under discussion is so narrow that little change is to be expected. But this does not counter the rebuttal that the 1957 White Paper discussions took place immediately thereafter and then there were major changes. Indeed, had the policy-maker who had fallen asleep in mid-1955 woken in mid-1957 he would have noted substantial changes in both the substance of policy, the process of decision-making, and the climate of opinion.

At the beginning of this study, the 'New Look' was defined as having two distinct components, one to do with the balance of nuclear to conventional power and the other associated with the purposes of the deterrent power itself. Having noted the difficulties encountered during 1955–6 with regard to reorientating force posture away from a stance of multiple capabilities, logically the next question becomes whether such difficulties were also accompanied by problems in the area of defining the objectives of Britain's deterrent. Specifically, did the 1957 stress on the independence of Britain's deterrent force have firm foundations in the evolution of policies during 1955 and 1956 or were the complexities and inconsistencies that manifested themselves in the conventional–nuclear balance discussions also present in this framework?

# 4

## The Nuclear Deterrent 1955–1956
### Moving Towards Independence?

BEFORE the House of Commons in March 1955, Prime Minister Churchill outlined the reasons why Britain required an independent deterrent force:

> Unless we make a contribution of our own . . . we cannot be sure that in an emergency the resources of other powers would be planned exactly as we would wish, or that the targets which would threaten us most would be given what we consider the necessary priority . . .[1]

Through this pronouncement Churchill was reflecting the continuity of rationale that had underwritten the acquisition by Britain of nuclear weapons for over a decade. In retrospect, it also seems to be one more declaratory step in the move to the Sandys 1957 White Paper's emphasis on Britain's independent deterrent posture. Indeed, it is on the basis of such statements that it is claimed in much of the existing writings on the 1957 White Paper that the emphasis of the document on the independence of Britain's deterrent was the culmination of processes and tendencies already prevalent in British strategic planning.

   While A. J. R. Groom has referred to the British tendency for conceiving of nuclear weapons separately from their delivery systems,[2] it was nevertheless clear to the Eden administration that deterrence was inextricably linked to the credibility of the delivery force. The problem was to determine the size and shape of that force during a period of economic stringency. Decisions had to be taken soon because in 1955 the first Valiants began entering service and the expectation was that the more capable Vulcans would be operational in 1957, and

---

[1] House of Commons, vol. 537, col. 1897, 1 Mar. 1955.
[2] A. J. R. Groom, *British Thinking About Nuclear Weapons* (London, 1974), 36–7.

the Victor squadrons combat ready in 1958.[3] Furthermore, this force would have to be integrated with the Blue Streak ballistic missile project, the roots of which could be traced to a 1954 agreement with the Americans. Thus, the period 1955–6 is a very good one to begin testing the validity of the hypothesis that there is a continuity in the purposes of British nuclear strategic planning during the mid-1950s and that this continuity is reflected in a consistent move towards an independent deterrent force posture.

The first problem to take note of is that of the difference between declaratory and procurement/action policy. For, while there was a growing declaratory emphasis on the importance of Britain's nuclear force in the context of her strategic planning, during the period of the Eden administration the planned deterrent force was drastically cut back with strategic considerations in many cases apparently subordinated to economic ones. Secondly, both on the declaratory level and in private there was often little agreement on the purposes of this deterrent power as reflected in the debates over what the size of Britain's bomber force should be and when and in what manner it could be employed. Central to these discussions was the actual meaning British policy-makers attached to the concept of independence with specific reference to the relationship of the United Kingdom's nuclear force and that of the United States.

The question is thus raised whether the available documents of the period are able to enlighten us as to some of the varied meanings British defence officials attached to the concept of independence. Also of interest is the issue of how these problems manifested themselves in the ongoing debates amongst the services and between the services and the Ministry of Defence.

## The V-bomber Debate

*Competing criteria for determining force size*

An analysis of the documents reveals that strategic and doctrinal guidelines for determining specific bomber force levels were not

---

[3] For general discussions of the V-bomber force see S. Menaul, *Countdown: Britain's Strategic Nuclear Force* (London, 1980) and A. Brookes, *V-Force: The History of Britain's Airborne Deterrent* (London, 1982).

always explicit and were often ambiguous and contradictory. In a JPS paper discussed by the Chiefs in July 1955, it was stated that the allied bomber force

must be sufficiently large to continue to convince the Russians that aggression would result in the devastation of their country. At the moment the whole Primary deterrent is provided by the United States Strategic Air Command. Our contribution should not absorb an undue share of the Defence Vote but it must be big enough for the United Kingdom to have a say in Allied strategic policy. The important thing is that allied research should always keep our means of delivery ahead of the enemy and of his means of defence, and that our selection of the means of delivery should be governed by its being the most effective and economical available.[4]

What can be noted is the presence of three competing criteria for determining force levels: (1) political criteria—the relationship between force size and political influence (the need to influence the United States and also to become a 'respected member of the H-club');[5] (2) military criteria—the relationship of force size to operational requirements; and (3) budgetary criteria—the need to secure financial savings. The potential for contradictory policies arose from the attempt to limit spending while at the same time maintaining an undefined level of military and political sufficiency.

At one stage military planners appeared to attempt to resolve this dilemma by claiming that if reductions were to be made in the planned force level, then cuts should be made in quantity not quality.[6] This solved little (numbers were not specified) and was questionable economically (it was debatable whether cuts in units deployed would secure greater savings than cuts in research and development) as well as militarily (if the growing Soviet defence systems were to be breached then numbers, too, were important). In addition, if Britain wished to maintain influence over the United States in the making of strategic policy and the taking of political decisions then, relative to SAC, Bomber Command force levels could not be allowed to drop, assuming—as British decision-makers seemed to assume —that the British nuclear force did, in fact, influence the

[4] DEFE 4/78, JP (55) 67 (Final) discussed at COS 60 (55) 2, 22 July 1955.
[5] DEFE 4/78, COS 56 (55) 1 discussion of JP (55) 61 (Final), 12 July 1955.
[6] DEFE 4/78, JP (55) 67 (Final) discussed at COS 60 (55) 2, 22 July 1955.

Americans. This was all going to be even truer if the goal was to move Britain's force from being simply a part of the allied deterrent to a more independent posture. Of course, had there been consensus that the sole objective of procurement and deployment policy was the establishment of a British finite deterrent force—that is a force with the ability to destroy a very limited set of Soviet cities—then the pressures of economic stringency and political/military sufficiency could have been satisfactorily resolved. However, an analysis of the available documents reveals that there was no agreement on the requirements of such a capability and, more significantly, British policy-makers were not willing to relate procurement and deployment solely to minimum countervalue objectives. As shall be noted, the ability to target a set of enemy military installations remained an important consideration in Britain's operational planning and targeting deliberations. This further helped complicate attempts to reduce the size of the planned bomber force.

The increased destructive power of thermonuclear weapons could have legitimized a reduction in V-bomber procurement. According to a study by Malone, in 1954 the British government determined that the advent of the megaton warhead allowed for a cutback in V-bomber procurement to 180 units.[7] However, as late as the end of April 1955, the Minister of Defence informed the Defence Committee that Air Ministry plans called for the purchase of 327 aircraft in order to build up a front-line strength of 240 by 1958/9. He stated that orders for 95 Valiants, 65 Vulcans, and 49 Victors had already been placed. To complete the build-up, the output of Vulcans and Victors would have to be increased from a combined figure of four a month (which would have resulted in a force of 144 by 1958) to one of nine a month.[8]

If thermonuclear weapons led British policy-makers to believe that the United Kingdom's strategic and political goals could be achieved by a smaller bomber force, then surely by April 1955 this view should have been increasingly reflected in interdepartmental discussions? After all, Eden claims in his autobiography that the decision to produce the H-bomb had

[7] P. Malone, *The British Nuclear Deterrent* (London, 1984), 88.
[8] CAB 131/16, DC (55) 7, 28 Apr. 1955.

been taken in 1954 and Pierre has shown that this decision was based on research going back to 1952. Nevertheless, in the summer of 1955, Selwyn Lloyd remained attached to the figure of 240 bombers. He told the Defence Committee in April 1955 that in order to maintain the flow of production, further orders for V-bombers would have to be placed within the next two months. He stressed that if the full Air Ministry plan was to be put into operation, 123 aircraft remained to be ordered. While he admitted that the Air Ministry and the Ministry of Supply did not wish to commit themselves to ordering 240 units, this was because of the prospect that more advanced versions of the aircraft might be developed. The Minister was convinced of the need to make a contribution to the deterrent as quickly as technical and production considerations permitted. Even more significantly, he stated,

It is possible to argue that the enormous striking potential of these aircraft armed with nuclear weapons is such that the effect of reducing the front-line below 240, either on the deterrent or on the power to influence American policy, would not be vital. In neither sphere, however, can we afford to take any chances . . . [The medium bomber force] is by far the most important feature of our deterrent strength. It would be inconsistent and illogical, as well as, in my view unwise, not to build it up as soon as possible to the maximum practicable size.[9]

Selwyn Lloyd was adamant that it would not be prudent to reduce the proposed force below 240 units. He informed the Defence Committee that numbers and efficiency would both count in the American assessment of the British contribution. It would also have to be borne in mind that both the Americans and SACEUR were, as a result of negotiations on the provision of US aid to the RAF, aware of the Air Ministry's plan to provide for a front-line strength of 240 medium bombers.[10] Any attempt to reduce this figure was bound to cause acute political embarrassment. Finally, since perceptions of force strength were regarded as such a crucial factor in determining potential political influence, it could not, according to Selwyn Lloyd, be forgotten that 'in the case of long range bombers . . . our position by comparison with Russia and the United States is much better than in fighter aircraft'.[11]

[9] CAB 131/16, DC (55) 7, 28 Apr. 1955.
[10] Ibid.       [11] CAB 131/16, DC (55) 19, 8 July 1955.

On the basis of purely military criteria, a reduction in the planned force size was even more difficult. While a substantial British nuclear threat to the Soviet homeland was still dependent on the future deployment of operational bomber squadrons, planning would also have to proceed and take account of the growing number of Russian targets whose destruction was necessary for the survival of Britain (though not necessarily of such great concern to the United States). In April 1955, Selwyn Lloyd told the Defence Committee that the first objective of the British medium bomber force was the destruction of Soviet air bases from which nuclear attacks on Britain could be launched. The second objective would be the retardation of any Russian land offensive in Europe. Finally, the target list would also include attacks on other nuclear forces within the Soviet Union, though this role was regarded as clearly subordinate to the destruction of Soviet air bases. Strikes against cities would be carried out in conjunction with SAC.[12] It was certainly evident from Lloyd's statement that Britain hoped to conduct her nuclear strike operations together with the United States.

Although by 1955–6 the extent to which actual joint targeting plans had been finalized with the Americans is unclear, throughout this period attempts had certainly been made to improve the prospects for joint strategic planning with the United States. Following a series of bilateral agreements signed in 1955—agreements which included the exchange of war planning information—Bomber Command had increasingly been privy to information on aspects of US strategic targeting. An agreement at the Chiefs of Staff level aimed at facilitating Anglo-American nuclear strategic co-ordination was reached at the end of 1956 and ratified by Duncan Sandys in early 1957.[13] The degree of finalized planning aside, what is important to recognize is that this planned primary goal of fighting in conjunction with the United States and of attacking specific (in this case, counterforce and other countermilitary) targets in the context of a joint allied mission represented only a limited degree of independence.

---

[12] CAB 131/16, DC (55) 7, 28 Apr. 1955.

[13] Brookes maintains that the 1955 agreements led to combined targeting plans (Brookes, *V-Force*, 80–1) though the finalization of these plans was not immmediate (Freedman, 'Britain's Nuclear Targeting', in D. Ball and J. Richelson (eds.), *Strategic Nuclear Targeting* (Ithaca, 1986), 115.

That this independence would be manifested in terms of a specific British target set during combined allied attacks makes the term 'independence in concert', applicable to such a preferred option. True independent deterrence based on unilateral targeting of Soviet countervalue targets during operations conducted by Britain alone—what is termed in this study 'unilateral independence'—remained a constant but subordinate option to the more strategically and politically realistic alternative of joint allied action and limited counterforce targeting.

With the above set of counterforce objectives in mind, the decision as to the final size of the force would have to take cognizance of the 1954 Swinton Committee's estimate that in four or five years' time Britain could be faced by a possible 850 jet bombers operating from 40 permanent airfields with the option of using 150 others.[14] Since detailed target plans are unavailable, it is difficult to assess how many of these 190 airfields were targeted and what percentage were assigned to Britain's Canberra light bomber force stationed in Germany. Certainly the Canberras must have been included in any planned strike against these airfields as the RAF believed that with a 75 per cent serviceability rate, the 200 V-bomber force could only drop one hundred bombs in the first sortie.[15]

The point here is that if the RAF was seriously considering a pre-emptive strike on those counterforce targets that constituted the gravest threat to Britain alone, they could not have with equanimity allowed their forces to be substantially reduced. Such a position would have, of course, remained constant if the then planned 240 bombers were being matched solely to a number of Soviet cities to be attacked unilaterally—though obviously with a lesser degree of legitimacy given the more ambiguous requirements related to such a task. It is, in any event, not surprising that the Secretary of State for Air constantly urged the Defence Committee to state categorically that it accepted the figure of 240 aircraft as the final size of the planned medium bomber force. The Committee remained hesitant about committing itself so unequivocally. In May 1955, the Defence Committee agreed that for purposes of personnel and organizational planning, a final strength of 240 units could be

[14] CAB 129/71, C 54 (329), 3 Nov. 1954.
[15] DEFE 5/69, COS (56) 269, 11 July 1956.

assumed—though it reserved the right to alter this decision at a later date.[16]

Consequently, the reductions that took place in 1955–6 in the planned medium bomber force were not based primarily on the RAF's strategic reasoning. Rather, the reductions that occurred resulted more from costing exercises to which certainly the counterforce criterion of 'independence in concert' (and again, any possible implicit or explicit finite deterrence criterion based on a 240 force) were often subordinated. While this does not prove that Britain was uninterested in moving towards a posture of 'independence in concert' or 'unilateral independence' in 1955–6, it does show up the ambivalence with which Britain's actual policy was proceeding. For it was one thing to allow economic considerations to play a part in determining force levels, but another thing to do so at the expense of some of those very military and political considerations which provided the independent deterrent with its rationale.

### 1955–1956: from 240 to 180[17] medium bombers

That economic considerations were paramount in the decision to move from a planned force of 240 to one of 200 is indicated by the fact that proposals for such a reduction took place not in the immediate wake of American and Soviet demonstrations of thermonuclear power, nor even in the aftermath of Britain's decision to build the H-bomb, but rather in the context of the 1955 LTDP.

The Air Ministry entered into the LTDP negotiation intent upon maintaining its planned expansion of the medium bomber force to 240 aircraft.[18] The Ministry of Defence, however, insisted that the defence budget should not rise above £1,600 million and it was stressed that the RAF projected allocation of almost £570 million for 1956/7 be reduced. This would have involved a reduction of Bomber Command front-line force levels by 25 per cent to 180 aircraft. In a memorandum from Powell to Selwyn Lloyd, the figure of 180 medium bombers was mentioned as a final force level, but no explanation was given as

[16] CAB 131/16, DC 2 (55) 5, 2 May 1955.
[17] In the documents the numbers 180 and 184 often appear interchangeably.
[18] DEFE 7/963, fo. 41a, 14 July 1955.

to how this would relate to military and political objectives. On the contrary, what was stressed was the contribution that such a cut would make to the objective of realizing savings early on in the LTDP exercise.[19] Again, in a memorandum from the Minister of Defence to the services on 2 August, Selwyn Lloyd reaffirmed that the major objective of the policy review would be economic savings and one of the means would be a reduction in the planned front-line medium bomber force to 180 aircraft.[20] In a directive from the Minister to the services on 17 August, it was stated that economies made necessary a reduction in the medium bomber force to a level of 176. It was the Minister's view that a fundamental re-examination must take place not only of the front-line strength of the force but also the planned apportionment between the Valiants, Victors, Vulcans, and a new supersonic bomber—with the object, no doubt, being the sacrifice of sophistication and capability for financial savings.[21]

At a meeting between Selwyn Lloyd and the service ministers four weeks previously, discussion had focused on the size of the medium bomber force. The CAS, Sir William Dickson, in the face of hostility from the War Office and ambivalence from the Ministry of Defence, defended the figure of 240 bombers by linking this number to the political requirement of influencing US strategic bombing policy and the military requirement of attacking those Soviet targets which during the initial stage of global war were beyond the power of SAC. He was adamant that Britain's proposed contribution of 240 bombers was 'the minimum necessary'.[22] In reply, the Secretary of State for War, Anthony Head, stated that he doubted whether any Russian decision to start a major war would be influenced one way or another by the size of the British deterrent and he questioned whether the deterrent should receive priority above conventional capabilities. Selwyn Lloyd appears to have remained silent on this issue but expressed his commitment to the centrality of nuclear deterrence within British strategic planning and the need to give it priority within the context of research and development expenditure.[23]

[19] DEFE 7/963, Misc/m (55) 76, 2 Aug. 1955.
[20] DEFE 7/963, fo. 56a, 2 Aug. 1955.
[21] DEFE 7/964, fo. 1, 17 Aug. 1955.
[22] DEFE 7/963, Misc/m (55) 69, 12 July 1955.          [23] Ibid.

This debate reflects most distinctly the type of discussions which took place throughout 1955 and 1956 on this issue. Head's motives were obvious as he was struggling to contain attempts to reduce Army capabilities. His arguments do not suggest that he was opposed to an emphasis on nuclear deterrence, but they do tend to reveal his lack of sympathy for the requirements of an independent deterrent as defined by the RAF. It is possible to accept the argument that a Soviet decision to go to war would not be influenced by the size of the British contribution to the allied deterrent, while at the same time recognizing that absolute size was important in influencing American policy, for carrying out independent counterforce strikes against targets that most threatened the United Kingdom and for destroying significant numbers of Soviet cities should Britain find itself facing the Soviets alone. These issues provided much of the *raison d'être* of the British nuclear force during this period—issues which Head failed to address.

When Selwyn Lloyd sought an RAF ceiling of £545 million for 1956/7 and 1957/8,[24] the Air Ministry found itself forced to state that such a limit would involve reductions which would have 'catastrophic implications for the RAF'.[25] However, by the end of September 1955, the Air Ministry was convinced that in the face of Ministry of Defence pressures, it would have to make concessions. It did this by presenting two alternative projections for 1958/9: one of £527 million and one of £600 million. The starting point for choosing between them was—according to the Air Ministry—the recognition that the growth of Soviet nuclear strike power and the increasing importance of decisive action in the opening hours of a future war made it imperative to strengthen the allied deterrent. The crucial issue was that Britain was the only power capable of adding to the strike potential of SAC which, given the increasing number of potential Soviet targets, would in point of time be inadequate by itself.[26] It was claimed that the V-bomber force was the 'cardinal element'[27] of the British deterrent and the Air Ministry would be prepared to accept 200 bombers—a force that could

---

[24]  DEFE 7/963, Misc/m (55) 76, 2 Aug. 1955.
[25]  DEFE 7/964, Misc/m (55) 91, 14 Sept. 1955.
[26]  DEFE 7/964, Misc/P (55) 47, 30 Sept. 1955.
[27]  Ibid.

be purchased with the £600 million budget. A budget of £527 million, which would only allow for the procurement of 176 aircraft, was simply out of the question.

The fact that the Air Ministry was willing to compromise on 200 bombers can of course be used as evidence of the inconsistent manner in which the Air Ministry calculated minimal requirements (if 240 was regarded so strongly as the minimum, how could 200 then be acceptable?). On the other hand, it also attests to the severe economic constraints within which the Air Ministry was functioning and the Ministry's realization that compromise was necessary if a far worse situation was to be avoided.

As a primary strategic alternative the Ministry of Defence appears to have gravitated towards a circumscribed version of 'independence in concert'. Here, any ambitious counterforce or countervalue requirements were subordinated to a more economical policy whereby Britain's nuclear deterrent was firmly embedded in the framework of US strategic nuclear power acting both as a deterrent and an instrument of counterforce war fighting or countervalue destruction. What was important was not so much the actual numbers of British aircraft but that enough existed for the Americans to take note of Britain as a significant strategic actor. Thus Selwyn Lloyd's support for a reduction to 200 aircraft must have reflected his very strong economic concerns, the judgement that in the context of the overall allied nuclear deterrent force a 40-unit reduction actually meant little, and the belief that, in the final analysis, the new force would still, if needed, represent a credible independent deterrent.

By the end of 1955, the Air Ministry had managed to get the Defence Committee to state that it was

. . . highly desirable that the planned front-line strength of the Medium Bomber force should not be reduced below 200 aircraft in view of [this force's] exceptional importance both practically and in the eyes of other countries . . . [28]

While the possibility of securing some savings was not ruled out, it seemed unlikely that further reductions in the force would take place. This certainly seemed the case in view of the

[28] CAB 131/16, DC 13 (55) 1, 4 Nov. 1955.

nuclear focus of the 1956 White Paper. There it was stressed that it was essential for Britain to contribute to the allied deterrent 'commensurate with our standing as a World Power'.[29] In late February 1956, the new Minister of Defence, Walter Monckton, reaffirmed this emphasis when he explained to the House of Commons that while the budget projections for the RAF were only £517 million (£23 million less than the previous year) it would be wrong to infer that there had been any lowering of priority of the RAF.[30] Monckton was supported by the Secretary of State for Air, Nigel Birch, who told the House that 'The V-bombers are the spearhead both of the deterrent and of defence. Therefore they are more important than anything else.'[31] The size of the force was of significance as well and he stressed that

our V-bombers are not only our contribution to the deterrent but also our best hope of defence if war should come, simply because our best hope of defence would be to knock out the bases from which we were being attacked. Therefore, it is a fact that the V-bombers must have the first claim upon our resources . . .[32]

Experience in 1955, however, had led the Air Ministry to view with some suspicion public declaratory pronouncements. The lesson that had been learned was that while the government was prepared to make favourable statements with regard to the deterrent and the need to strengthen the medium bomber force, it was also interested in reducing planned force projections in a manner which, according to the Air Ministry, ran counter to British political and military interests. Consequently, it is possible to note that in the discussions that led up to the 1956 White Paper, the Air Ministry sought to strengthen the idea that the numbers in the force were of extreme importance and should not be reduced arbitrarily. Thus, the Air Ministry sought an alteration in an early draft of the White Paper which stated that

[Britain] must make a contribution to the allied deterrent which is consistent with our standing as a world power

[29] *Statement on Defence, 1956*, para. 8(1).
[30] House of Commons, vol. 549, col. 1022, 28 Feb. 1956.
[31] House of Commons, vol. 549, col. 1728, 5 Mar. 1956.
[32] Ibid. col. 1725.

to

[Britain] must make a contribution to the allied deterrent sufficient in quality and size to maintain our standing as a world power.[33]

Even more specifically, the Air Ministry informed the Ministry of Defence that

We feel it is important that we should spell out 'quality and size' because these contribute so much to the say we have in Allied Councils.[34]

The Air Ministry's concerns were not without foundation. By the summer of 1956, a new attack had begun on the planned size of the medium bomber force. A figure of 200 aircraft, which in 1955 Selwyn Lloyd had stated was the minimum that should be procured, was now regarded as excessive.

In February 1956, Walter Monckton expressed his intention of proceeding with the costing exercises which had been suspended in December 1955.[35] One of the major objectives of this new exercise was an attempt to reduce the size of Britain's contribution to the deterrent. On 8 March 1956, Monckton stated that

The Air Ministry's arguments have, as we know, been designed to justify a figure which had already been decided on for other reasons ... A decision to reduce the V-bomber force to 150 would save a useful sum and would, one suspects, make little difference to its deterrent value.[36]

Here Monckton appeared to be rejecting the Air Ministry's attempts to secure what he considered overly expensive capabilities. Rather, he preferred to express confidence in a much smaller force, one, given the thrust of the Minister's arguments, which was still viewed as primarily existing in the context of the allied deterrent, but which clearly would not match the minimal requirements of the RAF.

Significantly, the Chiefs, under pressure from the Ministry of Defence and the Defence Committee to find savings, and also

---

[33] AIR 19/848, memo by Penny, 13 Jan. 1956.
[34] AIR 19/848, Broadbent to Hanna, 13 Jan. 1956.
[35] DEFE 5/64, COS (56) 44, 2 Feb. 1956.
[36] DEFE 7/966, fo. 34, 8 Mar. 1956.

under pressure from their own services to prevent reductions in conventional forces and capabilities, resigned themselves to finding cuts in the medium bomber force. Consequently, a number of studies were undertaken by the Air Ministry which included reports on the military and financial effects of reducing the size of the planned medium bomber force. Specifically, there were considerations of alternative levels of front-line strengths—180, 150, and 120 bombers respectively.[37] By mid-July, the reports were ready for consideration by the Chiefs.

The centre-piece of the Air Ministry's argument was a strong rejection of any attempt to reduce the medium bomber force. The Air Ministry cited military and political considerations— considerations which the government had only a few months previously regarded as demanding a minimum force of 200 bombers. It pointed to the fact that NATO had already been informed that the ultimate size of the medium bomber force would be 200 instead of 240 aircraft and it was hinted that an announcement of any further reductions would cause major political problems. Indeed, the warning was given that 'To propose any further reduction either in quantity or quality at this critical time would show beyond doubt that our defence policy is based not on new military thinking but on economic expediency.'[38] Consequently, it was stressed that the deterrent should be built up without delay and it was also claimed that such a force would allow for economies in conventional weapons and manpower. It was also pointed out that the slow build-up of the V-bomber force was well known, had attracted criticism at home and abroad, and had seriously hindered joint planning with the United States which was not prepared to discuss the allocation of targets with the UK 'until we had a worthwhile operational force'. The report was adamant that

[The Americans would not] give us nuclear bombs although they have large stocks now and will almost certainly have more than their own forces could drop in the vital initial phase of a global war. This lack of co-ordination seriously weakens the overall value of the deterrent and thus the defence of this country and reduces our influence in N.A.T.O. affairs . . . The Americans would undoubtedly

---

[37] DEFE 5/69, COS (56) 234, 14 June 1956.
[38] DEFE 5/69, COS (56) 269, 11 July 1956.

regard 200 V-bombers as a worthwhile contribution to the deterrent but a smaller force would lose military significance disproportionately.[39]

The Chiefs were informed that not only would it be dangerous militarily to phase back the production of V-bombers, but also that it would lessen Britain's chances of getting NATO to place more reliance on nuclear forces and thereby allow the United Kingdom to withdraw substantial numbers of troops from Germany. The military and political costs would be out of all proportion to the financial savings to be secured.[40]

Most of these considerations were again reaffirmed in a letter from Dickson to Monckton in July 1956. For the reasons mentioned in the Air Ministry studies, Dickson was certain that a force of about 200 bombers was 'as near the mark as anyone can hope to get' and that a force of below 200 'might well be the last straw in our current difficulties over US Aid . . . from a wider standpoint it would certainly increase American suspicions that the mainspring of our new strategy is not military thinking but economic expediency'.[41] He stressed that the growth of the Soviet air force would diminish the effective striking power of SAC. This would have the result of increasing the value of the British contribution to the deterrent. In addition, Dickson pointed out that the more NATO continued to base its strategy on the 'tripwire concept', the more important the perception that the deterrent was effective. He concluded that these were military considerations of the greatest importance and that they pointed to an increase rather than a decrease in the size of the planned V-bomber force.[42]

Throughout the summer of 1956 the Air Ministry defended a 200-bomber force in the face of a concerted effort by the Ministry of Defence to secure savings at the expense of the nuclear deterrent. Little effort was made, however, to challenge the assumptions upon which the Air Ministry based its arguments with discussions again tending to focus mainly on economic considerations. In July 1956 the Air Council complained that the Ministry of Supply did not appear to be fully aware of

[39] Ibid. The emphasis on the 'vital initial phase of global war' is further indication of the intention to strike at counterforce targets, there being no strategic imperative to destroy Soviet cities at the outset of conflict.

[40] Ibid.

[41] AIR 19/855, Dickson to Monckton—undated but during July.          [42] Ibid.

the military and political implications of slowing down the build-up of the bomber force and that delay in the production of the V-bombers would only postpone costs.[43] Air Ministry studies compared the financial gains of reducing the V-bomber force with the strategic implications which, the Air Ministry believed, would result from such measures. It was demonstrated that a reduction in the planned procurement would mainly effect the Victors and Vulcans, particularly the most developed versions of these types which would constitute the most valuable element of the force. In addition, any attempt to delay the build-up of the bombers by curtailing the planned rate of production would increase unit costs and reduce the effective life of the deterrent. Specifically, a reduction to 120 bombers would involve cancelling orders already placed for about 25 Victors and Vulcans with the result being that savings would be reduced due to redundancy charges.[44]

The most significant finding of the financial analyses was that if the planned procurement of V-bombers was reduced to 184 then the total savings over the period stretching from 1957/8 to 1962/3 would be £22.5 million. Finally, if 120 aircraft were purchased, the total would be over £127 million.[45] According to the Air Ministry, if the planned force was reduced to 184, savings would be marginal. In addition, when this saving was placed alongside another study which sought to demonstrate the difference in forces to be declared to NATO between 1955 and 1959 under the varying assumptions of 248 and 200 units, the problem was seen to be even more significant. For, if only 200 bombers were built instead of the original 248 promised to NATO, then in 1956 there would be 52 aircraft less than originally planned in the force; in 1957 there would be 80 bombers less; in 1956, 56 bombers less and in 1959, 40 planes less.[46] Clearly, with a 184-unit force, the situation would be far worse.

The Ministry of Defence and the Chiefs of Staff Committee duly took note of these reports.[47] The Chiefs informed the

[43] AIR 19/855, Conclusions of Air Council Meeting, 15 (56), 5 July 1956.
[44] AIR 19/855, Dickson to Monckton—undated.
[45] AIR 19/855, Penny to Dickson, 16 July 1956.
[46] AIR 19/855, Howell to Dickson, 9 July 1956.
[47] DEFE 6/37, JP (56) 131, 13 July 1956.

Ministry of Defence that they had considered the findings of the Air Ministry but

find ourselves unable to comment upon the size of the force proposed by the Air Ministry until we are in possession of more information on future defence policy and expenditure. It would be invidious to pass judgement upon a single element of one of our Services in isolation.[48]

They maintained that it would be preferable for a manpower ceiling, and if necessary, a financial ceiling for defence to be laid down prior to any statement on their part concerning the size of the medium bomber force. This assertion was most probably motivated not by a desire to achieve financial savings as much as because the Chiefs could not agree on any major reductions in the bomber force. They could not agree because: (1) the Air Ministry was strongly opposed to any cuts; (2) the study on the size of the deterrent was one of the first studies to be completed under the 1956 Policy Review and the Chiefs clearly did not wish to set a precedent for making cuts in other areas. They were prepared to state that a financial ceiling should proceed discussions on reductions because they wished to influence the final figure and, ultimately, the programmes and capabilities to be cut or retained.

Walter Monckton was, however, not so hesitant. On 3 August, he wrote to Nigel Birch and told him that because of the Ministry of Defence's attempt to limit spending for 1958/9 to £1,450 million and the RAF share for that year to £505 million 'sweeping changes in the plans for the forces would have to take place'.[49] This would have to include a retardation of the build-up of the bomber force. Monckton certainly had not been impressed by the Air Ministry's reasoning. He chose, once again, not to address the strategic uses as outlined by the Air Ministry and preferred instead to concentrate on economic concerns. He did not seek to challenge the Air Ministry's arguments but focused instead on the broader issues of reducing the defence budget.

The alarm with which the Air Ministry greeted Monckton's directive was manifested in a memorandum by the VCAS in which the implications of the Minister's reasoning were analysed.

[48] DEFE 5/70, COS (56) 276, 18 July 1956.
[49] AIR 19/855, Monckton to Birch, 3 Aug. 1956.

It was demonstrated that a costing exercise based on 184 bombers together with a deceleration of the rate of build-up would have to be based on £350 million for 1958/9 and that it remained to be considered 'how we should illustrate the effects of a further reduction to the £505 million that the Minister of Defence would allocate to us in 1958/9'.[50] The exercise would have to be based on a V-bomber force of 152 units and a Victor/Vulcan production rate of five a month. This, of course, did not imply that the Air Ministry would have accepted such a procurement target or that it preferred cuts in the numbers of the planned V-bombers to cuts in other areas; rather, the Air Ministry seems to have thought that by choosing V-bombers to illustrate the financial implications of the Minister's directive, the Ministry of Defence would be deterred by the apparent implications from proceeding with these ideas.

However, if the Air Ministry thought it could scare the Ministry of Defence by stressing the dangers that were being created for Britain's nuclear force, it had badly underestimated the Ministry's resolve. In the last quarter of 1956, there seemed little interest outside the Air Ministry in building up the medium bomber force to 200 aircraft. In a memorandum to Walter Monckton from the Minister of Supply, Reginald Maudling, the latter stated that

The main deterrent to global war is the American nuclear capacity and any addition we can make to this cannot be more than marginal. Clearly, if we are to continue to develop megaton weapons, we must have some means of their delivery, but at the present moment we appear to be pursuing a greater number of alternatives than can be justified by our financial and technical resources.[51]

Maudling suggested that research and development should only continue on one improved version of the V-bomber (either the Vulcan or the Victor). Though he did not state anything specific about the ultimate size of the V-bomber force, Maudling

---

[50] AIR 19/855, Memo by VCAS, 8 Aug. 1955. Within the Air Ministry it was also stated that it would be wrong to consider a 184 force after having stressed that a larger amount represented the only acceptable minimum. It was felt that to do so would give support to the view 'that it was only necessary to apply pressure to the Air Ministry to bring about reductions'. AIR 19/855, AC 20 (56), 13 Sept. 1956.

[51] AIR 19/855, Maudling to Monckton quoted in letter from Broadbent to Birch, 10 Sept. 1956.

gave the strong impression that he would be prepared to support Monckton's call for a reduction in the planned force size.

When the Air Ministry presented its £505 million costing exercise in September, it had managed, by including cuts in Fighter Command, to plan on the basis of a medium bomber force of 184 aircraft. Nevertheless, it was categorically stated that while the exercise followed the lines laid down by Monckton's directive 'it should not be supposed that they are acceptable militarily or easy.to justify politically'.[52] The plan was to budget for £529 million in 1957/8 and £509 million in 1958/9. The Air Ministry stressed that there was a large uncertainty about these figures. It assumed a Victor/Vulcan production rate of five a month with research and development leading to a phase two version of both types. However, it was claimed that by 1959 only limited financial savings could be secured by any further reductions in the medium bomber force 'which are remotely consistent with the deterrent policy which we have presented to the Americans and Canadians as the basis for a reappraisal of NATO strategy'.[53] The Air Ministry stated that the deterrent would have to be strengthened if cuts in conventional forces were going to be made. Moreover, if reductions in the number of planned bombers were carried out it was 'bound to reflect on the sincerity of our intentions'.[54]

Of equal concern at this stage was the attempt by the Minister of Defence to cut down on the improved versions of the Victors and Vulcans. In a meeting of the Air Council on 13 September, it was agreed that the elimination of one type of Mark 2 V-bomber would make it impossible to build up a 'worthwhile' force by the end of 1959.[55] On 26 September, Nigel Birch told Monckton that for purposes of deterrence it was essential to continue research and development into both the Mark 2 versions of the V-bombers. He stated that unless research continued in all these areas, the rate of build-up of the force would be 'intolerably slow' and there was no certainty

---

[52] AIR 19/855, The RAF Programme 1957/8 and 1958/9, Annex B to AC (56) 79, undated.
[53] Ibid.
[54] Ibid.
[55] AIR 19/855, Conclusions of Air Council Meeting 20 (56), 13 Sept. 1956.

that if one Mark 2 was chosen and another given up, that the right one would be developed.[56] These protests met with some success and at a meeting between officials of the Air Ministry, Ministry of Supply, and Ministry of Defence in September, Maudling agreed that since little saving could be secured in 1958/9 by cancelling one of the Mark 2s, the development of both should proceed.[57] The Air Ministry had won one small battle.

But in the context of the wider and certainly far more important debate over the ultimate size of the V-bomber force, the Air Ministry was not so fortunate. At the end of October 1956, and in the wake of the Suez crisis, the new Minister of Defence, Anthony Head, began to investigate the issue of the planned build-up of the medium bomber force. The Air Ministry became increasingly concerned with what it regarded as the new Minister's lack of understanding about the requirements of nuclear deterrence. Following a meeting between Head and Air Ministry officials, it was stated that Head,

> by the way he put his questions, did not obtain a clear picture of the utilisation of the bomber force . . . He appeared to rundown the importance of the Kiloton [weapons] and he argued that only a small number of Megaton bombs would be needed.[58]

It was pointed out to the Minister that for purposes of deterrence bombers were more important than bombs. Yet Head remained unimpressed and 'raised the question of the number of Megaton bombs that could be dropped in war without risk of world destruction'.[59] Clearly, the new Minister of Defence was not overly sympathetic to the Air Ministry's desire to build up the medium bomber force to 200 aircraft. It is also significant that Head appears—to the RAF's consternation—to be thinking primarily in countervalue terms ('only a small number of Megaton bombs would be needed'). His rejection of kiloton weapons may have been a reference to counterforce capabilities. When in charge of the War Office, Head had certainly not been overly sympathetic to the RAF's definition if it limited counterforce requirements.

[56] AIR 19/855, Birch to Monckton, 26 Sept. 1956.
[57] AIR 19/855, Misc/m (56) 129—undated.
[58] AIR 19/855, Melville to Boyle, 29 Oct. 1956.          [59] Ibid.

On 20 December, shortly before his replacement by Duncan Sandys, Head wrote to Nigel Birch and informed him that in view of the major change that would be brought about in the size and shape of Britain's armed forces, the planned medium bomber force would be built up to 184 aircraft only.[60] No mention was made of the strategic or political consequences of such a move or of the strategic and political motivations behind such a step. Once again, strong economic considerations and the view that in the context of the joint Anglo-American deterrent force a reduction of sixteen aircraft meant little and, finally, that in the worst case scenario a 184 force could still serve as a credible British deterrent, must have influenced the decision.

In fact, on 18 December, the Chancellor of the Exchequer, Harold Macmillan, demanded that the V-force be reduced to 100 bombers only (the number which was presently on order)—a demand that had been rejected not solely because of any strategic reasoning but because it would effect the morale of the armed forces. Moreover, the Chancellor also pointed out that such a reduction would make it more difficult for the RAF to accept that there would be no more expenditure on a number of projects including, significantly, a supersonic bomber[61]—an aircraft that would have been the long-term future mainstay of any nuclear capable bomber force.

## The Intermediate Range Ballistic Missile (IRBM):[62] 1955–1956

In the United Kingdom work had begun on missiles in 1947, but this had been mainly on the surface-to-air type. Difficulties had been anticipated in directing a long range missile to its target and refining the atomic bomb down to warhead size. Thus, in May 1954, the then Minister of Supply, Duncan Sandys, reached an agreement with the Americans on joint missile development. When British development of Blue Streak began in 1956, it was recognized to be based on the Atlas

---

[60] AIR 19/855, Head to Birch, 20 Dec. 1956.
[61] CAB 130/122, GEN 564/1st meeting, 18 Dec. 1956 and GEN 564/2nd meeting, 19 Dec. 1956.
[62] In the documents both the terms Intermediate Range and Medium Range are sometimes used interchangeably.

missile.[63] Blue Streak was designed to have a range of 2,000 nautical miles and it was planned to have 15–20 available by 1965. Development and production costs were projected to be £70 million but the US was going to pay 15 per cent of the project.

The government announced its decision to proceed with the development of a long range ballistic missile in the 1955 White Paper. The White Paper stated that while the prime means of delivering nuclear weapons remained the medium bomber, it admitted that one day manned bombers could be replaced by ballistic missiles and that Britain was 'therefore working on the development of such a rocket as an addition to our deterrent strength'.[64] The 1956 White Paper contained similar assurances and the Minister of Supply, Reginald Maudling, emphasized the importance of such developments when he stated in the Commons that

It seems fundamental that eventually it will be very difficult for any manned aircraft to penetrate enemy defences, and the real weapon is likely to be a ballistic missile. If we are to develop a warhead of any kind, there is no sense in doing that unless we have the means to deliver it . . .[65]

Yet, despite these statements, during the period immediately prior to 1957 not only did the issue of the IRBM remain relative peripheral to the debate on the size and role of the deterrent (not surprising since the IRBM was still in its early stages of development) but the Air Ministry tended to be most ambivalent about this future centrepiece of Britain's independent deterrent force. For the RAF's 'organizational essence' was not necessarily coterminous with the procurement of this unmanned system nor therefore arguably with the future independence of Britain's deterrent. While the relative marginality of the issue during 1955–6 ensured that it did not unduly inform upon the more central debate on the medium bomber force, an analysis of its content serves to cast doubt on the contention of a consistent move towards an independent deterrent and underlines some

[63] See Groom, *British Thinking About Nuclear Weapons*, 124–6.
[64] *Statement on Defence, 1955*, para. 74.
[65] House of Commons, vol. 549, col. 1226, 29 Feb. 1956.

of the discontinuities in both the Air Ministry and Ministry of Defence's stance across the 1955–7 period.

Indeed, at a meeting of the Air Council in mid-September, it was agreed that the development of Blue Streak would involve a 'tremendous scientific effort' which would be of no value in any other field; and while there was no call to reduce the Blue Streak programme, the view was expressed that the stand-off bomb was a better weapon.[66] On 26 September, Nigel Birch wrote to the Minister of Defence and informed him that the planned supersonic bomber was not an alternative to the IRBM. On the contrary, they were complementary weapons. He was adamant that

If [the air-to-surface Blue Steel] fails and if OR330 [supersonic bomber] is not developed, we will find ourselves with no effective deterrent power until Blue Streak is successively developed and deployed operationally . . .[67]

Again, at a later meeting at the end of September, it was concluded that if presented with a choice between the OR330 and the ballistic missile, the Air Ministry would prefer the bomber.[68] The Air Ministry seemed more interested in relying on the Americans for the provision of missiles, but while hope was expressed that in exchange for giving the United States the right to station missiles in the UK, they would provide Britain with an IRBM system, the Air Ministry did not choose to address the argument that only a totally produced British system could form the basis of a truly independent British deterrent.[69]

What is evident is that in the year immediately prior to the 1957 White Paper, the Air Ministry did not lobby as hard as it might have for this aspect of the future independent British deterrent. It was the Defence Research Committee (DRPC) under Sir Frederick Brundrett, and not the Air Ministry, that proved to be the strongest supporter of the Blue Streak project. In July 1956, Brundrett reported that it was clear

---

[66] AIR 19/855, 21 (56), 19 Sept. 1956.

[67] AIR 19/855, Draft Letter from Birch to Monckton, 26 Sept. 1956.

[68] AIR 19/855, Misc/m (56) 129—undated but during September.

[69] Ibid. Talks with the United States over the deployment of American IRBMs in Britain had been going on during 1956. For a discussion of this point see Ch. 6.

that unless we change our present policy of maintaining continuously in being an effective contribution of our own to the strategic deterrent, we must retain in the programme the medium range ballistic missile.[70]

The report referred to the increasing vulnerability of the V-bomber force and claimed that 'only the IRBM holds out the hope of remaining invulnerable by 1970'.[71] It warned that if the UK dropped out of IRBM research it would mean the end of ballistic missile research in Britain. Brundrett also considered the possibility of acquiring a missile force from the United States but claimed that the range of the American Jupiter would be too small for British purposes. While the range of the Thor would just suffice, it would still not be enough to cover all the targets that the UK would be interested in covering. Furthermore, while a British warhead could be fitted to an American missile, the weight of the British warhead would reduce the range of the weapon. Finally, even if financial difficulties could be overcome, the Americans could not supply the UK with complete missiles until the McMahon Act was altered. In short, the report emphasized that as long as Britain remained committed to contributing to the deterrent, investment in the development of the IRBM must be continued. Two weeks later Brundrett reaffirmed these ideas when he told the Chiefs that a discontinuance of the IRBM programme and total reliance on the United States would be 'catastrophic'.[72]

Yet, the former CAS, and now Chairman of the Chiefs of Staff Committee, Sir William Dickson, viewed these claims with some circumspection and preferred rather to reflect Air Ministry concerns that the IRBM would come at the expense of the supersonic bomber. At a meeting of the Chiefs of Staff Committee on 25 September, which focused on the research and development programme, Dickson cast doubt on the wisdom of investing heavily on the Blue Streak project since it was quite possible that Britain might get IRBMs from the United States without having to pay for them.[73] Moreover, the support of the Ministry of Supply, Reginald Maudling, for this position was also secured. Maudling concurred with the Air Ministry's

[70] DEFE 5/69, COS (56) 265, 10 July 1956.
[71] Ibid.
[72] DEFE 4/88, COS 71 (56) 8 discussion of COS (56) 265, 24 July 1956.
[73] DEFE 4/90, COS 95 (56) 1 discussion of DRP/P (56) 42, 25 Sept. 1956.

views when he stated that while he supported continued work on Blue Streak, he, too, preferred to underline the merits of the supersonic bomber. He underlined the limitations of IRBMs when he demonstrated that: (1) an IRBM could not be accurate enough with anything other than a megaton warhead and it therefore could not be used in a limited war; (2) reconnaissance of the results of a ballistic missile attack would have to be carried out by manned aircraft; (3) ballistic missiles could not be used to attack enemy fleets.[74] These views had also been expressed to Monckton when Maudling had written to him two weeks earlier that

We are some five years behind the American's development of ballistic missiles and it seems probable that they will ask leave to station some of their ballistic missiles in this country. In these circumstances, for us to go ahead with such missiles appears to be unjustifiable duplication of effort.[75]

Yet, in December 1956, Anthony Head appeared to have paid more attention to the urging of Sir Frederick Brundrett than to that of Dickson or Maudling. Thus, Head's December directive stated that research and development on the supersonic bomber would be discontinued while that on Blue Streak would remain in place.[76] The Ministry of Defence was here certainly faced with a problem, because, on the one hand, it seems to have recognized that in the long term the deterrent would have to be based on the IRBM, while on the other hand, it had to deal with an Air Ministry and Ministry of Supply which had a number of reservations about a project which interfered with its acquisition of its preferred *manned* bombers. At the same time, however, it is not clear whether the Ministry of Defence's attachment to continued IRBM research was primarily motivated by a clear commitment to procure a capability for 'unilateral independence' or simply because of some broad notion that missiles would in the future form the basis of a delivery capability—whether or not that capability would form part of a truly independent force. Once more, there appears in the 1955–6 period to have been less of an irrevocable move to acquire an

[74] Ibid.
[75] AIR 19/855, Maudling to Monckton, 10 Sept. 1956.
[76] AIR 19/855, Head to Birch, 20 Dec. 1956.

independent deterrent capability than a confusion of motivations.

## Defending the Deterrent? 1955–1956

While deterrence should not be defined solely by narrow
technical criteria, it can be argued that strategic stability is very
much a function of attacker to target ratios and the extent to
which a country's second strike force exceeds the minimum
considered necessary. These points were central to Albert
Wohlstetter's argument that deterrence is not automatic, that
it is essentially a very delicate process, and that the delivery of a
second strike could only be assumed through measures aimed
at decreasing the vulnerability of delivery vehicles.[77] Although
Wohlstetter's article, 'The Delicate Balance of Terror', was
only published in 1959, as Gray has demonstrated, there had
been an interest throughout the middle half of the 1950s in
the requirements of a stable strategic balance.[78]

In the United Kingdom this concern manifested itself on two
levels. First, there was a recognition that thermonuclear weapons
made the air defence of Britain more difficult; secondly, there
was a growing concern regarding the necessity of defending the
V-bomber bases so as to ensure a credible second strike force.
Strengthening the deterrent was then crucially bound up with
defending the deterrent. A central question is what was the
effect of these concerns on the procurement of fighters and
surface-to-air guided weapons (SAGW) during 1955–6? This is
significant as it can be argued that if Britain was intent upon
acquiring what has been termed in this book a unilateral
independent deterrent capability (which would have required
British countervalue attacks most probably in a second strike
mode), then it is reasonable to assume that the means to protect
the deterrent would have received growing attention and additional resources.

The 1955 White Paper mentioned the dilemmas facing the
UK when it came to the question of air defence. It stressed the

---

[77] A. Wohlstetter, 'The Delicate Balance of Terror', *Foreign Affairs*, 37, No. 2 (1959),
211–34.

[78] See C. Gray, *Strategic Studies and Public Policy: The American Experience* (Lexington,
1982), Ch. 5.

difficulties inherent in a defence against thermonuclear weapons (even if only a few enemy bombers got through, damage would be massive), but it also stated that attempts were being made to improve these defences through an increase in the proportion of the force's all-weather fighters and high priority research into guided-missile technology.[79] Subsequently, on 4 August 1955, the Chiefs discussed a report by the Air Defence Committee on the development of the UK air defence system from 1960 until 1970. Its starting point was the recognition of the impossibility of preventing serious damage to Britain, but also of the necessity of protecting Britain's ability to retaliate. The major threat was perceived to derive from low level attacks by manned bombers carrying megaton or kiloton weapons. Due to the difficulties that the Russians were expected to face in the development of a long range missile, such a weapon was not expected until 1965. The Air Defence Committee admitted that

We cannot at present, envisage a defence against the ballistic rocket, although there are some indications that such a defence may eventually be possible. A direct defence of the base against the flying threat is, nevertheless, essential, in order to give our counter offensive every chance of success and to force the enemy to adopt increasingly expensive and technically advanced methods of nuclear delivery. We believe that it is within our power to build such a level of defence.[80]

For this purpose, the Air Ministry regarded the projected allocation of 576 fighters as the minimum necessary.[81] This was to be complemented by the deployment of the Stage 1 SAGW which, it claimed would provide 'a worthwhile deterrent to the interim threat' and its later replacement by the more capable Stage 2.[82]

The Ministry of Defence, however, was not overly receptive to these ambitions. At the beginning of August 1955, Selwyn

[79] *Statement on Defence, 1955*, paras. 44, 74.
[80] DEFE 5/60, COS (55) 185, 4 Aug. 1955.
[81] DEFE 7/964, Misc/P (55) 47, 30 Sept. 1955. As a result of the 1954 defence review the projected build-up of fighters had been reduced from 792 to 576.
[82] There were four stages of SAGW under development: Stages 1, 1½, 1¾, and 2— with each successive stage representing a more capable weapon system. In 1954 the Chiefs had agreed that Stage 1 would be produced for training purposes only. This decision had been influenced by the cost of the system relative to its efficacy against a nuclear attack supported by extensive electronic counter-measures. DEFE 5/60, COS (55) 192, 9 Aug. 1955.

Lloyd maintained that in the context of cost-cutting, he was prepared to take risks in the field of fighter defences. Indeed, he informed service ministers that these defences would have to be reduced by 15 per cent.[83] Thus from August, the Air Ministry found its force limit reduced to 488[84] (a drop of nearly 100 on the previous year's plans and over 300 from the 1953 plans) and continued attacks on its SAGW budget. Selwyn Lloyd preferred to maintain that Britain's 'real defence was the existence of the medium bomber force armed with nuclear weapons'.[85] He therefore did not address the issue of enhancing the deterrent raised by the Air Ministry. The Minister demonstrated that for him, deterrence was anything but delicate and the mere existence of a nuclear armed medium bomber force was enough to deter the Soviets. Air defences could thus be reduced, notwithstanding Dickson's constant assertion that British air defences 'added to the deterrent . . . by protecting our own medium bomber force from surprise attack'.[86]

1956 saw little change in the terms of the debate with major gaps between declaratory and action policy and between the Air Ministry's and the Ministry of Defence's position. On the one hand, not only did the 1956 White Paper promise improvements in air defences, but a document on long-term programming drawn up in February, was unequivocal that

An effective Fighter Command is an indispensable factor in our national policy of 'deterrence' . . . It follows that the more effective the allied air defences are known to be, the greater the degree of uncertainty for the potential aggressor and the more effective is our deterrent policy . . . Thus, if our national deterrent policy is going to be effective, it must include in its composition an efficient air defence system because: (a) without it, allied nuclear strikes could not be launched in time; (b) it puts the problem of success or failure squarely to the aggressor.[87]

The government seemed to be taking these ideas to heart when the Policy Review Committee told the Air Defence Committee to focus its attention on the defence of the V-

[83] DEFE 7/963, fo. 56a, 2 Aug. 1955.
[84] DEFE 7/963, Misc/m (55) 76, 2 Aug. 1955; also see DEFE 7/965, Misc/P (55) 53, 13 Oct. 1955.
[85] DEFE 7/965, Misc/m (55) 128—undated.        [86] Ibid.
[87] DEFE 5/65, Annex 3 to COS (56) 74, 14 Feb. 1956.

bomber bases. Nevertheless, from the Air Ministry's perspective, strategic considerations were still being subordinated to
economic ones as the Air Defence Committee was instructed to
limit its investigations to force levels of 400, 350, and 300
fighters respectively.[88] The Air Ministry's completed report on
the defence of the V-bomber bases thus carried with it strong
justifications for both the SAGW and fighter aircraft components
of the air defence system. Its centrepiece was the contention
that since early warning would only allow a third of the
V-bombers to be scrambled, it was essential

> to provide a degree of the defence that will allow the highest proportion
> of 'V' bombers to take off in time. Without any defence system the
> enemy could attack our airfields at will with much less sophisticated,
> and therefore cheaper, aircraft and weapons . . . [British air defence]
> not only uses up [enemy] resources which would be diverted to other
> purposes, but also adds appreciably to the deterrent by making the
> enemy uncertain whether he can stop our 'V' bombers taking off on
> their missions.[89]

The report indicated that from 1958 the UK would be threatened
by short range ballistic missiles and from 1960 by the medium
range types. While there existed no defence against these
weapons, the report stressed that manned bombers would still
represent the main threat, and against it a defence was possible.[90]
It was stated that until 1960 the main bomber threat to the UK
would remain the subsonic bomber. It was estimated that the
number of bombers that could be used against the UK were 250
light and 275 medium bombers. From 1960, the Soviets would
have a new bomber with a speed better than Mach 1.5. By 1965
this would be the main threat to Britain. The manned bomber
threat would be intensified with the introduction of propelled
guided bombs. The proper long-term defence against manned
bombers, consisted of SAGW in combination with long range
fighters. The minimum number of fighters necessary was put at
three to four for every bomber that had to be attacked (though
this could be reduced to one fighter should that aircraft be
armed with air-to-air missiles). Consequently, it was the Air
Ministry's contention that 450 fighters would be needed to

---

[88] DEFE 7/965, Misc/m (55) 48—undated.
[89] DEFE 5/69, COS (56) 262, 10 July 1956.          [90] Ibid.

inflict a 'deterrent level of casualties'. Significantly, it was also added that as the number of fighters was reduced below 450, the defensive value of the air defence system would deteriorate more rapidly than the direct ratio of the numbers would indicate. This was because the system became less flexible and the danger of saturation at any point increased.[91]

Unfortunately for the Air Ministry, Minister of Defence Monckton, similarly to his predecessor, Selwyn Lloyd, seemed unimpressed with this line of argument for protecting the basis of a successful second strike. Much to the chagrin of the RAF, fears of a 'defence gap' were relegated because air defence continued to be viewed as neither totally viable or cost-effective. Thus, in his 3 August directive, Monckton demanded an RAF budget for 1958/9 of £505 million and that there be 'a large reduction in the front line strength of Fighter Command'.[92] The Minister called for the cancellation of the Thin Wing Javelin fighter, even though he admitted this would lead to a gap between the time when the existing Thick Wing Javelin became inadequate and when new aircraft capable of dealing with the estimated Soviet threat came in to service. Concomitantly, he instructed the DRPC to limit research and development expenditure in 1958/9 to £175 million. This would have included cuts in the development of SAGW, the planned supersonic fighter (the OR 329), and the Saunders Roe (P. 177). Here, Minister of Supply Reginald Maudling, while still interested in the continued development of the OR 329 and the P. 177, strongly supported Monckton in his efforts to cut air defence expenditure.[93] He stressed that Britain was

continuing to spend too much on marginal improvements to an air defence which in fact can never be more than fractionally effective . . . So long as we continue to devote so much of our effort to military purposes in general and within that main compass to defensive weapons in particular, we will in my submission be continuing to waste our precious raw material.[94]

---

[91]  DEFE 5/69, COS (56) 262, 10 July 1956.

[92]  AIR 19/855, Monckton to Birch, 3 Aug. 1956.

[93]  CAB 131/17, DC (56) 14, 28 May 1956. Maudling, however, preferred to continue development of the supersonic fighter.

[94]  Ibid.

Not surprisingly, the Air Ministry viewed these pronouncements with growing concern. In an examination of the implications of the Minister's 3 August directive, it demonstrated that with a budget ceiling of £505 million, front-line fighters would have to be cut from 480 to 350. It was resolute that it would not be able with £505 million to produce even a 'defensive' façade capable of inspiring doubt in the minds of the Soviets about their capacity to neutralize a substantial proportion of the bombers before they could take off. Nor would it force them to go to the expense of developing sophisticated weapons before they contemplated an assault on British bases or upon American bases located in Britain.[95] The Air Ministry emphasized that the elimination of the OR 329 meant that the Javelin would never be replaced in the all-weather force by a British fighter. Moreover, if manned fighter development ended with the Javelin, the P. 1 (the eventual Lightning) or the P. 177 (later abandoned), the air defence of the UK and overseas theatres would have to depend mainly on SAGW. Concomitantly, SAGW should not be abandoned after Stage 1—an option that was regarded as 'disastrous' because of that stage's limited range and low resistance to electronic counter-measures.[96]

The Air Ministry's attachment to the OR 329 and extensive SAGW development continued throughout the latter part of 1956, but to little avail. It was agreed that Dickson would try to secure agreement to reinstate the OR 329 into the budget.[97] In turn, Birch informed Monckton that manned aircraft were a vital ingredient of air defence and if money could not be found by an increase in the defence budget, it should come at the expense of other defence projects.[98] He stated that it was totally unacceptable to reduce air defence forces to 300 aircraft (which would be the result of a £505 million budget allocation for 1958/9). He stressed that the Air Defence Committee had demonstrated that in order to defend the V-bomber bases, a minimum of 450 fighters were necessary. If the number of fighters were reduced below this figure the aircraft would have to be equipped with more sophisticated weapons, and the SAGW system

[95] AIR 19/855, Annex B to AC (56) 79—undated.
[96] AIR 19/855, AC (56) 85, 17 Sept. 1956.
[97] AIR 19/855, Dean to Birch, 25 Sept. 1956.
[98] AIR 19/855, Birch to Monckton, 26 Sept. 1956.

would have to be developed still further. In these circumstances, a front-line force of 300 was not possible before 1963. Birch reinforced his arguments with the words:

It is hard to envisage any programme of discussion with our allies which could lead to early acceptance by them of reductions in our front line on the scale and with the rapidity which it has been necessary to assume.[99]

For the Air Ministry this line of argument was little influenced by the Suez crisis, and at the beginning of November, Assistant Under Secretary of State R. Melville wrote that a reduction in fighter strength to 300 'would throw out the defence so obviously and dangerously that the Russians would conclude that they could launch attacks on our deterrent bases with a good prospect of success'.[100] However, Minister of Defence Anthony Head had to take a broader view of the post-Suez strategic and economic environment—one that emphasized economic considerations as well—and in his December directive he maintained that the existing manned fighter defences would have to be halved.[101] Head would also not support the OR 329 and SAGW beyond Stage 1¾.[102] The Air Ministry's position looked bleak indeed as its arguments for defending the deterrent—and thus Britain's independent second strike capability—were brushed aside.

One of the main problems in assessing the degree of progression in terms of nuclear deterrent policies across the 1955-7 period is the definition that British policy-makers attributed to the word 'independence'. Not only were Sandys and his predecessors in 1955-6 ambiguous in the meaning they gave this term, but analyses in the secondary literature, too, do not attempt to tackle this point in a consistent manner. A definition is necessary, however, for otherwise it is difficult to determine in what there was or was not continuity.

Two competing definitions were put forward in this chapter: (1) 'unilateral independence' whereby Britain would seek to

[99] AIR 19/855, The RAF Programme 1957/8 and 1958/9, undated.
[100] AIR 19/855, Melville to Chilver, 2 Nov. 1956.
[101] AIR 19/855, Head to Birch, 20 Dec. 1956.
[102] For these points see AIR 19/855, AUS (A) to CAS, 29 Oct. 1956.

deter the Soviet Union independently of the United States through the maintenance of a capability to deliver unacceptable damage to the USSR in the form of nuclear strikes against her cities; and (2) 'independence in concert', whereby Britain would maintain the capability pre-emptively (or possibly even under attack) to destroy her own Soviet targets which were regarded as specifically threatening to the UK in the context of a joint allied attack. The Swinton Report of 1954 had identified just under 200 of these targets. In fact there existed a third approach, essentially a variant of (2), which reflected a more limited definition of 'independence in concert'. This was one in which Britain would retain a nuclear capability for political reasons (to influence the United States and reinforce the United Kingdom's world power status) as well as, in the context of joint allied operations, for attacking targets considered most threatening to her. However, there was in this approach a greater willingness to place trust in the capabilities of SAC for dealing in the future with an ever-expanding Soviet target set of all types. The difference between this approach and (2) was one of degree, but by being somewhat less attached to specific target sets (as was the RAF) supporters of this position (such as the various Ministers of Defence) had a greater tolerance for economies and cuts in the planned force.

To repeat, however, none of the latter two options involved the complete rejection of the alternative of 'unilateral independence'. For, in the final analysis—especially in a situation of the growing vulnerability of the United States to Soviet nuclear attack—Britain could never rule out the eventuality of having to face the Soviets alone. Given such a possibility it would only have been prudent to have prepared for this, the very worst case scenario.

While options were neither articulated so explicitly in these terms, nor were totally exclusive, they did, nevertheless, reflect different proclivities amongst decision-makers. Specifically, during 1955–6 the debate focused mainly within the parameters of various degrees of interdependence with the United States and not on the competing attractions of true independence— that is 'unilateral independence' and total subordination to the Americans, or for that matter no nuclear force at all. The predominance of economic concerns, the imposing presence of

America's deterrent and the vulnerability of the United Kingdom to even a small Soviet nuclear attack meant that a limited version of 'independence in concert' ended up being the option which was preferred by many as the first priority for British nuclear strategic planning.

This has direct implications for the content of continuity across the years 1955-7. For an analysis of the documents of the 1955-6 period reveals that Britain was not matching her declaratory move towards greater emphasis on the nuclear deterrent with a priority list that placed 'unilateral independence' above action in conjunction with the United States; nor was she even pursuing procurement policies which could have provided her with the forces the RAF considered necessary for what may be termed a posture of 'independence in concert'. Indeed, throughout the 1955-6 period, the size of the medium bomber force was often treated by policy-makers outside the Air Ministry as a dependent variable with economy representing a major determining factor. It seems in many cases to have been implicit (and sometimes explicit) in the arguments of those who favoured reductions that, in the context of the joint Anglo-American deterrent, these reductions counted for little. The fact that with every reduction a limited counterforce capability of the type favoured by the RAF seemed more and more out of reach (as, of course, did any finite deterrence posture based on a 240-bomber force) reveals that during 1955-6 military requirements were often not addressed by British defence officials to the satisfaction of the Air Force.

The Air Ministry did not help the case for its, at least, limited definition of independence, when during 1956 it sometimes proved somewhat ambivalent about a British IRBM because of that weapon's threat to the preferred manned bombers. Arguably, this was an example of a service's parochialism (if not nostalgia) winning out over coherent strategic thinking, as there was little disagreement that missiles would form the basis of a future deterrent, independent or otherwise. As shall later be noted, by 1957 these hesitations were to be quickly overcome.

On the other hand, the Air Ministry's attachment to extensive air defences was a reflection of this same desire to protect its self-interest, but now acting as a driving force behind moves for enhancing Britain's ability to deliver an independent second strike. Although this was an expensive option which could not be totally effective—factors not denied by the Air Ministry—if the government was so keen on moving towards a truly independent capability, then the defence of the bomber bases should have received far greater attention than it in fact attained. For even marginal improvements were of significance for so central a capability of such limited size. To repeat an earlier assertion, the government's attitude makes most sense if the British deterrent was primarily viewed as existing and acting in the context of the Anglo-American relationship—declaratory pronouncements aside.

Thus, if there is to be a case for continuity across the 1955–7 period, it must be a continuity that was reflected not in a continuous move to 'unilateral independence' as a primary objective of policy, but towards some position that lay within the confines of 'independence in concert'.

# 5

## The Sandys White Paper of 1957

THAT the 1957 Defence White Paper represented not some new strategic departure but rather a reaffirmation of existing trends well established in British defence policy has been the underlying theme of most analyses of this document.[1] Yet, at the same time, it is clear that between January and April 1957, the new Minister of Defence, Duncan Sandys, brought about a revolution in British force posture. Despite the fact that there was nothing essentially new in his proposals, the inability of earlier occupants of Sandys's post to override service preferences highlights the scale of his achievement. For, in the final analysis, not only did Sandys impose upon British defence policy a sharper declaratory focus, but more significantly, he presented the services with little option other than for a substantial withdrawal from a posture of multiple capabilities. His achievement was to be a British 'New Look'—a policy reflecting greatly reduced reliance on manpower and a strong declaratory emphasis on Britain's burgeoning nuclear deterrent.

### The Immediate Impetuses behind the British 'New Look'

The Suez crisis provided the immediate backdrop and impetus for the shift of strategic emphasis announced by the Macmillan administration. Certainly, the failure of the British and French operation against Nasser was accompanied by a major domestic and international crisis for the embattled Conservative government. Public divisions at home over Britain's policy in the Middle East paralleled pressures on the United Kingdom within the Commonwealth and the United Nations and a deterioration in the all-important relationship with the United

---

[1] See Introduction.

States. The inability of Britain's military to secure its objectives against what was considered a second rate foe underlined the frailties of the United Kingdom's conventional military power, while Bulganin's threats and the American unwillingness to provide generalized support seemed to many to highlight the importance of independent nuclear deterrence. Perhaps most significantly, the economic strains that attended the Suez crisis—specifically the run on the pound and the fall in reserves —made policy-makers aware that the budget in general and the size and shape of the defence budget in particular would have to be radically amended.

Combined, the various strains helped facilitate a flux in perceptions and attitudes—a flux that manifested itself both on the level of public opinion and government. Traditional images of Britain's role as a world power in the international arena had been rudely shaken as had the electorate's confidence in the competence of the governing party. It was the immediate objective of the new Prime Minister Harold Macmillan—who replace the battered Eden in January 1957—to secure both his international and domestic fronts by restoring public confidence in the Conservative government and overseas faith in Britain's willingness and ability to function as an important actor on the world stage. To do this he made economic reform his first target with strategic policy the umbrella for his plan of expenditure restraints. Such an approach was regarded as imperative if the United Kingdom was to retain some semblance of her traditional stature within the international community and the Conservative Party its now tenuous position in government.

It was indeed fortuitous for the Conservatives that their loss of face at Suez could at least be partially offset by the perceived prestigiousness of the upcoming British thermonuclear test planned for mid-May 1957 on Christmas Island. There had been exceedingly good progress between the decision to develop the H-bomb and the test series—a timescale made short by the political imperative of demonstrating a thermonuclear capability and completing a test series before an international test ban took hold.

The United Kingdom's growing atomic weapons design know-how helped form a foundation for the new project with the Blue Danube and Red Beard nuclear bomb programmes

serving as the basis for the new design concepts.[2] Following the
May test a number of further explosions took place in 1957.
During this test series a prototype H-bomb and other big yield
designs were analysed as well as detonation systems and explosive
techniques. According to Simpson the first fully successful
megaton test took place on Christmas Island on 8 November
1957.[3]

It is clear that Macmillan's emphasis on thermonuclear
weapons helped assuage the right-wing of the Conservative
party—especially that segment of the party which according to
Epstein remained 'essentially unreconciled to a second place in
an American alliance or to internationalism in general'.[4] Disquiet
at Britain's poor military showing in Egypt and anger at the
American refusal to be more supportive created a natural
constituency within conservative ranks for a policy that emphasized Britain's nuclear independence. However, at the same
time, there were many in the Conservative Party—especially
the large grouping of retired military officers—who viewed the
weapon as a dangerous means whereby the government could
legitimize the reduction of conventional forces. These forces,
which were to be informally led by the former Minister of
Defence Anthony Head, were to make their presence felt after
the publication of the annual Defence White Paper.

In the post-Suez aftermath, Macmillan was also quick to
recognize the political advantages that could be gained from
splitting the Labour Party over the H-bomb issue.[5] The front
bench of the Labour Party had supported the development of
the H-bomb and in the immediate aftermath of Suez, while
roundly condemning the government, spokesman on defence
George Brown remained committed to the view that

if we still have visions of retaining influence in the world, if we still
have visions of ourselves as the centre, if no longer the mother of a
great Commonwealth of nations, and if we see ourselves influencing
the circumstances in which the deterrent may be used, I do not see
how we can do without it.[6]

---

[2] J. Simpson, *The Independent Nuclear State* (London, 1983), 104.
[3] Ibid. 244–5.
[4] Leon Epstein, *British Politics in the Suez Crisis* (Chicago, 1964), 55.
[5] Alistair Horne, *Macmillan, 1957–1986* (London, 1989), 52.
[6] House of Commons, vol. 564, col. 1293, 13 Feb. 1957.

Concomitantly, in a House of Commons debate on 1 April 1957 Labour Party leader Gaitskill was of the opinion that the United States may not in all circumstances be prepared to support Britain against Soviet nuclear blackmail. Consequently it was necessary for Britain to possess a nuclear deterrent capability.[7] Gaitskill was soon to shift his position to support the left wing of his party and push for a ban on nuclear testing, though Labour unease and confusion was only to become more visible following the publication of the Sandys White Paper in April and the British thermonuclear explosion in May.

Disquiet amongst the press and military professionals with regard to the adoption of a British 'New Look' force posture was also adumbrated in the immediate post-Suez period. For example, an editorial in *The Times* criticized the 'hollowness' of the claims put forward by those who expressed attachment to Britain's nuclear deterrent. It was also stated that

As the nuclear stalemate between east and west approaches, the balance of power is likely to shift back towards conventional forces. In general, therefore, there is not time to make large reductions in our conventional strength . . .[8]

To the extent that these ideas were at the very least demanding a continuation of a posture of multiple capabilities with both a nuclear focus and large conventional forces, they could not be squared with Macmillan's and Sandys's emphasis on the need to achieve major economic savings.

Certainly, the exigencies of economic savings provided the most immediate and vital motivation. In his autobiography, Macmillan states that at the time of the formation of his administration he had come to the conclusion that a complete review of British defence policy was essential and that this review would have as its object the achievement of major economic savings. Already during the previous year he had warned that Britain was carrying 'two rifles' because compared to the continental European countries she was assigning about twice as large a share of her resources to defence.[9] During the

[7] House of Commons, vol. 568, col. 71, 1 Apr. 1957.
[8] *The Times*, 11 Dec. 1957.
[9] Speech before the Foreign Press Association in London, *Manchester Guardian*, 17 May 1956.

Suez crisis Chancellor of the Exchequer Macmillan reportedly presented the Cabinet with the alternatives of devaluation or cease-fire and in November the reserves fell by £100 million to stand at the end of the month at their lowest level since 1952.[10] On 4 November in order to restore home demand, the duty on petrol and diesel oil had been increased, a large drawing made on the UK quota with the International Monetary Fund, and further 'second line' reserves mobilized. While the drain on the reserves was halted, the economic survey for 1957 warned that the year would be dominated by balance of payments problems, that the current surplus was quite inadequate to enable the country to meet all its overseas commitments, that even if the terms of trade should improve, exports would still have to be increased, and that a considerable proportion of Britain's domestic product would have to be exported if the balance of payments situation was not to be worsened.

A major potential for exports was the metal producing industries which, as throughout the 1950s, were deprived of manpower and were having to devote a large part of their product to domestic military uses.[11] It was clear that this sector would have to be supplied with labour if Britain's balance of payments situation was to improve and her economy made more sound. That same month Macmillan had warned Minister of Defence Anthony Head in a November 1956 memorandum that Britain was facing the most difficult economic situation in her history and that substantial savings would have to be made in the defence budget. He reaffirmed the war planning priority list which placed emphasis on nuclear deterrence and the need to cut out 'all preparations for global war that we can without losing our power to influence world affairs or alienating our essential allies'.[12] Soon after coming to office the Prime Minister wrote to Lord Salisbury that discussions with the Governor of the Bank of England had made clear the necessity of reducing the defence budget in order to hold the value of the pound in the autumn. The point was that 'If we lose the pound, we lose

---

[10] For a discussion of the economic problems in the wake of the Suez crisis see A. Horne, *Macmillan, 1891–1956* (London, 1988), 442–3.
[11] For the economic survey produced at the beginning of 1957 see CAB 129/86, C (57) 65, 12 Mar. 1957.
[12] Quoted in Horne, *Macmillan, 1891–1956*, 47.

everything'.[13] The very day in January that Macmillan moved in to 10 Downing Street he demanded that Head agree to major economic and manpower cuts by that afternoon. Head's failure to do so allowed Macmillan to replace him with Churchill's son-in-law, the more aggressive Duncan Sandys.

In his earlier role as Minister of Defence and later as Chancellor of the Exchequer, Macmillan had witnessed the difficulties that the Ministry of Defence had encountered in imposing direction and discipline on service preferences. As noted, the 1955 and 1956 policy reviews had been long-running difficult affairs whose results were often ambiguous and whose implications were often less than decisive. A recognition of these problems had led the Minister of Defence, Anthony Head, to state just three weeks before his resignation in January 1957 that

> he was convinced that it was impracticable to achieve inter-Service agreement on a long-term programme. Attempts to do so in the past had merely resulted in short-term compromises which in the end had led to wasteful expenditure . . . In his view the outlines of a long-term defence programme and the allocation of resources between the Services should first be agreed by Minister of Defence with his senior colleagues . . .[14]

While the new Prime Minister did not have the time completely to overhaul the Ministry of Defence's position relative to the services, he was 'determined, by all the influence that I could bring to bear, to make the Minister of Defence's position as strong as it must be'.[15] The services were thus informed that Macmillan 'proposed to bring some reality to the task given the Minister of Defence under Section 1 of the Minister of Defence Act, 1946'.[16] On 18 January 1957, Macmillan issued a directive to the Chiefs and service heads outlining the responsibilities of the new Minister of Defence. It is clear from a reading of the document that the weight of influence in decision-making was being pushed decisively in the direction of the Ministry of Defence. It was stressed that the first goal of the Minister would be to draw up a new defence policy aimed at securing substantial reductions in both expenditure and manpower. He would then

---

[13] Ibid. 50.      [14] CAB 130/122, GEN 564/1st Meeting, 18 Dec. 1956.
[15] Macmillan, *Riding the Storm* (London, 1971), 245.      [16] Ibid.

have to prepare a plan which would reshape the armed forces in line with the new policy. The directive was furthermore explicit that the Minister of Defence would have authority to make decisions on all matters of policy influencing the shape, organization, size, and deployment of the armed forces. This would also apply to the issues of their supply, equipment, and pay as well as to research and development. Equally as significant was the point that if a service minister wished to make a proposal to the Prime Minister, the Defence Committee, or the Cabinet on any of the matters mentioned above, he would have to make it through the Minister of Defence himself.[17]

Sandys came to the post with a record indicating a predilection towards cost-cutting, reliance on nuclear deterrence and missiles, and a willingness to override service sensitivities. During the Second World War he had played a vital role in helping identify and destroy German missile sites. This experience had left a lasting impression on him to the extent that he considered himself well cognizant of the major changes taking place in the realm of military technology and aware of the natural conservativeness of the defence departments especially when it came to resisting change to their traditional and preferred roles and capabilities. During the Radical Review exercise of 1953 it was Sandys who had spearheaded the government's assault on the Navy's carrier fleet—an assault that may have succeeded had it not been for his ill health, but one which nevertheless left much ill feeling and resentment. Vice Chief of the Naval Staff, Sir William Davis, was adamant that Sandys had little appreciation of strategic problems and was out to secure rapid economic savings. He states that the new Minister of Defence had 'little underlying realisation of the strategical needs of the Country'[18] and that he did not 'have any strategical concept beyond the factor that in his opinion the atomic weapon was all important!'[19]

Davis's contention about Sandys's appreciation of strategic realities appeared to be only partly based on the fact that Sandys's strategic vision differed considerably from his. For Sandys's proclivity for quick results with the minimum of fuss

[17] CAB 131/18, D (57) 2, 18 Jan. 1957.
[18] *Unpublished Memoirs of Sir William Davis*, 787.
[19] Ibid. 789.

and opposition tended to indicate that he was often less concerned with the strategic coherence of his plans than that they should be quickly implemented. Indeed, it can be argued that throughout the period under study, it appears that Sandys's primary concern was not strategy as much as economy. For as A. J. R. Groom correctly notes, the decisions of this period were 'above all . . . motivated by notions of economy and prestige'.[20]

At a meeting of the Cabinet on 21 January, the Chancellor of the Exchequer, Peter Thorneycroft, forecast a budget deficit of over £500 million. He warned that Britain had mobilized nearly all the support for sterling which she could command and had very little left to meet future crises. Savings would immediately have to be sought in the fields of defence, civil, and public spending. The defence budget for 1957–8 was now projected at £1,550 million and it would have to be cut by a substantial amount at once. Sandys readily agreed with the view that the nation could not afford such a level of defence production and that it was crucial to reduce the burden it imposed on materials and skilled manpower. It was at this meeting that the new Minister of Defence promised substantial cuts in defence expenditure,[21] laying the basis for the British 'New Look'.

## The Nuclear Deterrent, Conventional Forces, and the 1957 White Paper Negotiations

While much of the focus of the secondary literature has tended to be on the aspects of nuclear policy in the 1957 White Paper, a reading of the relevant documents makes clear that manpower issues dominated discussions and it is there that the more revolutionary aspects of the Paper are to be found. Indeed, an analysis of the documentation concerning the nuclear deterrent in the context of the White Paper negotiations reinforces this assertion. While the Minister of Defence stated in a directive to the services in late February that Britain would play a part in preventing war 'by creating a British element of nuclear deterrent power',[22] there was no mention of the word independent or any

[20] A. J. R. Groom, *British Thinking About Nuclear Weapons* (London, 1974), 581.
[21] CAB 128/31, CC 2 (57) 3, 21 Jan. 1957; also see CAB 128/31, CC 5 (57) 2, 31 Jan. 1957 and CAB 128/31, CC 8 (57) 2, 2 Feb. 1957. [22] Ibid.

suggestion that the force be used in an independent manner. This whole area was left unexplored. Indeed, not only were discussions on nuclear weapons pushed to the side in the face of the far more pressing discussions on conventional force issues, but Sandys's approach to the subject demonstrated the Macmillan government's qualified attitude towards a British independent deterrent.

At the Defence Committee meeting of 27 February, Macmillan underlined the relative importance of conventional force issues as opposed to nuclear ones. Only following a lengthy discussion of manpower did the Prime Minister turn to the issue of nuclear weapons and then only to state that Britain would not use them other than in the context of a global war and in conjunction with the United States. In addition, Britain would not use tactical nuclear weapons except in wars in which the United States was engaged or was giving full support.[23] The Prime Minister thus clearly rejected the independent British use of nuclear weapons.

At the same time, he demonstrated the complexity of the issue at hand when he stated that 'We should, however, have within our control sufficient weapons to provide a deterrent influence independent of the United States'. The Prime Minister did not specify over whom this influence would be achieved or how the influence would be exercised though he did say that 'Our objective should be to remain a nuclear power and for this purpose we would need the capacity to make both atomic and hydrogen weapons and the means of delivering them'. Yet, when it came to actual force requirements he maintained that the number of kiloton and megaton bombs which we should produce 'would depend on further assessment of the costs involved'—an indication that economic as much as strategic considerations would determine the size of the force.

It is reasonable to assume that had Macmillan's and Sandys's focus been on further strengthening the nuclear deterrent at the expense of conventional force capabilities and conventional force levels (as opposed to allowing the importance of the deterrent to rise relative to conventional force levels merely as a result of cutbacks in the latter), then the Air Ministry would

[23] CAB 131/18, D 2 (57) 1, 27 Feb. 1957.

have greeted these ideas with satisfaction. Yet, the Air Ministry's attitude throughout the 1957 White Paper discussions was one of apprehension mixed with uncertainty. The problem was that for the Air Ministry, Sandys was not only intent upon seriously cutting back manned aircraft, but he also appeared in some instances to be weakening and not strengthening Britain's nuclear deterrent. If Sandys was keen on basing a new defence policy on the British deterrent he did not seem to be in a rush to bring these ideas to the notice of the services. Thus, at the beginning of March, Assistant Under Secretary of State for Air, R. H. Melville, complained to Powell that the Air Ministry was being asked to prepare a memorandum on the air estimates, but it had no idea what the Minister intended to say about the RAF's role in the White Paper.[24] In fact, when the first major draft of the White Paper was presented to the Chiefs and services on 12 March, while the manpower sections were there in detail, the paragraphs on the nuclear deterrent were as yet not ready.[25]

It appeared to the Air Ministry that Sandys was not intent upon shifting the focus from conventional forces to nuclear weapons, but mainly concerned with securing economic savings through a reduction of the former. Assistant Private Secretary K. C. Macdonald—who while not high on the bureaucratic chain was in this case setting out a position that was undoubtedly not confined to himself—wrote to Ward on 12 March expressing extreme displeasure with regard to Sandys's plans. Thus, according to Macdonald, the effect of the White Paper on the UK would be 'panic', on the services 'bad' and on the world 'shattering'. The only certain result of Sandys's ideas was that Britain would ultimately become a second class military, economic and political power. This perceived lack of interest on the part of the Minister of Defence in the nuclear deterrent was resulting in the defence of the UK being placed 'wholly in American hands'. It seemed to be Macdonald's view that Sandys was only implicitly relating nuclear weapons to conventional force levels. Consequently, there had to be a greater stress on nuclear weapons and this had to be tied to a time-scale

[24] AIR 19/849, Melville to Powell, 1 Mar. 1957.
[25] AIR 19/849, Draft B, 12 Mar. 1957.

of manpower rundown. The Assistant Secretary's warning was unequivocal:

A plan, better phased in manpower rundown and related in time-scale to new weapons would create [a] feeling of confidence. But even such a plan would require [a] most explicit demonstration that H.M.G. meant business both in going ahead with new weapons and improving conditions of Service people.[26]

These fears were reaffirmed by Air Ministry Permanent Under Secretary Maurice Dean, who told Ward on 14 March that nowhere in the present draft of the White Paper was there any mention of overall policy, priorities, or strategy.[27] As a result of this confusion the RAF was bound to suffer. Although the nuclear deterrent sections of the White Paper were still not ready, Assistant Chief of the Air Staff Earle was adamant that

It is difficult to know what general recommendation to make until we see the rest of the paper, but enough is already available to show that much of it is pretty puerile stuff which I thought would serve the Government badly with public opinion . . .[28]

In the second half of March, the Air Ministry found itself encouraging the Minister of Defence to strengthen further the nuclear focus of the White Paper. On 16 March, following a meeting between Ward and the Air Council, Ward's Private Secretary, Ewen Broadbent, wrote to the Ministry of Defence that paragraph B.17(a) of the 12 March Draft which stated that 'the reshaping and re-distribution of the armed forces, on the lines indicated above, will greatly reduce the military manpower required' was misleading because 'it is not reshaping or re-distribution but new policies and new scientific developments which will permit the major reductions in manpower to be made'.[29] Concomitantly, the Ministry of Defence was also informed that Sandys must strengthen his paragraph on the deterrent because the one the Air Ministry had seen gave the

---

[26] AIR 19/849, Macdonald to Ward, 12 Mar. 1957.

[27] AIR 19/849, Dean to Ward, 14 Mar. 1957. It is interesting to note that at this point Dean legitimized a British deterrent by stating that: 'Furthermore, the possession of nuclear strategic weapons and the means of delivering them may be the only means of preserving our superiority over the Germans'.

[28] AIR 8/2157, ACAS (P), 14 Mar. 1957.

[29] AIR 19/849, Broadbent to Forward, 16 Mar. 1957.

impression that Britain was almost wholly dependent upon the United States and 'it plays down the British element of the deterrent'.[30] This point was reaffirmed in discussions in March between Ward and Sandys, where once again, it was often the Secretary of State for Air, and not the Minister of Defence which appeared to underline the stress on Britain's deterrent and the independence of that deterrent. On 18 March, Ward wrote to Sandys that

You agreed at our meeting last Friday that we should strengthen [the nuclear deterrent paragraphs]. This has already been done to some extent but I still feel that in view of the importance of the deterrent as brought out in [the relevant paragraphs] and as also emphasised in all the recent talks with NATO, it is important not to play it down too much, I suggest therefore that we should delete the words 'an element of' and make the sentence read 'possess a nuclear deterrent of her own.'[31]

Arguably, the demand that Sandys should not 'play down too much' the focus on the deterrent does not seem to square with a view that his primary concern during the White Paper negotiations was to focus on nuclear deterrence and to emphasize Britain's independent deterrent capabilities. Of course, the Air Ministry could just have been overreacting to an aspect of policy that touched directly on its 'organizational essence'. Yet, at the same time, it should be recognized that Sandys was most concerned with getting his ideas on manpower accepted, and it was there that the main battles took place. For him, it was enough that the importance of the deterrent would rise relatively as the manpower basis of multiple capabilities was taken away. He had, however, no major disagreements with what the Air Ministry was saying and was therefore willing to accede to variations in declaratory intent. Thus, at least to an extent, the Air Ministry, by encouraging Sandys, helped strengthen the declaratory emphasis on independent nuclear deterrence.

The results of these discussions and the Minister of Defence's shifting position on the declaratory aspects associated with the deterrent can be noted in a comparison of a number of key

---

[30] AIR 19/849, Broadbent to Forward, 15 Mar. 1957. This draft could not be found at the Public Records Office.

[31] AIR 19/849, Ward to Sandys, 18 Mar. 1957.

paragraphs circulated before and after discussions and correspondence between Ward and Sandys in mid-March:

1. In a draft circulated for Cabinet discussion on 15 March,
Sandys and Powell had written:

(7)c Now and in the foreseeable future, the free world is almost wholly
dependent for its protection upon the nuclear power of the United
States.[32]

By 26 March, this had been replaced with the words

The free world is to-day mainly dependent for its protection upon the
nuclear capacity of the United States.[33]

The replacement of 'foreseeable future' with 'to-day' can be
seen as a shift away from the impression that the United States
would always provide such a capability and that Britain would
always reside under the US deterrent umbrella.

2. A draft circulated on 15 March stated that Britain should
'possess an element of nuclear deterrent power of her own'. By
26 March this had been replaced with the stronger sentence, 'it
is generally agreed that she should possess an appreciable
element of nuclear deterrent power of her own'.[34] Here Sandys
had gone some way towards meeting Ward's criticisms, but not
all the way. While no documents are available indicating that
Ward's demands that the White Paper include the sentence
that Britain must 'possess a nuclear deterrent of her own'[35] was
rejected this did not appear in Cmnd. 124. Arguably, such a
sentence would have greatly underlined the independence of
Britain's deterrent for the word 'element' tended to indicate
that Britain's deterrent was but part of a greater whole—in this
case the allied deterrent. Why Sandys did not include this
sentence is unclear but perhaps he rejected such an explicit
statement of independence because it was not in line with his or
Macmillan's thinking as expressed at the 27 February Defence
Committee meeting. This would support the contention that
during the White Paper negotiations, the Air Ministry was
sometimes more concerned about laying declaratory stress on
nuclear deterrence and unilateral independence than Sandys.

---

[32] CAB 129/86, C (57) 69, 15 Mar. 1957.
[33] CAB 129/86, C (57) 79, 26 Mar. 1957; also see Cmnd. 124, para. 15.
[34] Ibid.          [35] AIR 19/849, Ward to Sandys, 18 Mar. 1957.

3. Air Ministry pressure was also responsible for expanding the 15 March draft sentence that 'the means of delivery for these weapons is provided by the V-class' to that of

The means of delivering these weapons is provided by medium bombers of the V-class whose performance in speed and altitude is equal to that of any bomber aircraft now in service in any other country.[36]

Here the credibility of Britain's nuclear contribution was definitely reinforced.

4. Although it is difficult to assess from where the impetus derived, the following sentence appeared in the 26 March draft and not that of 15 March:

. . . in assessing the value of military effort, it must be remembered that, apart from the United States, Britain alone makes a contribution to the nuclear deterrent power upon which the peace of the world so largely rests.[37]

Again the aspect of independence received a boost with the result that at an Air Council meeting on 27 March, Ward could state that the latest proof was a 'considerable improvement'.[38]

5. The Air Ministry, however, did not give up in its attempt to lay added emphasis on the independence of Britain's nuclear force. There was still concern about the manner in which Sandys was presenting the Thor and Blue Streak missile issues in the White Paper.[39] In a meeting with Powell only two days before the White Paper was published, Ward told him that language must not be used in the White Paper which implied that Britain would look solely to the United States for ballistic rockets.[40] Powell appears to have agreed to this Air Ministry suggestion and he convinced Sandys to broaden the sentence dealing with missiles to read that 'agreement in principle for the supply of some missiles of the ballistic type had been reached with the United States'.[41] The key word here was 'some' which implied that not all weapons of this type would be acquired from the United States. The Air Ministry could thus be assured that the Blue Streak project was still secure.

[36] CAB 129/86, C (57) 79, 26 Mar. 1957.
[37] Ibid.
[38] AIR 19/849, AC (57) 8, 27 Mar. 1957.
[39] See next chapter.
[40] AIR 19/849, Ward to Boyle, 2 Apr. 1957.
[41] See Cmnd. 124, para. 16.

Two basic issues can be gleaned from the debate on the nuclear deterrent in the context of the White Paper discussions: (1) there seems to have been a difference of emphasis between what the Prime Minister and Minister of Defence were saying in the privacy of the Defence Committee and what was being said on the declaratory level of policy concerning the future independent role of Britain's nuclear deterrent; (2) there was an attempt by the Air Ministry to shift the focus of the declaratory expressions towards a greater emphasis on independent nuclear deterrence (unrelated to how that independence was actually defined).

It was because of Sandys's tendency to focus on the reduction of manpower spending without clearly elucidating how and when nuclear weapons would fill this gap that the Air Ministry, theoretically the greatest beneficiary of Sandys's nuclear focus, expressed deep concern over the wording of the White Paper. The wording of paragraphs and their inclusion was viewed as a matter of great significance as it was believed that declaratory expressions could ultimately help influence action policies. Certainly the shifts described above were not great and it can be reasonably argued that the differences were ultimately not large. However, on the level of declaratory policy—as the services and Sandys clearly recognized—each nuance carried with it the possibility for far broader implications on the level of procurement policy. Here, the Air Ministry thought it was strengthening the nuclear deterrent and the independent deterrent focus of the White Paper, while in fact it was merely broadening the gap between declaratory and action policy. That Sandys was prepared to accede, at least partly, to Air Ministry pressures, is testament to his desire to avoid extra battles with the service departments which were peripheral to the more pressing issues of economic savings and manpower reductions.

It must be recognized that Sandys approached the White Paper with the prime intention of setting out the basis for securing savings through manpower reductions. Of course he accepted that there must be a shift in stress from conventional to nuclear forces but he did not consciously attempt to unite the two major aspects of his policy into a consistent whole. From the papers available at the Public Records Office it appears that the focus on nuclear deterrence was sometimes more implicit than explicit in the 1957 White Paper negotiations and that Sandys seemed relatively uninterested at this time in outlining a coherent and systematic policy of British nuclear deterrence linked to other levels of British defence policy.

Arguably, given his style and approach to defence planning he would have reduced manpower anyway—nuclear weapons notwithstanding. This approach differed somewhat from the declaratory level where the link between manpower reductions and the focus on the nuclear deterrent was made more explicit. In a speech in the House of Commons on 17 April 1957 Minister of Labour and National Service Ian Macleod stated that, 'If we refuse to rely on the deterrent we cannot at the same time urge the abolition of National Service'.[42] This was reaffirmed by Macmillan who on the same day stressed that 'the end of conscription must depend upon the acceptance of nuclear weapons'.[43]

Yet there is little evidence that at the beginning of the White Paper negotiations there were major dicussions of the relation between the timing of British nuclear weapons deployment and cutbacks of conventional forces. Nor does there appear to have been a strong interest in the Ministry of Defence during 1957 for further increasing the *absolute* power of Britain's deterrent force beyond that already planned. On 28 February, for example, Powell spoke of the need for a 'moderate size [V-bomber] force (number undecided)'[44] but made no mention of the requirements of independent deterrence. Again, while he stated that the V-bombers would ultimately be replaced by ballistic missiles, he stressed that Britain would continue only a modest research programme into her own Blue Streak missile, while Thor missiles would be supplied and controlled by the United States. Moreover, despite attempts by the Air Ministry in 1955 and 1956 to stress the link between defence of the V-bomber bases and the credibility to the British deterrent, the Permanent Secretary warned that air defence forces would be reduced from 480 to 280 aircraft.[45]

---

[42] House of Commons, vol. 568, col. 1958, 17 Apr. 1957.
[43] House of Commons, vol. 568, col. 2040, 17 Apr. 1957.
[44] Ibid.
[45] 2nd TAF would also be reduced from 466 to 104 by 1961. See AIR 2/14712, Review of Defence Plans—Note by Minister of Defence, 22 Feb. 1957.

On 20 February, Powell underlined the main focus of the White Paper when he told the Permanent Under Secretaries of the defence departments that Sandys would attempt to terminate national service and set the total manpower ceiling at 380,000.[46] Again, following a special Cabinet meeting at Chequers on 23–4 February at which Sandys sought Cabinet approval for his defence plans, the services were issued with a directive in which it was apparent that the first goal would be the termination of national service—an objective to which all else would be subordinate. This would have direct economic implications in itself, as well as serving to undercut the basis on which conventional capabilities were constructed. Sandys was, as usual, direct:

In reviewing our defence plans, my starting point has been the Government's declared intention to end National Service as soon as practicable. For the purposes of this review, I have assumed that there would be no call-up later than 1960 and that consequently the last national serviceman would leave the forces in 1962.[47]

The target was to reduce spending from the total of £1,600 million in the defence estimates of 1956/7 to an annual figure of around £1,300 million. Although Sandys admitted that the costs of his reduced programme had not yet been established, he warned that if drastic economies were not instituted, defence spending would shortly rise to £2,000 million. 380,000 troops would have to suffice, this despite the fact that—as the Minister admitted—'[it] would appreciably affect our ability to exert military power in distant parts of the world and would inevitably reduce our influence in NATO, SEATO and the Baghdad alliance'.[48] The Minister was not explicitly arguing that nuclear weapons would fill this gap.

There was a similar thrust in the presentation given by Powell to the Permanent Under Secretaries of the service

---

[46] AIR 19/856, Extract from Minutes of Meeting of Permanent Secretaries, 20 Feb. 1957.

[47] AIR 2/14712, Review of Defence Plans by Minister of Defence, 22 Feb. 1957. Although this directive is dated 22 Feb., Sir Richard Powell is adamant that it was not sent to the services and Chiefs until after the meeting at Chequers on 24 Feb. or possibly after the Defence Committee meeting on 27 Feb.

[48] Ibid.

departments on 28 February.[49] A reading of this presentation
indicates that the proposed order of battle did not in itself mean
that Britain was to rely more heavily on the nuclear deterrent
other than in a relative sense—that is, there was still no clear
linkage between specific force reductions and numbers of nuclear
weapons and the timing of their deployment. While a balancing
of the one with the other would be too simplistic a formula to
measure the strategic coherence of Sandys's plans, the point is
that the two issues did seem very loosely connected. The
services were thus made well aware that the focus of the
forthcoming White Paper would be a reduction in manpower
and that their task would be to make use of the reduced force to
attain the old objectives. Before the Defence Committee on 27
February, Macmillan reaffirmed that the main objective of the
new defence policy was the reduction of the regular forces to
380,000 by the earliest practical date and that the economic
objective was an annual defence budget of £1,450 million, not
taking into account any contribution from the United States or
Germany.[50]

Nuclear issues continued to remain peripheral to the manpower debate and to the degree that it was included, the
services seemed to have reservations about the idea that nuclear
could replace conventional fire-power. Thus towards the end of
January, the Chiefs wished Sandys to be informed that even the
figure of 450,000 men for the armed forces (that is Minister of
Defence Anthony Head's plan presented towards the end of
1956) was not based on any study of strategic requirements.[51]
He was told that the Chiefs believed that while there might be
economic reasons for reducing the order of battle, 'in our
opinion there are no military or strategic grounds which justify
considerable reductions from the resources at present devoted
to United Kingdom defence'.[52] They went on to warn that the
reduction of Britain's forces to approximately half what they
were in 1954 would involve the country in serious risk.

In fact, despite the care and time the Chiefs allocated to the
Head plan during the first weeks of 1957, Sandys seems to have

---

[49] AIR 19/856, Extract From a Meeting of the Permanent Secretaries, 28 Feb. 1957.
[50] CAB 131/18, D 2 (57) 1, 27 Feb. 1957.
[51] DEFE 4/95, COS 8 (57) 4, 21 Jan. 1957.
[52] DEFE 5/73, COS (57) 34, 5 Feb. 1957.

ignored these studies and presented his February directive calling for a 380,000 force level on the basis of minimal consultation, let alone negotiation, with the Chiefs and service heads.[53]

The Chiefs appeared, in turn, to reaffirm their lack of confidence in the efficacy of nuclear weapons as replacements for conventional forces and their 'serious concern on the effect which [conventional force reductions] would have on the NATO, Baghdad Pact and the SEATO'. Concern was also expressed about the implications of a termination of national service on Britain's European allies.[54] The War Office also rejected out of hand the claim that with a figure of 165,000 men the United Kingdom could contribute 50,000 troops to BAOR in 1961— 43,000 being the more likely number.[55] The VCIGS, Sir William Oliver, also maintained that he was opposed to an early draft to the White Paper which he had seen because it made no mention of the Army's role in limited war, 'nor does it refer to their ultimate task of playing a part in global war should the deterrent fail'.[56] Indeed, even in the midst of the Sandys onslaught, the Army and the Navy remained attached to a concept of a long global war—the emphasis on nuclear weapons notwithstanding.

By the middle of March, Sandys and Powell were busy presenting the Chiefs and service heads with draft after draft (ultimately 13 major drafts) of the White Paper. At this stage, service and Chiefs of Staff opposition to the Minister's plans focused almost exclusively on the manpower issue with little attention being focused on Britain's nuclear weapons. The Chiefs preferred to attack the basis of Sandys's 'New Look' with the claim that the draft White Paper gave the impression that there were strategic reasons to support the government's proposed reductions when in fact this was not so and the motivations were primarily economic.

On 21 March, Dickson met with Sandys and expressed the Chiefs' dissatisfaction both with the substance of Sandys's proposals and the manner in which the Minister was going

---

[53] For Sandys's early presentation of his ideas to the House of Commons see House of Commons, vol. 564, cols. 1302–15, 13 Feb. 1957.

[54] DEFE 5/74, COS (57) 47, 22 Feb. 1957.

[55] AIR 19/849, War Office comments on the White Paper, 20 Mar. 1957.

[56] WO 32/17171, fo. 18a—undated.

about his task. Dickson explained to the Minister that the Chiefs regarded themselves constitutionally as the expert military advisers to the government—the clear implication being that they were not being treated as such. The Chairman of the COSC then painted a grim picture of the world situation and demonstrated that Sandys's proposed manpower cuts were extremely dangerous. He pointed to the growing Soviet and Chinese military potential and the increasing threat to all of Britain's alliances. Dickson also warned that the UK would have to take cognizance of growing threats to purely British interests. Finally, he once more reaffirmed the Chiefs' attachment to a 450,000 force armed with 'modern weapons'[57] thereby indicating that he would prefer both large nuclear *and* conventional forces.

True to form, Sandys quickly dismissed Dickson's complaints. He told him that British defence requirements could be divided into two parts: the first was the defence of purely British interests; the second was the contribution that the UK had to make to her defensive alliances. Sandys believed that the 380,000 force would be adequate for the first category; with regard to the second requirement, the Minister maintained that Britain's final force contribution would have to be determined in negotiation with her allies and that while 'military considerations come into this . . . the decision must be made on political and economic grounds'.[58] Sandys went on to state that he regarded a 375,000 force as being 'fair' and effective when compared with the military and economic potential of Britain's allies. Dickson was left with the clear impression that despite his objections, Sandys intended to proceed on the basis of a 380,000 force. Here, the Minister was clearly subordinating even his own strategic premisses to economic considerations.

On 27 March, Sandys made an effort to convince the Chiefs of the merits of his proposed order of battle—though it was evident from the outset that this was not a search for compromise on his part but a reaction to the criticisms that he had been ignoring the Chiefs. The basis for discussion was provided by the fifth proof of the White Paper which stated that the government believed that Britain could discharge her responsibilities

---

[57] ADM 205/114, Dickson to the Chiefs, 21 Mar. 1957.
[58] Ibid.

with an all-regular force but no mention was made of the Chiefs' lack of agreement.[59] Sandys informed the COSC of his confidence in an all-regular force of 375,000 being able to defend British colonies and protected areas, take part in limited overseas operations (i.e. in support of the Baghdad Pact or SEATO allies) and to 'make a fair contribution to the joint effort of NATO'. As far as Sandys was concerned, if NATO was to be strengthened conventionally, then the other partners must begin to carry a greater burden. He maintained that he did not think the conventional effort that Britain was now making would in any way determine whether a third world war would start or not. Then the Minister went on to state that although the resulting NATO force

would not be regarded as enough for safety, in his view they were sufficient to deter Soviet Russia from starting a nuclear war since she could attain her ends in other ways at much less risk to herself, e.g. by subversion in the Middle East and South East Asia. However, a greater probable danger was the potential commercial threat from Russia since, with her form of Government she could easily undertake a trade war.[60]

The Minister's ideas were here certainly somewhat confused. On one level he seemed unclear as to what he considered was actually deterring the Soviets from starting a global war: was it allied conventional or nuclear forces? Nor did he attempt to separate out the British and American nuclear contributions. On another level, he appeared to equate Soviet goals in the Middle East and the Far East with those in Europe, and he seemed to blur the Chiefs' careful distinctions between cold, limited, and global war. Here it must be recognized that what undoubtedly drove Sandys was not so much an explicit strategic formula as much as the issue of financial savings—thus his concern about a trade war. Consequently, while he patiently listened to the Chiefs' views, he was not prepared to change his approach. For him, the problem was now one of wording and presentation, not strategic rationales. He could only assure the Chiefs that it was not his intention to implicate them in the decision to terminate national service and reduce the armed

[59] ADM 205/114, C (57) 79, 26 Mar. 1957.
[60] ADM 205/114, COS 5 (57) 1, 27 Mar. 1957.

forces to 375,000. The wording of the White Paper could therefore be adjusted, but the Chiefs' appeals had otherwise fallen on deaf ears. Furthermore, the battle over the wording was not yet over and the Chiefs continued to believe that Sandys was still attempting to create the impression in the White Paper that there was general acceptance that Britain's commitments could be sustained with a 375,000 force.

Sandys, however, sought to move away from giving the impression that economic considerations came at the expense of military ones. Thus, the Chiefs' statement on the predominance of economic factors was ultimately replaced with the sentence,

Britain's influence in the world depends first and foremost on the health of her internal economy and the success of her export trade. Without these, military power cannot in the long run be supported. It is therefore in the true interests of defence that the claims of military expenditure should be considered in conjunction with the need to maintain the country's financial and economic strength.[61]

The Chiefs were furious that even their compromise position on the presentation had been ignored. At 3.30 p.m., 45 minutes before the Cabinet meeting on 28 March began, they met to discuss the matter. Mountbatten stressed how seriously he viewed the efforts 'to avoid the point the COS were making'.[62] At that meeting, Dickson did not relate the cuts to any increased emphasis on the strategic deterrent or tactical nuclear weapons but stated that

a reduction in the total strength of the forces to 375,000 could not be justified on strictly military grounds. The threat of communism had in no way diminished, and since the planned reduction in British forces would not, in the event, be counter-balanced by any comparable increases in the forces of the other countries in the Western Alliances, the total forces available for the defence of the free world would be reduced. Though no precise estimate could be given of the forces required for sound military planning, the further reduction now proposed . . . would result in a disproportionate loss of fighting units. The Chiefs of Staff therefore considered that it should be made clear

---

[61] Cmnd. 124, para. 6.
[62] ADM 205/114, COS 25 (57) 1, 28 Mar. 1957 in the White Paper discussions summary.

in the White Paper that the decision to reduce the forces eventually to 375,000 was dictated primarily by economic needs.[63]

Though the available documents do not describe any tensions at the Cabinet meeting, these must have been strong, because the Prime Minister, once having admitted that the question of manpower was the most important feature of the White Paper, stated that he, himself, would draft the relevant paragraphs, taking account of the concerns of the Chiefs of Staff.[64] To the satisfaction of the Chiefs, the problem seemed to be taken out of Sandys's hands. Consequently, a proof of the White Paper issued on 30 March stated in paragraph 46 that 'in the light of the need to maintain a balanced distribution of the national manpower, regular forces [of 375,000] constitute the objective which [the government] should seek ultimately to attain'.[65] At a meeting of the Chiefs of Staff Committee on 1 April, it was concluded that while this paragraph was far from satisfactory, it was open to different interpretations, and if the Chiefs were asked 'if they agreed with the paragraph they should be at liberty to say they did not'.[66]

Yet, by the 11 a.m. Cabinet meeting on the following day, it appears that Sandys had once again altered the relevant paragraph which now stated that the regular strength of the armed forces would by 1962 be between 350,000 and 400,000 men. Moreover, no mention was made of the relationship of economic to military criteria in determining this force level. The Chiefs reacted angrily, but once more to no avail.[67] At 5 p.m. on 3 April it was discovered that in the latest version of paragraph 46—a version which Sandys had no intention of circulating for agreement and of which there was only one copy in his private office—the sentence 'In the light of the need to maintain a balanced distribution of national resources . . .' had been omitted. It seemed that the Minister of Defence was continuing to circumvent the Chiefs' demand that they be distanced from the manpower proposals. At 5.30 p.m. Mountbatten made an

---

[63] ADM 205/114, the Defence White Paper discussions summary.
[64] Ibid.; also see CAB 128/31, CC 26 (57) 1, 28 Mar. 1957.
[65] CAB 129/86, C (57) 84, 1 Apr. 1957.
[66] ADM 205/114, the Defence White Paper discussions summary.
[67] ADM 205/114, CM 28 (57) 2, 2 Apr. 1957 in 1957 White Paper discussions summary.

urgent phone call to Dickson and demanded that the matter be investigated. Sandys, whose plans were now uncovered, agreed to alter the wording so as to imply that economic as much as strategic motivations lay behind the decision to cut manpower and terminate the national service programme. This was reflected in the final draft of paragraph 46 which appeared in Cmnd. 124.[68]

### The Navy, Nuclear Weapons, and Preparations for War during the 1957 White Paper Negotiations

During the White Paper negotiations of 1957, the services continued to attempt to contain Sandys through influencing the wording and inclusion of paragraphs in the White Paper. Thus, there was a long but losing battle supported by the Navy and fought by Chairman of the COSC Sir William Dickson to prevent the inclusion of paragraph 13 which stated that 'the overriding consideration in all military planning must be to prevent war rather than to prepare for it'[69]—thereby indicating the Navy's continued commitment to global war capabilities and its less than unqualified commitment to a policy primarily based on the threat of massive retaliation.

This rejection did not imply that the Navy—especially Mountbatten—was during 1957 uninterested in also moving towards a nuclear role in terms of propulsion or strike capabilities. Indeed, the Navy evinced a preference for pursuing such an option independently of the Americans. The staff requirements for a British nuclear submarine had been concluded in February 1957 with agreement reached with Vickers and investigations into enriched uranium cores begun at Harwell. By September, much to the RAF's consternation, the Navy was requesting reactor fuel for its programme from the same stock that was supplying the Air Force with its fissile material. Progress, however, remained slow but the Admiralty remained hesitant

---

[68] See Cmnd. 124, para. 46. As a result of these cuts, the Army would be reduced to 165,000 by 1962 of which 50,000 men would be in Germany, 12,000 in the Middle East (Cyprus, East Africa, and the Persian Gulf), 14,000 in the Far East (Malaya, Hong Kong, and Singapore), 8,5000 in transit, and 80,500 in the UK (of which 27,500 would be designated for the mobile strategic reserves).

[69] Cmnd. 124, para. 13, a point made by T. C. G. James.

about seeking help from the Americans as this they believed would jeopardize the independence of Britain's submarine programme.

However, in the context of Sandys's economic strategy of cost-cutting and his political strategy of closer alliance with the United States the Navy's independent pretensions, too, gave way to greater co-operation with the Americans. In June, twenty-five British engineers and nuclear scientists associated with the submarine project visited the United States. During First Lord Selkirk's visit to Washington in October, Admiral Rickover—in charge of America's nuclear submarine programme—gave the impression that the sale of US nuclear propulsion technology to the United Kingdom might be possible. The following month Rickover stated that the Royal Navy had to decide whether it was more interested in satisfying its pride with an independent project or moving as quickly as possible towards deploying a nuclear submarine.[70] Mountbatten was by now apparently convinced that co-operation with the Americans held the key to the future of Britain's naval nuclear programme and he readily agreed with Rickover that co-operation would be best for both countries.

Despite this interest in nuclear propulsion, in the context of the 1957 White Paper negotiations and throughout 1957, the Navy seemed more concerned about defending its conventional forces than about agreeing that a nuclear emphasis enabled conventional force reductions or even about pushing for itself a nuclear strike role. On assuming office in January, the new First Lord, Lord Selkirk, wrote to Sandys what in retrospect can only be regarded as a very optimistic brief.[71] The thrust of Selkirk's arguments was that Head's call for a 90,000 strong Navy (the so-called 90 Plan)—which the Navy had accepted—was itself problematic. Ships of all classes would be reduced, and significantly—from the point of global war capabilities—the supplementary and extended reserve fleets would be abolished by 1960/1. The First Lord went on to warn that such an inbalance was legitimate only because the Ministry of Defence's directive made the assumption that conventional preparations for global war were of a low priority. Selkirk

---

[70] E. Grove, *From Vanguard to Trident* (London, 1987), 231–2.
[71] AIR 19/856, Selkirk to Sandys, 14 Jan. 1957.

stressed that this was not a view held by the Navy and he was adamant that 'the only circumstances in which there will be no survival are if we plan on the basis that there can be none'.[72] Clearly, the Navy's commitment to the nuclear focus of the 1957 White Paper was less than unreserved—at least in terms of bargaining tactics.

The Navy also faced problems in relation to how the nuclear deterrent was being presented in the White Paper and the way that this related to their concept of broken-backed warfare. Prior to Macmillan's meeting with Eisenhower in March[73] Dickson circulated a draft paper to be used at the conference which stressed the centrality of the British contribution to the deterrent in the context of the Anglo-American relationship. Consequently, the Navy Director of Plans, E. D. G. Lewin informed Mountbatten,

If you agree with the proposition which [Dickson] makes you will be underwriting the importance of the . . . deterrent in a much more forthright manner than you have ever done before. If you consider that there is a chance of the President suggesting to the Prime Minister that we should drop out of the deterrent market, it would, from the long term Naval point of view, be very damaging if you were on the record as supporting our share of the deterrent as 'the most appropriate and effective' contribution which we could make with our limited resources.[74]

Lewin pressed this point home on 1 April when he wrote to the Navy's Parliamentary Secretary, Christopher Soames, that as a result of the large number of drafts of the White Paper, the connotations of the word 'deterrent' had become confused. He pointed out that in paragraph 1 it was stated that Britain must make a fair contribution to the allied deterrent to global war and to discharge her responsibilities in many parts of the world. Lewin maintained that here it was not clear whether what was meant was nuclear deterrence or nuclear forces plus conventional forces.[75] If it was only .nuclear deterrence then the statement, according to Lewin, was indefensible, since conventional forces which contributed to the prevention of global war could also be

---

[72] Ibid.  [73] See next chapter.
[74] ADM 205/114, Memo to Mountbatten, 21 Mar. 1957.
[75] ADM 205/114, Lewin to Soames, 1 Apr. 1957.

used in conventional operations during global war. Lewin was here supporting a broken-backed capability.

Equally as significant, it can be argued that if Sandys's focus in the White Paper negotiations had been primarily on the nuclear deterrent, then surely this should have been clear to all by the beginning of April. Indeed, it is possible to claim that Sandys must have made the nuclear deterrent focus plain by now, but the Navy refused to accept it and pleaded ignorance as to the meaning of the White Paper—ignorance that would have allowed it later to make claims for conventional global war preparations. Lewin admitted that in paragraph 20 it was stated that the possession of nuclear power was not itself a capable deterrent. However, he maintained that this paragraph came so far after paragraph 1 that the common usage of 'deterrent'—namely 'nuclear deterrent'—was likely to be assumed to be that put forward at the beginning of the paper.

Lewin also objected to paragraph 24 in which it was said that naval forces did not contribute directly to the deterrent. He maintained that if the deterrent was defined broadly (that is to include non-nuclear forces) then the paragraph was unacceptable because the Navy did contribute—the implication here being that if it was defined narrowly (including only nuclear power) then it was acceptable. This reinforces the argument that during the White Paper negotiations the Navy was concerned about contributing not so much to the nuclear deterrent to global war but to conventional preparations should that war be fought. At the same time, the Navy certainly did not wish to foreclose its options. Consequently, the sentence stating 'naval forces do not for the most part contribute directly to the deterrent' was dropped by the time the White Paper was published, though it was continued to be stressed that 'the role of naval forces in total war is somewhat uncertain'.[76]

While the Navy, no doubt, felt that it had secured a victory because a threat to its global war preparations had been removed, it is not clear whether Sandys attached similar meaning to the removal of this paragraph. It is unlikely that he did, given his antipathy towards conventional global war preparations. Possibly, he took the narrow interpretation of the deterrent as

---

[76] Cmnd. 124, para. 24; also see ADM 205/114, Abraham to Soames, 2 Apr. 1957.

his starting point and saw the deletion of the sentence merely as a recognition that the Navy had little to contribute to the nuclear deterrent.

This measure of ambiguity made it easier for the Admiralty to go along with the White Paper—and allowed Sandys to press on with his manpower objectives. Amongst the Board of Admiralty there was still uncertainty and much displeasure about the wording of the paragraphs defining the intentions of the government as to the final size of the forces,[77] but there was cause for optimism as well. Thus, on 3 April, naval commanders were informed that with regard to the Navy's role in nuclear war,

The relevant paragraph in the White Paper tries to face this problem frankly for the first time and comes to the conclusion, precisely because the course of nuclear war can never be predicted, that the country must maintain such Naval Forces as, in co-operation with the NATO Navies, will constitute a vital piece both of the overall deterrent and of our preparations for total war.[78]

The Admiralty was firm in its belief that a 'costly programme of re-equipping the Navy with up-to-date weapons lies ahead'. The key words in the 3 April letter were 'overall deterrent' (which demonstrated that the Navy was giving deterrence the 'broad interpretation') and the explicit statement of 'preparations for total war'. The Navy was in no way giving up its commitment to broken-backed warfare—a fact that the Air Ministry had long recognized: only two weeks previously, Assistant Chief of the Air Staff, A. Earle, had written to Boyle that the Navy was perpetuating what Earle regarded as the old fallacy that following the thermonuclear exchange phase, a battle would have to be conducted against the Soviet submarine fleet.[79]

Clearly, there was still much confusion and incoherence and it seemed inevitable that another crisis would arise later when the implications of Sandys's manpower proposals began to inform themselves more directly on ambiguous declaratory policy. Yet, this was still in the (albeit near) future. While

---

[77] ADM 205/114, Minutes from Admiralty Board, 28 Mar. 1957.
[78] ADM 205/114, Admiralty: General Message Home and Abroad, 3 Apr. 1957.
[79] AIR 8/2157, Earle to Boyle, 14 Mar. 1957.

Ziegler is correct in his interpretation that the statement of the Navy's role in global war being somewhat uncertain 'was a phrase that struck a chill into every sailor';[80] the Navy also often seemed intent upon seeing its glass as half full.

Even in the wake of the 1957 White Paper, the Navy remained attached to the concept of conventional preparations for global war. In July, the First Lord had hinted at the need for global war forces when he stated that Sandys's planned cuts would lead to Britain losing all standing in NATO (an essentially political justification for these forces) and that NATO would become a 'hollow deterrent' (the military justification for global war forces).[81] The statement in the White Paper that Britain must make her contribution to NATO on a reduced scale[82] was thereby in practice strongly opposed. First, the Minister's attempt to cut forces based on a war preparation priority list (which placed global war preparations at the bottom) was strongly resisted on the basis that the Navy order of battle could not be broken up into these specialized functions. Secondly, Sandys's claims that global war was unlikely was rejected with the statement that 'NATO policy to which Her Majesty's Government is committed, is that global war is possible, and that the alliance must be prepared to fight it'.[83]

Concomitantly, it was Selkirk's view that (1) vast quantities of hydrogen bombs in the UK could not make her influence felt overseas; (2) the Commonwealth was built on sea-power and the 80 Plan (that is, an 80,000 Navy), by undermining naval manpower, would undermine the Commonwealth; and (3) the strength of NATO would be seriously impaired and 'without Nato our hydrogen deterrent becomes a hollow straw, a mere bluff which the most gullible communist could not fail to see through'. Selkirk went on:

In my view, therefore, we should be seen, in the eyes of the Commonwealth, of NATO, and especially America, and of the world at large, to be abdicating our position as a naval world power. This is not a question of pride or sentiment. Our friends will be discouraged; our enemies will take heart. Thus the balance of cold war may be expected to swing against us, and the outcome may be very serious.[84]

---

[80] Ziegler, *Mountbatten* (London, 1985), 582.    [81] Ibid.
[82] Cmnd. 124, para. 24.    [83] CAB 131/18, D (57) 29, 15 Nov. 1957.
[84] AIR 19/856, Selkirk to Sandys, 21 June 1957.

In this regard Selkirk received strong support from Mountbatten. Indeed, throughout 1957, the First Sea Lord remained adamant that the White Paper would be incompatible with the promises of the Navy to NATO. It was, according to Mountbatten, impossible to estimate for how long after the nuclear exchange Soviet submarines would endanger shipping and, consequently, there would be a need to provide for global war anti-submarine forces.[85] Here Selkirk was more specific and maintained that the growing strength of the Russian fleet meant that it could function for six months to a year after a nuclear exchange whatever the outcome. The First Lord stated that

In global war itself, it has been possible to claim with some plausibility that a Navy provided for peace and the cold war would put up an adequate showing in the unpredictable circumstances of global war. I have in fact made such a claim in my own Explanatory Memorandum this year [but in view of the increase in Soviet naval strength] I would no longer be able to do so.[86]

On top of these anti-submarine requirements, Mountbatten and Selkirk continued to press for a major convoy role for the Royal Navy. Mountbatten stressed that in the event of global war occurring, SACLANT would need to get supplies into Western Europe, and the only way this could be done would be to fight a 'monster convoy' through the Atlantic.[87] In turn, Selkirk reaffirmed the Navy's focus on anti-submarine missions, but also stated that with the forces projected in the White Paper, the Atlantic could not be kept open—a situation he termed militarily disastrous.

In discussions between the Minister of Defence and the Chiefs of Staff on 19 February, the Chiefs had withstood an onslaught by the Minister as he attempted to rid the Navy of all its aircraft carriers. Mountbatten united the Chiefs of Staff Committee behind the JPS report that

We conclude there is a need to retain the Fleet Air Arm because it provides a means of applying air power in areas where other means cannot be efficiently or economically used. We consider that, in the

[85] DEFE 4/96, COS 24 (57) 1, 28 Mar. 1957.
[86] AIR 19/856, Selkirk to Sandys, 21 June 1957.
[87] DEFE 4/100, COS 72 (57) 2, 23 Sept. 1957.

strategic circumstances with which we are faced, the carrier is the most flexible and valuable unit of the Fleet and that, if economies in Naval forces have to be made, these ships should be the last to be reduced.[88]

The Chiefs were here legitimizing the need for carriers in terms of cold and limited war roles and not as a global war capability. This possibility stemmed not only from a belief in the necessity of such forces but also from the recognition that Sandys, unlike his predecessors, would not diverge from the set of war preparation priorities which placed global war at the tail-end, nor would he succumb to the attractions of a Strike Fleet role—a role, after all, to which he had never been particularly partial.[89] The Chiefs were more concerned to secure the ships rather than to convince the Minister about a controversial rationale for their use. In addition, support for the Navy's position could be more easily mustered in the Cabinet if it was framed in limited and cold war terms.

Thus, Mountbatten's lobbying soon brought strong support for his and Selkirk's attempts to alter Sandys's position. For example, on 22 August, the Secretary of State for Commonwealth Relations, the Earl of Home, presented a report to the Defence Committee on the 'Implications for the Commonwealth of Proposed Naval Reductions' in which Sandys was taken to task for endangering Britain's position in the Far East and South Atlantic. It was the Secretary of State's view that everything must be done to avoid the impression being created that Britain was starting a process of general withdrawal from South East Asia. The independence of Malaya would be endangered and Australia and New Zealand isolated, with the latter two countries being pushed towards greater co-operation with the United States. The most significant factor in Britain's power in these areas was the British naval contribution and the Secretary doubted whether the Australian and New Zealand governments would regard the presence of a carrier group east of Suez as adequate compensation for reductions in the ships based in Singapore to as few as two frigates. It was crucial that the base at Singapore be retained with a substantial naval presence because for Auckland and Canberra, the base still represented

[88] DEFE 4/95, JP (57) 20 (Final) discussed at COS 14 (57) 1, 19 Feb. 1957.
[89] Grove, *Vanguard to Trident*, 91–3, 98, 102, 105, 107, 110–14.

a 'visible, vital and essential link with the UK'. Concomitantly, Sandys's reductions would adversely influence Britain's security in the South Atlantic by prejudicing her ability to defend the sea routes around southern Africa. In short, while Sandys's 'New Look' may have realized substantial economies, the implications for foreign policy and military objectives were entirely detrimental.[90]

To reaffirm this position, in September the Admiralty, with the Chief's backing, presented a paper (the so-called 'Autumn Naval Rethink') on the Navy's role in global war, cold war, and especially limited war and its need for carriers—a case, according to Mountbatten, that was so convincing that he was certain Sandys would give the Navy extra men and money.[91] These ideas were reflected in a report presented to the Defence Committee by Selkirk on 15 November. It is significant that the Navy's position had altered little from June. When it came to cold and limited war capabilities, the report repeated the Navy's earlier assertion that the 1957 White Paper had recognized the need for forces to meet both these requirements; however, now manpower and financial cuts made it impossible to do so. It was stressed that under Sandys's reductions, the Navy was being pressed to a point where vital interests were being liquidated. The Admiralty proposed that Sandys agree that the absolute minimum forces necessary for cold war duties include—in addition to the carrier task group east of Suez—sixteen frigates of which six would be in the Far East, six in the Persian Gulf, four in the South Atlantic, and two in the American and West Indies Stations.[92]

In the face of this constant and unrelenting pressure, the Minister of Defence moved some way to the Navy's position. In mid-November, Sandys presented his own paper to the Defence Committee on the role of the Navy.[93] In it he agreed that because the Navy could recruit more than 80,000 men, the Navy manpower limit could be allowed to rise to 88,000.[94]

[90] CAB 131/18, DC (57) 21, 22 Aug. 1957.
[91] Ziegler, *Mountbatten*, 553 and Grove, *Vanguard to Trident*, 210.
[92] CAB 131/18, D (57) 29, 15 Nov. 1957.
[93] CAB 131/18, D (57) 28, 14 Nov. 1957.
[94] For Sandys's attempt to get the Navy to replace the Army in Gibraltar and Malta see PREM 11/1998, Macmillan to Denny, 12 Nov. 1957; PREM 11/1998, Macmillan to Sandys, 12 Nov. 1957.

Sandys also agreed to a fourth carrier (to be held in reserve), but on the proviso that it make no extra demands on money or manpower. At the same time, he told the Admiralty to cut back on aircraft production, a reduction which would involve cancelling as many Scimitars as possible, a slowdown of the planned production of Sea Vixen and that if the NA 39 was to be produced, the RAF would first have to accept it as a successor to the Canberra. In other words, what the Minister was giving with the one hand he was taking with the other. His compromises were certainly not unconditional ones and a return to the pre-1957 force posture of multiple capabilities seemed out of the question.[95]

## The V-Bomber Force Debate during 1957

Similarly to the pre-1957 V-bomber force debate, economic concerns played a major role in determining the size of the planned V-bomber force—a tendency that was made possible by a greater willingness of those outside the RAF to, at least implicitly, and often explicitly, rely on the deterrent power of SAC. Although in the available documents of the 1957 period the sub-theme of 'unilateral independence' informed strongly on arguments for the preferred V-bomber order of battle, unilateral action continued to be regarded by Sandys and Macmillan as a remote possibility and reductions in the planned force were also demanded on financial grounds and legitimized by the fact that Britain would most likely only act in conjunction with the United States. The theme of nuclear strategic concert continued to remain a firm foundation on which policy was based.

The Army and Navy thereby sought to prevent the expansion of the planned V-bombers beyond the 184 announced by Head

[95] The Navy was clearly subordinating its interest in a nuclear capability to the maintenance of conventional forces. Indeed, when asked whether during this period Mountbatten was arguing for nuclear capabilities for the Navy, Sir Richard Powell maintained, 'I don't think he was at that time demanding a nuclear role' (King's Conference on the Sandys White Paper). The Admiralty's preference to frame its requirements in conventional terms most probably reflected the necessity of defending, in the face of Sandys's onslaughts, what already was in the Navy's possession. Furthermore Sir William Davis is explicit in his memoirs that at the beginning of 1957 'all ideas of reorientating the Navy in part to a Nuclear Role were set aside'. Unpublished Memoirs of Sir William Davis, p. 790.

in December 1956, while at the same time holding out the possibility that the force would be reduced still further. Thus, in discussions in January over joint nuclear strategic planning with the Americans, Templer and Mountbatten only agreed to accept the American proposals provided that such co-ordination did not serve to push up UK bomber force numbers. Mountbatten argued strongly that it be made very clear to Washington that agreement to their proposals did not commit Britain to a specific size of the bomber force.[96] Similarly to the pre-1957 period, these services continued to accept the declaratory focus on nuclear deterrence but not the implications of that focus for their conventional forces. This rejection did not subside as 1957 progressed. In July the First Lord, Lord Selkirk, wrote Sandys a letter concerning the Admiralty's view on the size of the V-bomber force in which he stated that while the Admiralty supported the broad principle of contributing to the deterrent, neither the Admiralty nor the Chiefs of Staff had ever agreed that a sensible defence policy could be maintained with forces of 375,000 men. Moreover, the possibility of basing a sound policy on this manpower was not influenced by the size of the bomber force except to the degree that the bombers and the conventional forces became competitors for financial resources. For Selkirk, the nuclear deterrent did not legitimize smaller forces and, indeed, the smaller the order of battle, the more necessary became their equipment. If the V-bombers and their nuclear ordnance absorbed an excessive proportion of defence resources it would be more difficult to develop a policy designed to protect Britain's alliances and world-wide interests.[97] The Navy thus rejected any link between a reliance on nuclear weapons—whether used independently or in concert with the United States—and conventional force levels. This was a position once more supported by the Army when in October 1957 Sir Gerald Templer was adamant that with costs of forces steadily mounting it might be necessary to give up the deterrent.[98]

As for Sandys and Macmillan, from the beginning of 1957, they seemed ambivalent about the future size of the V-bomber force. On 27 February, Macmillan told the Defence Committee

---

[96] DEFE 4/94, COS 3 (57) 7 discussion of COS (56) 451 (closed), 8 Jan. 1957.
[97] CAB 131/18, D (57) 18, 29 July 1957.
[98] DEFE 4/101, COS 81 (57), 21 Oct. 1957.

that on present plans, by 1960 there would be 184 V-bombers of which 120 would be Mark 2s. If existing orders were completed and no more were placed, there would ultimately be a front-line strength of 176 of which only 40 would be Mark 2s. He preferred to maintain that the final number was still under consideration.[99] From this discussion it was apparent that primarily economic and not strategic requirements would determine the final force size. This was reaffirmed in a letter from Powell to Dean in which the latter was told that for costing purposes 'assume whatever pattern not exceeding a front-line of 184 medium bombers you would regard as sensible'[100]—not exactly a very strategically rigorous method of addressing the issue of bomber strength.

Yet, while often unclear as to the purposes of their nuclear deterrent force, the Air Ministry, in the face of Army, Navy, and Ministry of Defence objections, clung tenaciously to the 184 figure (of which 120 would be Mark 2s which could deliver Blue Steel). In the face of a possible further assault on the size of the force, it was the Air Ministry's plan to attempt the fastest build-up manageable. This would mean accepting a larger proportion of the less capable Mark 1s but 'on present plans [this] would appear the better alternative—a very slow build-up may well invite a reduction in the size of the force'.[101] This was a surprising strategy since the Air Ministry itself admitted that without Blue Steel (which would be carried by the Mark 2s) the V-bombers would become extremely vulnerable to Soviet air defences. Consequently, it was stated at the same time that if the Minister of Defence succeeded in cutting the V-bomber force below 184 'it would be better to procure more Mark 2s in order to get better quality in the reduced force'.[102]

In a paper presented to Sandys by the Air Ministry on the size and composition of the medium bomber force on 15 May, the efficacy of the Mark 2s was stressed and the impotence of Britain's V-bomber force underlined if this type were abandoned. It was demonstrated that: (1) from 1957 to 1961 when the V-bombers would carry free-falling bombs only, the

[99] CAB 131/18 D 2 (57) 1, 27 Feb. 1957.
[100] AIR 19/856, Powell to Dean, 27 Feb. 1957.
[101] AIR 8/2155, Provisional Plan L: Brief for the CAS, 7 Feb. 1957.
[102] Ibid.

superior performance of the Mark 2s would make the force less vulnerable to enemy defences and enable it to penetrate and attack a larger selection of key targets; (2) between 1960/1 and 1963/4, Russian targets would be defended by SAGW and successful delivery would require Blue Steel; (3) after 1963/4 the Soviet SAGW would improve in quality and the maintenance of the deterrent would depend on the improved air-to-surface missile, the OR 1149. Both Blue Steel and the OR 1149 could be carried on Mark 1s but only with the penalty of reduced operational effectiveness. Consequently the Air Ministry believed

the force should contain at least 120 B.2 aircraft in order to make it an effective deterrent in the eyes of the enemy, since this would depend upon his assessment of our ability to penetrate deeply into his territory and render vulnerable a large proportion of his key areas.[103]

Here Sandys concurred that

in order to exercise any serious deterrent influence upon the Kremlin we should need to have not less than 15 squadrons (i.e. a front-line of 120), equipped with aircraft capable of launching propelled bombs (i.e. Vulcans and Victors of the Mark 2 type).[104]

Yet, his acceptance of the Air Ministry figures was couched in terms that expressed the limitations he imposed on the concept of 'unilateral independence' and adumbrated his later willingness to tolerate further reductions to the force. Thus while agreeing with a total of 120 Mark 2s, his support of it was guarded. Indeed, he added the rider that 'it is generally accepted that financial reductions make some appreciable reductions [in the planned V-bomber force] inevitable'[105] and that

Since the possession of a British element of nuclear deterrent is a central feature of our defence policy, and since it is one of the main justifications we have advanced for the reduction in our contribution of conventional forces to N.A.T.O., I am sure we should not hesitate to order the extra 95 Mark 2 aircraft which, at relatively small cost, would so appreciably increase our military power and influence.[106]

[103] AIR 2/14699, Misc/m (57) 71, 15 May 1957.

[104] CAB 130/122, Strategic Bomber Force Memo by Minister of Defence, 27 May 1957.  [105] Ibid.

[106] Ibid. The 95 aircraft (53 Vulcans and 42 Victors) together with the existing orders for a front-line of 6 Mark 2 squadrons (based on orders of 49 Mark 2 Vulcans and 29 Mark 2 Victors) would result in a total front-line of 120 Mark 2s.

Strategic reasoning was matched here by political justifications and economic considerations. For the Air Ministry, the strategic rationale of independent deterrence was the sufficient condition for determining the force size; for Sandys it was just one factor (irrespective of whether it was to be taken at face value or not). His position was thus inherently more flexible—a flexibility demonstrated by his readiness to bow to Thorneycroft's demands for securing more savings through reductions in the V-bomber force—even if this clashed with what the RAF felt was the minimum necessary for a unilateral deterrent stance.

In reply to Sandys's request for 95 extra Mark 2s, the Chancellor of the Exchequer presented a paper on 29 May entitled 'The Deterrent and the Defence Budget' in which he refused to commit himself to such a procurement for fear that it might overstrain the economy.[107] Thorneycroft did not reject the request outright but wanted to see how Sandys's other plans for savings unfolded. In a meeting with Sandys on 30 May, Thorneycroft said that before he committed himself to any final bomber force size he wished to see what the total RAF expenditure would be. All he was now prepared to say was that the total medium bomber force should be between 120 and 184 of which 80 would be Mark 2s.[108]

Thorneycroft made no attempt to relate these figures to strategic requirements or, more specifically, to Sandys's statements concerning the necessary numbers needed to 'exercise any serious deterrent influence upon the Kremlin'. Even more significantly, the minutes of the meeting do not reveal that Sandys was interested in referring to his earlier arguments. In his discussions with Thorneycroft he preferred to express most concern with regard to the fact that continual procrastination over the final size of the V-bomber force would harm the ongoing talks with the Americans over co-ordinated strategic strike plans. Thus, for the Minister of Defence, what was significant here was the implications of uncertainty for Anglo-American strategic co-ordination and not the issue of requirements for independently deterring the Soviet Union. Once Thorneycroft managed to convince him that relations with the Americans and NATO would not be adversely influenced by

[107] CAB 130/122, GEN 570/1st meeting, 29 May 1957.
[108] CAB 130/122, GEN 570/2nd meeting, 30 May 1957.

the postponement of the procurement decision for a few months, Sandys was willing to accept—at least until July when force costings were to be ready—planning on the basis of a front-line force of only 80 Mark 2s.[109] Sandys's later willingness to countenance a total of 144 medium bombers was most probably a result of Thorneycroft's arguments (arguments with which he did not strongly disagree), his conception of strategic concert with the United States which meant that sufficient Soviet targets were in any event covered by the combined force, and the fact that even with these reduced numbers Britain could, if the worst came to the worst, independently attack enough countervalue targets necessary to deter the Soviet Union by itself.

While at the end of July, Sandys told the Defence Committee that he still regarded 184 medium bombers as the minimum procurement target,[110] on 2 August he told the committee that there 'could be no arithmetical proof that this was the right figure'.[111] It was then agreed that further orders for V-bombers would be limited to the number of aircraft required to bring the front-line strength to 144. When reservations were expressed about the reductions, these were framed not in strategic terms but in political ones. It was stated that

the recent White Paper has emphasised that our future defence policy would be based on the deterrent and there might be unfortunate repercussions if we now announced that reductions were to be made in our provision for the deterrent.[112]

Furthermore, the Defence Committee went on to reaffirm these considerations and attachment to a measure of 'independence in concert'. They therefore pointed out that the difference between a force consisting of 96 and 120 V-bombers would be £54 million over a five-year period and that in view of the fact that

our investment programmes as a whole were already imposing a severe strain on the economy and since we should never, in practice expect to challenge the Soviet Union alone, some reduction in the total cost of the V-bomber force should be accepted. An appropriate

[109] Ibid.
[110] CAB 131/18, D (57) 15, 26 July 1957.
[111] CAB 131/18, D 7 (57) 2, 2 Aug. 1957.      [112] Ibid.

compromise would be to provide for a total front-line strength of 144 V-bombers.[113]

Here the V-bomber force was once more reduced in size on the basis of economic considerations, and this time accompanied with an explicit rejection of a preference for unilateral nuclear strategic actions. A comparison of the 1955—6 period with that of 1957 reveals no inconsistency on this score.[114]

## The Problem of Air Defences

Throughout 1957, the Air Ministry—similarly to the 1955–6 period—continued to reaffirm the point that the defence of the V-bomber bases was an integral part of the deterrent. The link between survivability and credibility was recognized in the White Paper. In paragraph 17 it was stated that

Since peace so largely depends upon the deterrent fear of nuclear retaliation, it is essential that a would-be aggressor should not be allowed to think he could readily knock out the bomber bases in Britain before their aircraft could take off from them. The defence of the bomber airfields is therefore an essential part of the deterrent and is a feasible task.[115]

The object of this section is to answer the question of whether the 1957 debate differed in any significant manner from that conducted in 1956? Specifically, in view of the greater declaratory focus on nuclear deterrence and independent British nuclear deterrence, was there now a greater sensitivity on the part of those outside the RAF to the necessity of air defences for the V-bomber bases? In other words, was Sandys interested in taking his own declaratory statements about defending the V-bomber

---

[113] CAB 131/18, D7 (57) 2, 2 Aug. 1957. Another squadron of Mark 2s was soon added bringing the total to 104 aircraft. Thus when completed, the force would be made up of three squadrons of 24 Victor Mark 1s, two squadrons of 16 Vulcan Mark 1s, five squadrons of 40 Victor mark 2s, and eight squadrons of 64 Vulcan Mark 2s. AIR 2/14699, Memo by R. C. Kent, 23 May 1957.

[114] The bombers would be armed with Blue Steel Mark 1 which would have a range of 100 miles, a speed of Mach 2.5, be deployable by 1961/2 and be capable of penetrating Soviet air defences until 1964/5. This weapon would then be superseded by a Mark 2 version with a range of 600 miles, though interest was then expressed in acquiring a more sophisticated weapon from the Americans. CAB 131/20 D (58) 55, 3 Nov. 1958.

[115] Cmnd. 124, para. 17.

bases seriously, or did his reservations about the efficacy of such defences and the need to secure financial savings in the RAF budget militate against such a step? Finally, is it possible to deduce anything about Sandys's attitudes towards independent deterrence in general from his approach to air defences?

The 1957 White Paper admitted that the size of Fighter Command would be reduced,[116] but it stressed that the remaining force would be adequate for the defence of the V-bomber bases. This was a claim bitterly contested by the Air Ministry. On 1 March, the Air Defence Commander, Sir Thomas Pike, wrote a letter to Dermot Boyle in which he pointed out that acceptance of Plan L would involve a reduction in front-line Fighter Command from 780 aircraft (including the auxiliaries) to 280 aircraft by June 1959. He agreed that, partly for reasons of economy and partly for reasons concerning the future deployment of SAGW, this was acceptable, but he expressed concern that the rundown in fighters and the build-up of the SAGW system would not be co-ordinated. A special committee set up by Boyle on SAGW deployment had concluded that an adequate defence consisting of 300 SAGWs armed with atomic warheads would only be ready by 1961/2. However, Pike considered the deployment date optimistic and he warned, 'I do not think that anyone could pretend that we should have a worthwhile defence/deterrent in 1959 with only 280 fighters and one very doubtful SAGW station'.[117] The crux of the matter was that from the end of 1958 until the nuclear SAGW was in place, a defence gap would open up. Unfortunately for the Air Ministry, Sandys did not appear to have related much to this criticism. Arguably, for him, the defence gap was irrelevant as the combined Anglo-American nuclear force was credible enough to deter war and

[116] At this stage Fighter Command was planned to be run down from 28 squadrons of 488 aircraft at 1 April 1958 to 21 squadrons of 296 aircraft by April 1960, and to a final figure of 292 by April 1961. The P. 1 was planned to come into service in 1960 and to reach 164 units by April 1962 and progressively replace the Hunter. The remainder of Fighter Command would consist of 112 Javelins. No more Javelins would be ordered and by 1962 they would begin to waste. By April 1963 it was planned to have 13 SAGW stations with 672 launchers and 825 missiles. Stage 1 Bloodhound and Thunderbird would be deployed by the end of 1959; Stage 1½ Green Flax would be deployed by the end of 1962. Sandys had cancelled the OR 329 and the P. 177 even though the Air Ministry was against completely terminating these projects. See AIR 2/14712, Ward to Sandys, 3 Apr. 1957.

[117] AIR 8/2155, Pike to Boyle, 1 Mar. 1957.

was insensitive to fluctuations in the level of defences surrounding the British V-bomber bases. Also, arguably, had Sandys been primarily interested in the British nuclear force as a 'unilateral independent' deterrent capability, he would have been more sensitive to the Air Ministry's complaints: if Britain was unilaterally to deter the Soviet Union then a defence-gap would have far-reaching consequences for deterrence credibility, not to mention the implications if Britain actually found herself forced to attack in a second strike mode. Thus, Sandys told Ward that there would be no war within the next five years because the Soviet Union would not have ballistic missiles to attack the United States. According to the Minister of Defence, the Air Ministry's case was further weakened by the fact that fighter aircraft could not obtain 100 per cent immunity against a thermonuclear attack delivered by bombers and were useless against a missile attack.[118] Ward strongly disagreed with Sandys's arguments but the Minister of Defence was dismissive of Ward's 'verbal démarche'.[119]

Sandys therefore pressed forward with his search for economies and was not overly attentive to the problems of vulnerability. Pike was informed by the Vice Chief of the Air Staff (VCAS), Sir Ivelaw Chapman, that while Pike's concerns were not without foundation and the level of fighter defences included in Plan L were not without risk, he would just have to accept it as the Air Ministry was having difficulty in convincing Sandys to accept even this attenuated force. Ivelaw Chapman complained that the Minister of Defence was avoiding the fact that war was unlikely because of the deterrent but that this situation could only continue so long as the deterrent was relatively invulnerable.[120] Yet, Ivelaw Chapman's argument would only have carried weight with Sandys if the Minister had been intent upon viewing deterrence in purely British terms. For, to repeat, in the context of Anglo-American deterrence, the combined nuclear force was not vulnerable enough to undermine allied threats of nuclear reponse. Consequently, from the Air Ministry's point of view, the second half of 1957 posed more problems than the first.

[118] AIR 19/856, 12 Mar. 1957.
[119] AIR 2/14712, Memo by Broadbent, 12 Mar. 1957.
[120] AIR 8/2157, Ivelaw Chapman to Pike, 11 Mar. 1957.

In his search for savings, Sandys cut the V-bomber force to 144, thereby making the task of air defence even more difficult as the target presented to the attacking forces was now considerably smaller. The Air Ministry was then forced to defend the number of planned V-bomber bases against attempts by Sandys to secure savings in this area. On 16 August, the Minister of Defence was informed that for a front line of 144 medium bombers, the minimum dispersal scale that was acceptable to the Air Council consisted of six main bases from each of which eight aircraft would operate in war; twenty-four dispersal bases at which four aircraft would be based and a main base for the two photo-reconnaissance squadrons, 50 per cent of which would be dispersed to two bomber dispersal airfields. It was stressed that 'smaller forces means more compact targets and suggestions that we can do with less are without foundation'.[121]

As the year progressed, Sandys became more open to suggestions that dispersal was a significant issue[122]—but this apparently only because he and Macmillan were interested in totally abolishing Fighter Command—an issue that caused major tensions between Sandys and CAS Sir Dermot Boyle.[123] On 31 December, Macmillan told the Defence Committee that it was his and Sandys's view that the expenditure involved in providing for fighter aircraft was no longer justified, that the only defence was nuclear counter-attack, and that it would be wiser to use the £100 million a year which was then devoted to fighters to

---

[121] AIR 2/14699, 16 Aug. 1957.

[122] The following year saw studies and trials focusing on the subject of bomber dispersal. On the assumption of seven days' warning and forty minutes tactical warning, during the working week 20 per cent of V-bombers could be ready in two hours and 75 per cent ready in twenty-four hours. Once warned, the squadrons would be dispersed and brought to readiness. They could then be launched within a forty-minute radar warning and maintain this state of readiness for up to a month. It was stressed, however that 'since the principal assumption on which our plans are based is the *seven day warning*, no attempt is presently made to maintain bomber stations on an operational basis during week-ends'. AIR 2/14872, Operational Readiness of Bomber Command, 21 Feb. 1958; also see AIR 2/14872, Measures to Improve the Operational Readiness of Bomber Command, 21 May 1958.

[123] According to Boyle, 'I was totally opposed to Sandys's sudden policy of no more manned fighting aircraft and I left him in no doubt about my views at that time . . . History has also proved that his policy was wrong. Perhaps the most useful lesson to learn from this episode is the amount of damage which such quick . . . decisions by those in high places can cause to the national institutions involved' (letter from Sir Dermot Boyle to Professor L. Freedman, 18 May 1988).

provide more bombers or to build up other deterrent forces.[124] Macmillan, however, argued that fighters could still make it more difficult for a bomber force to carry out their attack, and until this role had been taken over by the SAGW, fighters should be retained. This, of course did not indicate that Macmillan or Sandys had been won over by the Air Ministry's reasoning. Indeed, Macmillan preferred to express most concern about the 'psychological' impact on Britain's allies and her own domestic opinion of abandoning fighter defences.[125] To this Sandys added his view that in the light of the expected diplomatic problems arising out of the abolition of Fighter Command, he would accept that its total abolition was out of the question. Yet, he added, this decision would have to be reviewed at a later date[126] and thus the option of terminating Fighter Command was left open and the issue of the potential defence gap left unresolved.[127]

Consequently, the 1957 White Paper's focus on Britain's nuclear deterrent did not reflect itself in concern for the defence of that deterrent. While arguably the contribution of fighters to the defence of the air bases was marginal (an argument that the Air Ministry did not totally accept), if the deterrent was so central to Britain's defence policy then surely, in terms of

[124] With regard to other 'deterrent forces', the 1957 papers indicate the existence of an interest in the possibility of anti-ballistic missile systems. In his paper on fissile material for nuclear weapons presented to the Defence Committee on 27 July, Norman Brook stated that 'Though it is not possible to be so definite about the prospects of deploying a defence system against ballistic missiles, we believe that a substantial measure of defence could be achieved by 1967'. See CAB 131/18, D (57) 14, 27 July 1957.

[125] CAB 128/31, CC 86 (57) 5, 31 Dec. 1957.

[126] CAB 131/18, D 14 (57) 3, 31 Dec. 1957. On the other hand, Thorneycroft remained adamant that fighter defences would only provide marginal security and that any attempt to provide against all potential threats would lead to economic disaster. The Chancellor also suggested that the P. 1 be abandoned and that Fighter Command be equipped with Javelins which were then being produced. This would save between £200 million and £240 million over the next five years including £11 million over the next financial year. This was rejected by the Defence Committee.

[127] By the end of 1958 little further had been concluded. On 14 November, Sandys reaffirmed once more that Fighter Command, which stood at 480 front-line aircraft at the end of 1957, would be cut to 280 by mid-1959 and he also warned that 'If, however, some major economy in defence expenditure is essential, the possibility of reducing the fighter defence of the deterrent bases may have to be re-examined'. CAB 131-20, D (58) 61, 14 Nov. 1958. The RAF's concern was that Sandys was envisaging a Fighter Command reduced to only 12 squadrons armed with Red Top and Genie air-to-air missiles. AIR 8/2220, D (58) 26, 18 Nov. 1958.

Britain's total defence posture, this was more than a marginal issue.

## The Wider Internal Debate

The opening up of the strategic debate in Britain both in Parliament and outside also manifested itself in the, albeit muted, response to the Sandys White Paper. Similarly to the bureaucratic debate described above, attention was focused on the sagacity of emphasizing massive retaliation, of defining independent deterrence, and of cutting back on conventional forces.

Sandys's explanation in the House of Commons of the meaning and implications of the British 'New Look' helped reflect a measure of ambiguity especially with regard to the degree to which the logic of the 'New Look' strategic formulation was to be pursued. This was most evident when it came to the issue of limited war in Europe. Speaking on 16 April the Minister of Defence had stated that

Limited and localised acts of aggression . . . by a satellite Communist State could, no doubt, be resisted with conventional arms, or, at worst with tactical atomic weapons . . . If, on the other hand, the Russians were to launch a full-scale offensive against Western Europe, it would . . . be quite unrealistic to imagine that the issue could be fought out on limited conventional lines and according to rules.[128]

The view that an outbreak of hostilities on the central front need not escalate from the theatre nuclear to the central nuclear level, or even from the conventional to the theatre nuclear level itself, appeared to undercut the declaratory reliance on massive nuclear response.

The Conservatives' ambivalence about terminating national service, reducing manpower, and cutting back on conventional capabilities—especially among the retired servicemen who were strongly represented on the back benches—therefore found an opening within the Minister's own arguments as Sandys seemed to be admitting that conventional capabilities and manpower could not be entirely disregarded. At the Conservative Party conference in October, while the government's

---

[128] House of Commons, vol. 568, col. 1765, 16 Apr. 1957.

emphasis on nuclear weapons was supported, it was also warned not to cut back so greatly on conventional forces.[129] This was a refrain soon taken up with added vigour by former Minister of Defence Anthony Head—a man who had resigned in January 1957 after being presented with the new plans— when he claimed that with growing super-power strategic parity, the readiness to use tactical atomic weapons would decline. This would result in the only remaining responses being on the one side the use of conventional forces for what he termed 'minor matters' and for holding territories, and on the other, the ultimate sanction of nuclear weapons.[130]

While Head appears to have been Sandys's most vocal critic in the Party, major criticism also emanated from those ministers with responsibilities which called for British political and military presence overseas such as Colonial Secretary Lennox Boyd, Foreign Secretary Selwyn Lloyd, and the Commonwealth Secretary, Lord Home. Indeed, they continually expressed unease with Sandys's conventional reduction plans. On the other hand, those ministers with their sights on economic savings such as Chancellor of the Exchequer Peter Thorneycroft demonstrated most support for Sandys's plans. Thus, on this level of decision-making, political and economic rather than strategic issues determined the position of both supporters and opponents of Sandys's plans.

Similarly to the Conservatives, the Labour Party was also caught between on the one hand a desire amongst a number of their senior defence specialists to place less reliance on what was perceived to be in many instances an incredible threat and on the other the need to avoid reverting to electorally unpopular conscription and economically expensive conventional forces.

In April 1957 Labour Party leader Hugh Gaitskill supported Sandys's emphasis on independent nuclear deterrent as he believed that in certain circumstances the United States would not be prepared to extend her deterrent so as to protect the British Isles.[131] In turn, John Strachey—one of Labour's tradi- tionally strongest supporters of an independent British deterrent

---

[129] National Union of Conservative and Unionist Associations, 77th Annual Con- ference, 10–12 Oct. 1957, 26.

[130] For Debate see House of Commons, vol. 577, cols. 395–401, 7 Nov. 1957.

[131] House of Commons, vol. 568, col. 71, 1 Apr. 1957.

—told the Labour Party conference of 1957 that without a nuclear capability Britain would not be able to follow policies regarded as unfavourable by the Americans.[132]

Concomitantly, the growing strength of the Campaign for Nuclear Disarmament—a movement which had gained impetus following Britain's nuclear test in May—reinforced splits within the Labour Party over nuclear issues. Already prior to the publication of the 1957 White Paper approximately 100 Labour MPs had indicated their desire to stop all nuclear tests, and by the middle of the year an H-bomb Campaign Committee had been formed.[133] By April, Gaitskill himself, taking note of these pressures, was supporting a moratorium on nuclear testing,[134] although the implications of CND for Labour Party politics had in 1957 yet to be fully realized. Indeed, by the Labour Party conference in October, even Aneurin Bevan had come around to support the British nuclear deterrent and at the 1957 TUC conference there was little union support for unilateral nuclear disarmament.

However, attacks on Sandys's stance also came from the more conservative wing of the Labour Party. For example, MP Richard Crossman felt that the paper represented a 'reckless gamble' and presaged the undermining of the UK's ability to defend itself 'in the only kind of war this country could wage'.[135] He believed that Britain should renounce a nuclear capability—leaving it solely to the Americans—and focus on conventional forces alone. He was later to go on to throw light on the questionable strategic logic of Sandys's plan by pointing out that there was, in any event, a major time lag between planned theatre nuclear weapon deployment in Europe and planned reductions in BAOR.

Crossman's arguments were taken further by Dennis Healey who criticized Sandys 'for basing the whole of alliance strategy on the limited use of atomic weapons [in which] they really do not believe . . . at all',[136] and by using it mainly as a means for legitimizing reductions in conventional forces. Rather, Healey preferred the creation of a conventional buffer which could allow

---

[132] Report of the 56th Annual Conference of the Labour Party, London Transport House 1956, 177.

[133] Groom, *British Thinking about Nuclear Weapons*, 301.

[134] Horne, *Macmillan, 1957–1986*, 52.

[135] Quoted in Groom, *British Thinking about Nuclear Weapons*, 213.

[136] For Head's speech see House of Commons, vol. 577, cols. 416–21, 7 Nov. 1957.

for conventional responses to military challenges. While, similarly to Sandys, the Americans saw limited war in nuclear terms, Healey placed emphasis on constraining responses, if possible, to the non-nuclear level. Unfortunately this still begged the question of how troops would be found and where the money would come from—a criticism that those opposed to Sandys would still have to address.

Outside these political circles, responses remained generally tempered. Some observers reacted to the emphasis Sandys was placing on massive retaliation as opposed to limited war, others responded to the cutbacks he was making to Britain's conventional forces. Liddell Hart, for example, maintained that while the paper did not go as far as he would have liked 'It was quite as good as I expected, and nearly as good as I hoped.'[137] On 14 February he had told Sandys that his speech in the Commons on the new defence plans was 'the most realistic appreciation of the problem that has come from any official quarter'.[138]

Nevertheless Liddell Hart was later to warn that 'the White Paper also shows a continuing trust in the saving grace of tactical atomic weapons, and that tends to confuse its own conclusions'. He later questioned whether the pursuit of an independent British deterrent would not subtract from her resources needed for 'brush-fire' wars and add to the risks of world war by encouraging other NATO countries (especially Germany) to acquire their own nuclear weapons.[139] Thus in spite of his initial favourable response, by the end of 1957 Liddell Hart was questioning the two major pillars of the paper—conventional cutbacks and the independent nuclear emphasis.

Buzzard, on the other hand, from the start deplored the thrust of Sandys's reasoning, perceiving him as attempting to negate all that he felt made necessary the adoption of a policy of graduated deterrence. At the beginning of March 1957, following a speech by Sandys in the House, the Admiral had written to Liddell Hart stating that Sandys

[137] Liddell Hart to Post 12 Apr. 1957, 1/621, Correspondence with Duncan Sandys. Liddell Hart Papers, Liddell Hart Centre for Military Archives (LHCMA).

[138] Liddell Hart to Sandys, 14 Feb. 1957 1/621, Correspondence with Duncan Sandys. Liddell Hart Papers (LHCMA).

[139] Notes on the 'White Paper on Defence', Apr. 1957, 10/1957/20, Liddell Hart Papers, (LHCMA).

has missed the point completely, that if only he would concentrate thoughts and resources on deterring and suppressing limited war he would not only be dealing with the real threat, but also be doing the best possible to prevent global war, since that can now only happen if we fail to deter or suppress limited war.[140]

Conversely, the strong proponent of Britain's nuclear deterrent, Sir John Slessor, who generally was to welcome the paper, felt that the long war–short war dichotomy had been fudged, and preferred to denounce the 'nonsense' of graduated nuclear deterrence he felt implicit in parts of the paper.[141] He also was prepared to admit that cuts in the conventional forces had gone very far.

Nevertheless, Sandys proceeded with his cuts ignoring internal criticisms both from government and opposition as well as experts and press.[142] He was not to shift tack when it came to dealing with the very negative foreign responses to the British 'New Look'.

## The Wider External Response

The far-reaching nature of the changes in force structure sought by Sandys and Macmillan is underlined not only by the reactions of the Chiefs, service heads, the broader British political leadership and domestic expert opinion but also by those of Britain's allies in NATO and the WEU. Throughout the period of the White Paper negotiations and in the months thereafter, Britain's representatives in these two organizations reported on the unease that the news of Sandys's plans was causing. In March 1957 Sir Frank Roberts at the UK Permanent Delegation in Paris wrote to the Foreign Office that the statement in the White Paper which maintained that 375,000 regulars would be sufficient to effectively replace the present strength of 700,000 troops, would have a 'shattering' effect on NATO. He went on that 'the mention of the figure of 375,000 will also at once revive questions about our capacity and intention to

---

[140] Buzzard to Liddell Hart, 1/140/63, 4 Mar. 1957, Liddell Hart Papers (LHCMA).

[141] 'Sir John Slessor Comments on 1957 White Paper', Slessor Papers, Air Historical Branch, Ministry of Defence, London—Section III, Folder I, 'Global Strategy'.

[142] For a discussion of press reaction see for example A. Pierre, *Nuclear Politics* (London, 1972), 109.

maintain even 50,000 men plus the reduced 2nd TAF on the Continent'.[143]

Service objections were mirrored by allied responses, but Sandys remained relatively undeterred by either. For the Minister of Defence what was of greater concern was the issue of BAOR's cost.[144] Indeed, the Minister of Defence made little attempt to dispel fears that

the impression is bound to be created that, whatever the opinion of our allies, consultation is a formality and we have again taken an unilateral decision part of which will involve unlimited further cuts in BAOR.[145]

Yet, for Macmillan and Sandys, the issue could now be only one of packaging and not one of concessions or alterations in policy. While Foreign Secretary Selwyn Lloyd reported that Britain's proposals to reduce her troops on the Continent had been received without enthusiasm[146] and that both the French and German governments had been disturbed by the reductions planned in BAOR, it was Macmillan's view that the British case would 'need to be developed with skill and firmness; and in the meantime we should do nothing to imply that we had doubts that it would be accepted'.[147] Consequently, when French Foreign Minister Mollet informed the British that France attached great importance to 'la présence humaine', that modern weapons were no substitute for men, and that in certain circumstance a strategy of massive retaliation lacked credibility,[148] he was told that Britain recognized that there was a balance of risks involved but the pressures on her economy were very great.[149] In turn, when Chancellor Adenauer com-

[143] AIR 8/2157, Roberts to Foreign Office, No. 108, 27 Mar. 1957. It should be noted that 2nd TAF was also to be reduced from 33 squadrons of 466 aircraft to 18 squadrons of 216 planes by March 1958. This would then be cut back to 10 squadrons of 102 fighters by 1961. Light bombers were to be reduced from 17 squadrons of 170 aircraft to 5 squadrons of 80 aircraft by March 1958. These were then to be cut to 4 squadrons of 64 aircraft by March 1960.

[144] See for example CAB 131/18, DC 2 (57) 2, 27 Feb. 1957.

[145] AIR 8/2157, Steele to Foreign Office, No. 263, 31 Mar. 1957.

[146] PREM 11/1842, CC 14 (57) 1, 28 Feb. 1957.

[147] CAB 128/31, CC 12 (57) 1, 28 Feb. 1957.

[148] PREM 11/1847, Jebb to Macmillan, 18 Feb. 1957; also see NA, RG 59, 741.5/4-2457, 24 Apr. 1957.

[149] PREM 11/1847, Foreign Office to Paris, No. 422, 21 Feb. 1957; also see AIR 2/14712, record of discussion between Bourges Manoury and Sandys, 14 Feb. 1957.

plained that reductions in BAOR would lead to a chain reaction of reductions in other NATO countries, he was told by Ambassador Sir Christopher Steele that in the event of a major Soviet aggression, nuclear retaliation would follow within hours and that the combat efficiency of Britain's remaining conventional forces would, in any event, be greater in the future than at present.[150]

The Americans, too, were left in no doubt that Britain would not alter its course because of allied pressures. In January 1957, when Ambassador Caccia told US officials that tactical nuclear weapons would increase the firepower of Britain's remaining forces, he did not suggest there would be a linkage in timing between reductions and tactical nuclear weapons deployment.[151] According to American Ambassador Whitney, the fact that Sandys was cutting British troops in Europe before tactical nuclear weapons were in place meant that the Minister of Defence's policy rested on an implicit assumption that the Soviets would not attempt for the next few years to extend power by direct military means and that a 'major factor is reliance on [the] US nuclear deterrent'. Thus American concern was not that Britain would go off on its own in terms of nuclear power and deterrence but that it was too willing to rely on the nuclear arsenal of the United States.[152]

In correspondence between Sandys and Dulles, the Minister of Defence maintained that while he hoped that Britain's troop cuts would not adversely influence NATO, they would, he stressed, be carried out irrespective of NATO demands.[153] Even when President Eisenhower told Macmillan at the Bermuda conference in March that Britain's new policy reminded him of the US 'New Look', 'an idea which, however, had been considerably affected since its formulation a few years ago by political considerations around the world',[154] Macmillan

---

[150] PREM 11/1829A, Bonn to Foreign Office, No. 382, 6 May 1957; also see NA, RG 59, 741.5/5-1357, Embassy London to Department of State, Embtel. 6144, 10 May 1957.

[151] NA, RG 59, 741.5/1-1157, 11 Jan. 1957.

[152] NA, RG 59, 741.5/3-357, Whitney to Dulles, No. 4619, 3 Mar. 1957.

[153] Eisenhower Library, Dulles Papers, 1952–9, General Correspondence and Memorandum Series, memos of Conversations-General-S(1) 30 Jan. 1957.

[154] Eisenhower Library, Office of the Staff Secretary, International Trips, Box 2, The Bermuda Conference 21–3 Mar. 1957.

remained unimpressed and unwilling to alter the direction of policy laid out by Sandys in the White Paper. Public Pentagon statements about UK claims that the British Isles was indefensible in the thermonuclear age represented a 'defeatist military attitude'[159] were also ignored.

By the time of the NATO heads of government meeting in Paris in December 1957, the British had managed to gain NATO acceptance of a reduction in BAOR of 31,500 men to approximately 63,000–64,000 to be reached by 1 April 1958. In the autumn of 1957, they had emphasized their inability to meet the costs of British troops in Germany after March 1958 and their continued interest in reducing BAOR by another 13,500.[156] While in October the British were prepared to concede that 5,000 men of the strategic reserve be left on the Continent, this was only dependent on future German aid, and the other 8,000 men of the second 13,500 'slice' remained non-negotiable.[157]

In Paris, Macmillan stressed the UK responsibilities outside NATO and made a plea for the concept of balanced collective forces within the organization. He called for the pooling of resources and the designation of specific tasks to various members.[158] With the emphasis on Britain's nuclear contribution, there was no attempt to moderate her position on force reductions. Indeed, in a meeting with Dulles and the Secretary General of NATO, Sandys emphasized 'the importance as he saw it of planning massive retaliatory action if there were any armed attack in Europe', and he criticized Eisenhower's speech at the conference for undercutting this impression through the

[155] 'Britain to Rely on Nuclear Arms, End Draft, Cut Sea and Air Units; Pentagon Sees Move as Defeatist', by James Reston, *New York Times*, 4 Apr. 1957.

[156] NATO was not yet informed of Britain's interest in reducing her forces in Germany to below 50,000. Throughout this period Powell appears to have remained convinced that NATO should not be made aware of the full scope of Britain's ultimate force cuts and should be told that 'the changes produced by the White Paper were such that we were not able yet to forecast up to 1962 and are still working out the details'. DEFE 4/97, COS 35 (57) 1, 10 May 1957. The Permanent Secretary was obviously concerned that knowledge of these cuts would create further opposition to Sandys's plans.

[157] NA, RG 59, 741.5/10-2257, Elbrick to Dulles, 22 Oct. 1957.

[158] *Foreign Relations of the United States*, vol. iv, 1955–7, No. 75, US Delegation at the NATO Heads of Government Meeting to the Department of State, 17 Dec. 1957.

statement that Soviet aggression would be met with 'all appropriate force'.[159]

Although the Americans had been informed by a senior British official 'close to Sandys' that the Minister's 'thinking had changed in recent months so that Sandys no longer relied so heavily or almost exclusively upon [the] concept of massive retaliation to deter war',[160] the statements of the Minister at the conference did not indicate a major shift in British force planning. Rather, Sandys and Macmillan remained intent upon pushing a strategic concept that allowed for large reductions in British troop deployments. Although not everyone at the conference was impressed with the strategic logic of the British arguments, few could have left believing the British would alter their position.

While according to Andrew Pierre the significance of the White Paper 'lies in the practical conclusions for the military services and the economy which were drawn from its strategic assumptions',[161] it would possibly be more accurate to explain that it was the practical consequences for strategy and force posture that were drawn from the White Paper's economic foundations that are of note. Indeed, even Sir John Slessor, in commenting on the White Paper, admitted that the main rationales behind the document were not strategic considerations but the objectives of securing financial savings and reaping the political rewards of terminating national service.

A number of important factors can be gleaned from the debate on the White Paper that reflected on thinking concerning British nuclear strategy in the mid-1950s. The manpower issue was recognized by both Sandys and the Chiefs as being more fundamental than anything else in that it impinged both directly and indirectly on roles and capabilities. However, similarly to the 1955–6 discussions on national service, only limited reference was made either by the Ministry of Defence or the Chiefs of Staff to massive retaliation strategy and/or tactical nuclear deploy-

[159] Eisenhower Library, John Foster Dulles Papers 1952–9, General Correspondence and Memoranda Series, Box 1, Memos of Conversation-General-S(1), Memorandum of Conversation with The Right Honourable Duncan Sandys, 17 Dec. 1957.
[160] NA, RG 59, 741.5/11-957, London to Secretary of State No. 2972, 9 Nov. 1957.
[161] Pierre, *Nuclear Politics*, 96.

ments as means for cutting back on manpower requirements. That nuclear weapons would replace conventional forces was always an accepted concept but it was rarely fleshed out in the sense that timing of deployment and numbers of men to be removed and weapons to be deployed were not often clearly linked—though, admittedly, a definite link in terms of numbers would have been difficult to secure. However, it should be recognized that the shift away from conventional forces was primarily a result of a conscious effort by Sandys to reduce manpower and secure savings. Indeed, he often appears to have approached the problem independently of an overall strategic conception, with the conventional and the nuclear components of his strategy not related other than in an implicit manner. Thus, the achievement of a strategically consistent balance between a declaratory stress on nuclear deterrence and a cutback in conventional global war preparations was as much a result of economic as strategic reasoning.

Concomitantly, the emphasis on independent deterrence in the context of the negotiations over the White Paper seems less forthright than appears reasonable to assume in the light of the admittedly very general declaratory statements concerning the independent role of Britain's nuclear force. Indeed, there seemed to be a *continuity* in strategic rationales underpinning the acquisition of a British nuclear deterrent that focused primarily on interdependence with the United States in terms of strategic planning. Certainly in this sense, the British 'New Look' was anything but new. This is a subject that will be investigated in greater depth in the next chapter.

The 'newness' of the British 'New Look' must rather rest on the uniqueness of Sandys's contribution in 1957 and the changes he brought about in conventional forces. Clearly, Sandys's approach was crucial to the outcome of the debate as he ignored and overrode service objections and predilections that led them to prefer a posture of multiple capabilities. He refused to get embroiled in interminable negotiations and instead sought to impose his own solutions. Thus the first stage of the White Paper debate dealt with the actual reductions of manpower. The word debate is, in turn, most probably inappropriate as Sandys pushed ahead relatively independent of any outside suggestions. During the second stage—which involved the wording of the White Paper and the implications of responsibility —Sandys appeared more amenable to pressure, but his style could only have caused tensions which further poisoned relationships. By the first week of April Sandys had achieved his goals as far as manpower was concerned and was in a good position to undercut service roles and capabilities.

With 1957 representing a turning point in policies concerning the size of Britain's conventional order of battle and the balance between her nuclear and conventional forces, it is clear that this year straddles a major *discontinuity* in British strategic planning —even though the pressures for such changes had long been existent. It is certainly significant that by terminating national service[162] Sandys had altered the balance between nuclear and conventional fire-power and not only on the declaratory level. The proposed force structure embodied in the paragraphs of the 1957 White Paper reflected a strategic coherence that was lacking in defence policies prior to 1957. The paper represented a shift away from an attachment to multiple capabilities to a greater emphasis on nuclear weapons at the expense of conventional forces. In this sense it was internally consistent. Consequently, it can be argued that the 1957 White Paper was truly the British 'New Look'. As Liddell Hart told the Minister of Defence, his task was to tackle ' "vested interests in vanished dreams" ',[163] and this Sandys succeeded in doing where others before him had faltered.

[162] Towards the end of the following year, Sandys was to be very optimistic about recruitment prospects indicating that the size of the Army could be raised to 180,000 and that he had 'every reason for confidence in our ability to carry through our plan to end National Service in 1962'. There would thus be no return to the large formations extant prior to 1957.
[163] Liddell Hart to Sandys, 14 Feb. 1957, 1/621, Liddell Hart Papers (LHCMA).

# 6

## The Independent Deterrent and Anglo-American Co-operation, 1957–1958

THE Suez débâcle highlighted most acutely the problems of independent British military and political action and brought to the fore debates as to the role of Britain in her relations with both the United States and Western Europe. The crisis certainly served to inform upon a major reassessment of Britain's strategic policy, but this was expressed somewhat differently on the levels of declaratory and action policy.

For reasons of international prestige, party politics, and the more specific need of seeking to address any future Anglo-American split, Britain's independence was often stressed, an independence which for strong economic reasons had to be framed in nuclear deterrent terms rather than those of conventional power. However, on the level of actual foreign policy, the Prime Minister, Minister of Defence, and Foreign Secretary were unequivocal in their search for greater American co-operation. This reflected their view that in the new strategic environment of the post-Suez world—an environment in which the limitations of British power were more than ever apparent—Britain's defence interests would best be served by *rapprochement* with the Americans and co-ordination with that country's military and political might. By so doing, economic imperatives could be addressed while the inevitable negative military consequences of financial cutbacks would be ameliorated. Independence would of course have to be subordinated, declaratory intent notwithstanding. When viewed against the backdrop of pre-1957 attempts to integrate nuclear planning with the United States, and the omniscience of the theme of the 'special relationship' in the decade following the end of World War II, qualitatively little had changed.

## The Context for Strategic Planning: The Move towards Interdependence and the Amendment of the 1954 Atomic Energy Act

If in the wake of Suez the procurement of a force posture so capable of large-scale independent military action was the main objective of British policy-makers, then there was little sense in cutting back on conventional forces. For many, the lessons of Suez did not point to cuts in manpower and conventional capabilities and an increased focus on the deterrent. For example, even as strong a supporter of the deterrent as Sir John Slessor was of the opinion that 'The aftermath of Egypt is going to mean that it will be crazy to reduce our real fighting strength probably for years to come'.[1] Yet, these ideas could not be squared with Macmillan's and Sandys's thinking which in the post-Suez environment was strongly influenced by the perceived necessity of tackling economic issues (a tendency exemplified in the White Paper discussions) and questions of prestige.

While economic concerns militated against too strong a conventional force focus, nuclear weapons touched at the heart of questions of status. Thus, for British Ambassador to the United States, Sir Harold Caccia, for whom the United Kingdom's international prestige seems to have been a major goal, Britain's acceptance as a great power now rested to a large extent on having a military nuclear programme.[2] The Ambassador also seems to have recognized that prestige necessitated a greater co-operation with the most powerful country in the world—a co-operation that would be enhanced once Britain demonstrated her ability to produce a wide range of nuclear weapons including the H-bomb. Clearly, he was confusing objectives of nuclear independence and interdependence. Indeed, the prestige argument took Caccia a step further to argue that nuclear weapons were necessary because Britain might find herself standing alone against the Soviet Union:

Apart from these considerations our recent experience over Suez also brings out [the] danger involved if we are ever to leave our nuclear

[1] Slessor to Hore Belisha, 8 Dec. 1956, Julian Amery Papers (LHCMA).
[2] FO 371/126682, Caccia to Foreign Office, No. 3, 1 Jan. 1957.

protection to the United States alone and the price to the United States were a risk of Soviet retaliation against them.[3]

Yet, it is significant to note that, despite Caccia's expressed concerns, in the wake of the Suez crisis the perceived need for acquiring a 'standing alone' capability was not regarded as important as the needs to address economic and political vulnerabilities through greater co-ordination with Washington. This point was clearly brought out at a Nuclear History Project Oral History Conference on the 1957 White Paper held at King's College London in July 1988, where participants were unequivocal in minimizing the significance of British isolation from the United States in the face of Soviet nuclear threats:

*Question.* How seriously was the risk of nuclear blackmail taken in the aftermath of the Suez crisis?

*Sir Richard Powell (Permanent Secretary, Ministry of Defence).* Not in my recollection.

*Sir Richard Way (Deputy Secretary, Ministry of Defence).* No.

*Powell.* No, we felt that Russian policy was essentially a defensive policy, and not a blackmailing or offensive policy.

*Question.* Did Bulganin's nuclear threat leave any impression at all?

*Way.* I would have thought that Suez made no difference at all.

*Powell.* I don't think so.[4]

Thus, while the 'standing alone hypothesis' was stressed on the declaratory level as a rationale for a British independent nuclear capability,[5] it was not regarded as the major objective, nor, as noted in the previous chapter, overemphasized on the operational level to the detriment of combined planning which remained the primary goal. Macmillan, of course, clouded the issue when on 27 February 1957 he told the Defence Committee that Britain should seek to attain 'independent deterrent influence'. However, when rooted in the context of discussions in 1957 and

---

[3] FO 371/126682, Caccia to Foreign Office, No. 3, 1 Jan. 1957.

[4] Conference held in the Department of War Studies, King's College London on 'The Sandys White Paper of 1957', 1 July 1988.

[5] See Sandys's speech in the House of Commons during the 1957 White Paper Defence debate in House of Commons, vol. 568, cols. 1758–1878, 16 Apr. 1957 and cols. 1930–2059, 17 Apr. 1957.

1958, what the Prime Minister was expressing was his interest in 'influencing' the Soviet Union to desist from attacks on the UK and 'influencing' the Americans to co-operate more fully with Britain's strategic planning. The former type of influence addressed issues of prestige (in that Britain could be seen as a world power intent upon independently deterring the Soviet Union) without the necessity of relating declaratory policy very closely to actual intent (the Soviets could never be certain whether Britain would use her nuclear weapons independently of the Americans); while the latter form of influence sought to make certain that in the event of Western resolve actually being tested, America's fate would be closely bound up with that of Britain's. As the 1958 White Paper was to go on and state: 'If the full benefits of collective defence are to be obtained, the members of the alliance must be prepared to accept they will inevitably become more and more inextricably dependent on one another . . .'.[6]

Thus in the wake of the Suez crisis Macmillan seems to have been most interested in using the deterrent as an incentive for further American co-operation through which, in the final analysis, both deterrence and joint operational planning would be strengthened. It was all well and good to speak of Britain's independent nuclear deterrent capabilities, but in a time of real crisis, American deterrent and war fighting capabilities would be what was needed. Here, the existence of a British independent nuclear force was not insignificant as it could not be ignored by American policy-makers who would have to find some way of integrating it into American strategic planning. This definition of independence was indirectly but clearly recognized by the Directors of Plans in October 1957 when they maintained that what Britain was seeking was an Anglo-American global understanding similar to that which had existed during the Second World War. In this regard it was important to recognize that Britain's importance in American eyes derived from her nuclear weapons rather than her conventional forces, which were being run down in line with the policies announced in the White Paper.[7]

---

[6] *Report on Defence 1958*, Cmnd. 363, Feb. 1958, para. 24.
[7] DEFE 6/48, JP (57), Note 12, 21 Oct. 1957.

It was this understanding of Britain's intentions that allowed the US to view statements on independence with some equanimity. For example, in May 1957, a British representative at the Western European Union stated that Eisenhower felt that the White Paper 'represents an effort to bring our military establishment into line with the military facts of today'.[8] Privately, the Americans recognized that there was a wide gap between declaratory and action policy, that there was a realization in London that 'the UK [was] no long able to [be] an independent military power [and that] . . . this means, though not so stated, acceptance [of a] supplementary role in collective defence under US leadership'.[9]

Throughout 1957 and 1958 Britain certainly made plain to the Americans her desire to further co-operation with them on as many levels as possible. Sir Harold Caccia, indicated this British preference when he informed the Foreign Secretary, Selwyn Lloyd, of his view that

I assume it to be our object to re-establish our relations [with the US] on their previous footing and to recover all of our special position. While the Communist threat remains, nothing else makes sense, in dealing with a country whose power is likely to increase in relation to our own.[10]

Churchill and Eisenhower were at this time also exchanging letters expressing their concerns about the need to improve co-operation and their—in Churchill's words—'unfaltering conviction, that the theme of the Anglo-American alliance is more important today than at any time since the war'.[11] The recognition that there was a need for Anglo-American co-ordination as opposed to independent action was thus widespread. Consequently, prior to Sandys's visit to Washington in January, he was informed by Selwyn Lloyd not to appear too anxious in securing American goodwill, but also to be careful not to appear overly resentful with regard to past American actions.[12] The image of independence was to be fostered, but

---

[8] ADM 205/114, Meade to Foreign Office, No. 29, 6 May 1957; also see FO 371/126684, Caccia to Foreign Office, No. 1846, 14 Sept. 1957.

[9] NA, RG 59, 741.5/4-957, No. 5488, Whitney to Dulles, 9 Apr. 1957.

[10] PREM 11/2189, Caccia to Lloyd, AU 1051/53, 1 Jan. 1957.

[11] J. Baylis, *Anglo-American Defence Relations, 1939–84* (London, 1984), 88–9.

[12] FO 371/126707, Logan to Forward, 23 Jan. 1957.

the goal was to be the provision of American Thor missiles, the further amendment of the McMahon Act, and an improved appreciation by the United States of Britain's global position.

It is evident that the climate was not one in which Britain was seeking to stress its independence from Washington. By the end of January relations had improved so dramatically that on the 29th of that month Macmillan was able to inform the Cabinet that he had been invited by President Eisenhower to meet in Bermuda and that 'the invitation was a welcome sign that the United States government were now prepared to resume friendly relations with this country'.[13] It was Sir Harold Caccia's view that the meeting would provide the impetus needed to reinvigorate the alliance,[14] and indeed, Macmillan wrote back to the Cabinet from the conference that Eisenhower appeared to be 'genuinely anxious' to restore the traditional relationship between the United States and Britain.[15] In his opening statement to the conference Macmillan stressed that no single country alone could defeat communism, while Eisenhower in his statement maintained that the object now 'was to strengthen to the greatest extent the closest co-operation between the two countries'.[16]

The steady improvement of relations during 1957 meant that following the Soviet launch of Sputnik in October,[17] the United States and Britain could push ahead with further co-operation in the fields of weapons systems and nuclear energy. Long-held British aspirations for greater collaboration in the fields of nuclear information exchanges as well as strategic planning seemed now more than ever possible. Sandys demonstrated a recognition that the Sputnik launch afforded such an improvement in relations when he informed the Conservative Party Conference in October 1957 that Britain would readily respond

---

[13] CAB 128/31, CC 4 (57) 8, 29 Jan. 1957; also see CAB 128/31, CC 10 (57) 3, 11 Feb. 1957.

[14] FO 371/126684, Caccia to Foreign Office, No. 309, 11 Feb. 1957.

[15] CAB 128/31, CC 22 (57) 3, 22 Mar. 1957.

[16] PREM 11/1838, BC (P) 1st, 21 Mar. 1957.

[17] For US attempts to get Britain to launch her own satellite the following year see NA, RG 59, 741.56301/9-2558. Discussion between Murphy and Powell, 25 Sept. 1958. For UK rejection and its expression of the need to examine 'just how such a venture would relate to basic decisions now being taken regarding the future of an independent UK ballistic missile' see NA, RG 59, 741.56301/10-1558, US Assistance for UK Satellite Launching, 15 Oct. 1958.

to any American attempts to improve collaboration in the nuclear field. Concomitantly, Macmillan wrote to Eisenhower that 'countries of the free world should try to pool their resources to meet the increasing threat'.[18] Prior to Macmillan's meeting with Eisenhower in October 1957, Powell told the Chiefs that future Anglo-American relations would be based on: (1) closer consultation and co-ordinated action in military, political, and economic fields; (2) the sharing of information on the availability of nuclear and other modern weapons; and (3) improvements in other efforts such as balanced collective forces.[19] Macmillan, in turn, informed the Cabinet that his objective in the forthcoming discussions would be to broaden the repeal of the McMahon Act so that the technical resources of both countries might be organized to 'effect a genuine policy of collective defence and that the demands on our economy might be reduced'.[20] Clearly, by the end of the year, co-operation rather than independence remained the key word.

The British were at this stage intent upon securing data on both the design and production of nuclear and hydrogen bombs. With such information British scientists could, it was hoped, develop nuclear warhead designs for thermonuclear bombs without further testing, thereby saving millions of pounds and circumventing the difficult issue of a possible moratorium on testing. While naturally keen on fostering nuclear co-operation, when in Washington in October 1957, Macmillan had still been surprised with the readiness of Eisenhower to call for the repeal of the 1954 McMahon Act and push forward with nuclear collaboration.[21] The demonstration of Soviet missile capabilities had driven Washington further to the recognition that nuclear co-operation with allies promised greater security benefits than nuclear isolation. Thus following the October Washington summit Macmillan reported that he and Eisenhower had concluded that no country could face the communist menace alone and that the ' "Declaration of Common Purpose" agreed to with the Americans . . . was in effect a declaration of

---

[18] H. Macmillan, *Riding the Storm* (London, 1971), 315.

[19] DEFE 4/101, COS 81 (57), 21 Oct. 1957.

[20] CAB 128/31, CC 74 (57) 2, 21 Oct. 1957.

[21] A. Horne, *Macmillan 1957–1986* (London, 1989), 57.

inter-dependence.'[22] He went on to tell his Cabinet that 'it had been agreed that the United States and the United Kingdom should regard the possession of nuclear weapons as a trust for the defence of the free world'.[23] Co-operation was certainly to receive a boost as a result of the Washington meeting. Two joint US-British committees were set up, one dealing with nuclear co-operation between the two countries, including exchanges of nuclear data, and the second, chaired by Sir Richard Powell, specifically covering the subject of nuclear weapons including missiles. The areas of future co-operation between the American and the UK nuclear programmes rapidly became apparent to British policy-makers on the two committees. During meetings begun immediately after the Eisenhower–Macmillan discussions and continuing into November and December, the Americans demonstrated a willingness to transfer certain nuclear materials for military and non-military uses together with non-nuclear components associated with nuclear weapons. Specifically, the United Kingdom would import U-235—needed for the manufacture of thermonuclear warheads as well as the construction of a nuclear submarine fleet—in exchange for British produced plutonium. Britain could also be supplied with non-nuclear components for fission weapons. The Americans also expressed a readiness to discuss measures mutually to enhance the design, development, and production of nuclear weapons and there was agreement to the transfer of information to America's allies which would enable them in the event of war to place US warheads on their own delivery systems. This was of interest to the United Kingdom which recognized the advantage of receiving certain American warhead designs rather than investing in an independent effort. Consequently, Britain expressed agreement not to manufacture nuclear warheads for American supplied artillery rockets, or produce her own nuclear artillery shells or all its requisites for nuclear depth charges or bombs. In return the Americans promised that in the event of a conflict Britain would be supplied with these weapons under existing NATO procedures. In the long term Britain would receive data related to any type of nuclear or thermonuclear weapon she had under

[22] CAB 128/31, CC 76 (57) 2, 28 Oct. 1957; also see Eisenhower Library, Telephone calls of John Foster Dulles, Smith to Dulles, 24 Oct. 1957.
[23] CAB 128/31, CC 76 (57) 2, 28 Oct. 1957.

development in exchange for the supply to the Americans of information on her own weapon designs. Both countries could monitor the progress of each other's delivery systems and could if they so desired seek to procure systems or components. Finally, Washington expressed its amenability to delivering to the United Kingdom military nuclear power plants together with associated components. Here, in exchange for the transfer of certain information on the Calder Hall nuclear reactor, Britain was to receive a submarine reactor and fuel from the United States.[24] The impending legislation clearly allowed for an interdependence in areas prohibited under the 1954 legislation and bound up the British further than ever before in American military and civil nuclear planning.

Disputes between the US Atomic Energy Commission and the Joint Committee on Atomic Energy over the issues of funds to purchase British plutonium, the transfer of components for nuclear weapons, the apparent one-sidedness of the exchange agreement, the dangers of potential major British commercial benefit, and the procedures whereby the JCAE could review the Agreements for Co-operation, slowed but did not substantially impede the general co-operation.[25] Additional complications were associated with American concerns over the amount of information to be passed to Britain concerning thermonuclear weapons,[26] the problem of a nuclear test moratorium, and, as shall be noted in a later section, the debate over control arrangements concerning US IRBM deployments in Britain.

Yet by the end of 1957 the talks on nuclear and military co-operation had resulted in agreement on US supply of uranium to Britain after 1962. Less progress was realized on the issue of British use of American nuclear test sites, though Admiral Rickover's agreement to allow the British Navy to purchase a submarine reactor from Westinghouse was obviously encouraging. Difficulties over the command and control of Thor were

[24] For a more technical discussion see J. Simpson, *The Independent Nuclear State* (London, 1983), 131–4.

[25] Hearings before the Subcommittee on Agreements for Co-operation of the JCAE. Amending the Atomic Energy Act of 1954—Exchange of Military Information and Material with Allies, 85th Congress, 2nd Session 1958, 104, 187, 196, 229–30, 298.

[26] For an extensive review of the American side of the negotiations see T. J. Botti, *The Long Wait: The Forging of the Anglo-American Nuclear Alliance, 1945–1958* (Connecticut, 1987), Chs. 22, 23, and 24.

slowly resolved and last minute hitches revolved around the issue of the submarine–Calder Hall linkage with the British government not wishing to be the subject of domestic criticism that she was giving up commercial objectives for information on nuclear weapons. With regard to this latter issue, Macmillan told the Cabinet on 1 July 1958 that at this late stage the US government sought to include in the preamble to the treaty 'words defining its purpose as the promotion of the maximum advantage to both countries in the application of nuclear energy to both civil and military purposes'. It was the Prime Minister's view that the reference to civil use was unacceptable because it could provide the Americans with the means for pressurizing the UK to disclose information on the civil nuclear programme.[27] Fortunately for Macmillan, the Americans were prepared to accede to this request.[28]

Prior to the bill's enactment, Congress amended the new Bill such that the executive would not transfer non-nuclear components of nuclear weapons to countries other than Britain and that non-nuclear parts of thermonuclear weapons would not in the near future be transferred. The amending bill was discussed between Eisenhower and Macmillan in Washington on 7–8 June and a provisional military agreement was reached which would be presented to Congress once the bill had been passed. On 3 July 1958 an *Agreement for Co-operation on the Uses of Atomic Energy for Mutual Defence Purposes* was signed between the United States and the United Kingdom which allowed for the exchange of information concerning both the production and design of nuclear warheads as well as the transfer of fissile material.[29] This agreement was supplemented the following year by a further agreement which allowed for Britain procuring component parts of nuclear weapons as well as complete systems and facilitating the uranium 235–plutonium exchange.[30] Clearly, the degree of Anglo-American nuclear interdependence had

---

[27] CAB 128/32, CC 51 (58) 2, 1 July 1958.

[28] CAB 128/32, CC 52 (58) 3, 3 July 1958.

[29] Cmnd. 537, *Agreement . . . for Co-operation on the Uses of Atomic Energy for Mutual Defence Purposes*, Treaty Series No. 41 (1958).

[30] Cmnd. 859, *Amendment to Agreement between the Government of the United Kingdom of Great Britain and Northern Ireland and the Government of the United States of America for Cooperation on the Uses of Atomic Energy for Mutual Defence Purposes*, Treaty Series No. 72 (1959); also see Simpson op. cit.

reached a new level and independent British nuclear production and research was very much subordinated to the economically more attractive objective of nuclear collaboration with the United States.

## The Test Moratorium in the Context of Amending the McMahon Act

One of the more immediate impetuses behind Britain's interest in a quick revision of the 1954 Amendment was the looming danger of a nuclear test ban moratorium. Increasing public and Soviet pressure for a test ban and the fact that Macmillan had been informed that the earliest date for a British thermonuclear test of a weapon which was both resistant to technical counter-measures and also reliable would only be in September, made the British very eager for aid from the United States and very impatient with slow passage of the bill through the American legislative system.[31] This issue of the test moratorium served to highlight the inherent tensions between Britain's desire for independence as well as interdependence with the Americans.[32]

In a presentation of a set of Foreign Office proposals on disarmament at the Defence Committee on 17 March 1958—a package which included a temporary suspension of nuclear tests independent of other types of arms reductions—Foreign Secretary Selwyn Lloyd appeared to indicate that the policy was less of a serious proposal than a negotiating tactic. He pointed out that the West would only agree to suspend nuclear tests if the Soviet Union expressed willingness to allow for an effective system of inspection against surprise attack as well as external control over the cut-off of the production of fissile material for weapons purposes. But he admitted that 'the Soviet Government are not much more likely to accept the new package than the old one, and thus the practical risk of embarrassment to our nuclear weapons programme is scarcely greater

---

[31] Macmillan, *Riding the Storm*, 474.

[32] For a detailed discussion of this issue including the role of the disarmament commission, the move from the complete to a partial goal of disarmament, and the Conference on the Discontinuance of Nuclear Weapons Tests see J. P. G. Freeman, *British Nuclear Arms Control Policy in the Context of Anglo-American Relations, 1957–1968* (Basingstoke, 1986). For another perspective see R. Divine, *Blowing in the Wind: The Nuclear Test Ban Debate 1954–1960* (New York, 1978).

than before'.[33] In any event, it was the COSC's view that nuclear tests should not be suspended until the United Kingdom had completed her own essential tests. It was stressed that 'We do not regard it as satisfactory to have to rely on United States information.'[34] Moreover at a COSC meeting at the beginning of March 1958 the view was expressed that 'It was also essential to us that we should receive from the United States before the cut-off date either sufficient weapons to fulfil our requirement or sufficient fissile material for our own weapons.'[35] Britain's independent programme would therefore not be impeded, though clearly that would have to depend on a measure of co-operation with the United States. This was a tendency demonstrated in a subsequent Defence Committee discussion in which it was pointed out that the Americans were considering a suspension of nuclear tests and that this could limit Britain's ability to produce new weapons and maintain an independent deterrent unless the United States provided Britain with the necessary help. It was stressed that 'Our acceptance of any proposal for the suspension of tests should, therefore, be conditional upon the United States undertaking to help us . . . if the suspension came into effect.'[36] With her independent test series not yet completed and the substance and progress of future interdependence with the Americans stemming from a future McMahon Act Amendment still unsettled, the British government was to come under further pressure when the Soviets announced their unilateral decision to suspend nuclear tests in March 1958. At a Cabinet meeting on 1 April it was pointed out that it would be extremely difficult for the United Kingdom to give up testing until the substance of the amendment to the McMahon Act was clarified. Instead the UK would have to stress publicly that a Russian test series had just been completed and that an American test series was about to begin while the British series was not yet finished. Also it had to be emphasized that the Four Power Working Paper which included a provision for the suspension of nuclear tests had been rejected by the Soviet Union in 1957. The British intention to stall was further indicated by the

[33] CAB 131/19, D (58) 12, 17 Mar. 1958.
[34] CAB 131/19, D (58) 15, 18 Mar. 1958.
[35] DEFE 4/105, COS 22 (58) 2 discussion of JP (58) 26, 7 Mar. 1958.
[36] CAB 131/19, 5 (58) 2, 20 Mar. 1958.

suggestion that the topic should be discussed at a future meeting of all relevant heads of governments.[37]

Much to British consternation, by the end of April the Americans were indicating that they were considering suspending at the end of their current series further testing for about six months so as to allow discussions to proceed with the Russians on an adequate system of control.[38] The Americans were then quickly informed that Britain was strongly opposed to such a move and that there should be no departure from the previous policy which linked suspension of tests with on the one hand the cut-off, and on the other, conventional disarmament. The Americans were then told that Britain was only prepared to contemplate the suspension of nuclear tests after 31 October —when her own test series was completed—provided that no final decision be taken before the Prime Minister visited Washington in early June. It was further demanded that the suspension of tests apply only to megaton explosions with a kiloton ban awaiting further negotiation. Also, in their own discussions, the British stressed that

the Americans accept that our agreement to a suspension of tests would be conditional on their making available to us under the terms of the revised McMahon Act the information needed to replace that which we could get by continuing testing; this means that we cannot finally adopt this course until we know what will be available to us under the revised McMahon Act.[39]

This need to be interdependent with the Americans in order to facilitate Britain's independence was reaffirmed in terms of the issue of fissile production cut-off where the British demanded that any agreement on this subject was dependent not only on an accepted system of international inspection but also on the provision that 'the Americans are ready to provide us with the material needed to complete our weapons programme'.[40]

The thrust of these proposals was reaffirmed to the Americans just prior to Macmillan's visit to Washington in June 1958.[41] It was becoming increasingly clear that the British were intent

[37] CAB 128/32, CC 28 (58) 1, 1 Apr. 1958.
[38] CAB 130/147, Washington to FO, No. 1031, 30 Apr. 1958.
[39] CAB 130/147, FO to Washington, No. 3161.        [40] Ibid.
[41] CAB 130/147, GEN 649/2/1, 4 June 1958.

upon using their position on a test ban as an incentive for a favourable amendment of the McMahon Act. Unfortunately, the Americans were at this stage moving away from the idea that it would be possible to pass information to the British on the subject of hydrogen bombs and their associated components and thus Botti is correct in stating that 'the British found their early June 1958 discussions with the Americans less fruitful than they had hoped'.[42] Britain had therefore no other option and was forced to carry out her test programme with megaton explosions on Christmas Island in April, August, and September 1958. But with her test series complete and her improved interdependence with the Americans firmly secured, Britain was then able to relate much more positively to the test ban moratorium proposals and negotiations which began at the end of October.

Thus according to Freeman,

Britain was, by the end of 1958, in a position to satisfy a number of superficially incompatible objectives: first, to utilise US knowledge so as to make rapid progress to the achievement of what was judged an adequate national nuclear stockpile; second, to forestall a growth in the number of weapon states by a [Comprehensive Test Ban Treaty] (and possibly a 'cut-off' proposal); and third, to pursue any arms control agreement which would inhibit a move on the part of the two super-powers to achieve any nuclear weapons advances that might threaten Britain's nuclear deterrent policy.[43]

Thus when the Soviet Union announced in the Autumn of 1958 that it considered itself unbound by its earlier promise of unilateral test restraint and free to match any Western tests, the United Kingdom joined the United States in terminating its test series. As Freeman goes on to state, 'In essence the Anglo-American relationship with regard to a test ban was now settled for the next three, and even perhaps five, years'.[44]

[42] Botti, *The Long Wait*, 232.
[43] Freeman, *British Nuclear Arms Control Policy*, 90.
[44] Ibid.

Independence and Interdependence in Planning and
Targeting: 1957–1958

While the 1958 White Paper stated that Britain was making an
increasingly important contribution to the Western deterrent,
this was only expressed after an explicit statement that the
allied defence system 'continues to rest primarily upon the
strength and constant readiness of the American Strategic Air
Command'.[45] Clearly the definition that British policy-makers
were prepared to give to 'independence' was still very circumscribed. From the available documents it is clear that in 1958
the paradoxical objectives of an emphasis on maintaining an
'independent' British nuclear force and the recognition that the
major thrust of policy must be directed towards a deterrent
posture in conjunction with the United States, remained constant. The need to secure interdependence with the Americans
while at the same time demonstrating a capability to act alone
was increasingly driven by improving Soviet technology—as
witnessed in the Sputnik launch—and projections as to that
country's future deployments. Doubts that had arisen following
Suez as to future American willingness to support Britain with
credible nuclear guarantees were further exacerbated by
America's increasing vulnerability to the USSR's burgeoning
nuclear capability.

In 1958 the COSC paid much attention to the concept of
'nuclear sufficiency' which they defined as being reached 'when
the U.S.S.R. has sufficient nuclear warheads and effective
means of delivery to allocate to the targets which she would
wish to destroy in global war'.[46] It was the Joint Intelligence
Committee's view that the Soviets would obtain this capability
by 1960–2.[47] Consequently, the Chiefs saw the major implications of this capability revolving around the questions of whether
the United States was now more unlikely to risk nuclear
destruction; whether the Soviets would be more inclined to take
chances in areas of the globe which they did not believe the
Americans would consider vital; of what proportion of British

[45] *Report on Defence 1958*, Cmnd. 363, Feb. 1958, para. 29.
[46] DEFE 4/111, COS 77 (58) 1, 3 Sept. 1958.
[47] DEFE 5/82, COS (58) 39, 13 Feb. 1958.

resources would have to be devoted to the Western deterrent and what to conventional forces as well as tactical nuclear weapons; and whether in this context Britain should maintain an independent deterrent and if so what 'would be the smallest deterrent which would make Russia think twice before risking war with the United Kingdom'.[48]

In January 1958, during a COSC deliberation on a JPS paper entitled 'The Effect on Soviet Policy of the Attainment by the USSR of Nuclear Sufficiency', it had been argued that the Soviet perception of 'the firmness of purpose shown by the United States Government at present or in the future might not be shared by the American people'.[49] In September 1958 there was further general agreement that the Soviet achievement of 'nuclear sufficiency' would make the Americans more reluctant to risk global nuclear war, the Russians more likely to risk escalation in areas not considered vital to American interest, and that tactical nuclear weapons would be needed to offset adverse balances of manpower and deter limited war. However, it was stressed that Europe would only be considered vital to the US if American troops were stationed there—the need for which was therefore underlined.[50]

In the context of nuclear sufficiency, according to the CIGS, Sir Gerald Templer, the Russians by taking quick action might present the West with a *fait accompli* before it had time to react—an argument supported by Sir Richard Powell, who pointed to Berlin as such an area where the credibility of the deterrent could be tested due to the lack of a shield force. The general dangers were additionally acute because if attempts were made to keep a war with the Russians limited—a possibility according to Sir Dermot Boyle if both East and West agreed to such a limitation—the West would, the CAS believed, lose.[51] War, nevertheless, was perceived to be more likely as a result of miscalculation than from conscious Soviet design. It was the Joint Intelligence Committee's view that 'if global war comes it is most likely to do so as the result of some miscalculation on

[48] DEFE 4/111, COS 77 (58) 1, 3 Sept. 1958.
[49] DEFE 4/103, COS 6 (58) 1 discussion of JIC (57) 120 (Final), 17 Jan. 1958.
[50] DEFE 4/111, COS 77 (58) 1, 3 Sept. 1958.
[51] DEFE 4/103, COS (58) 6 discussion of JIC (57) 120 (Final), 17 Jan. 1958.

Russia's part',[52] though the contingency of surprise Soviet attack—an increasingly easier option for the Russians as their bomber bases multiplied and there was less need for redeployment before attack—had also to be planned for.

When it came to the role of Britain's nuclear deterrent the meaning of independence fell again under the spotlight. CIGS Sir Gerald Templer stressed that while he agreed that Britain should make a contribution to the Western deterrent,

He disliked the phrase 'an independent contribution' since it would give the impression that Her Majesty's Government might wish to use it independently and offensively. He did not believe that any British Government would do this.[53]

Earlier that year Templer had in a discussion on the subject of 'nuclear sufficiency' used an appreciation of the new strategic condition to attack the concept of '*Independent*' (his italics) UK deterrent and to question 'the thesis that the validity of the Deterrent remains unchanged in the era of Nuclear Sufficiency'.[54] In September, however, he agreed that the deterrent must be *capable of being used* unconditionally in defence of the United Kingdom or in retaliation if the United Kingdom were attacked. His emphasis here was on the ability to control the weapons independently not on the object of actually using them unilaterally.

In turn, CAS Sir Dermot Boyle stressed that it was imperative that Britain's contribution to the Western deterrent be completely independent unless she was prepared to 'accept a further reduction in military status in comparison with other powers'. He maintained that 'Although in fact we might never intend to use it offensively, it was important that the Government should have unfettered control of the weapon.' It was Boyle's belief that if the Americans retained the 'key of the cupboard' of nuclear warheads, it could not be guaranteed that even if the UK was under attack she could obtain these weapons without American approval.

While Boyle was of the opinion that unlike the Soviet Union the Americans were devoting much effort to defence and survival

[52]	AIR 8/2220, D (58) 26, 18 Nov. 1958.
[53]	DEFE 4/111, COS 77 (58) 1, 3 Sept. 1958.
[54]	DEFE 5/82, COS (58) 39, 13 Feb. 1958.

under nuclear attack, thereby reinforcing the credibility of the deterrent, First Sea Lord Mountbatten contended that the United States would be most reluctant to use nuclear weapons except in self-defence. He doubted whether they would use them if faced with a *fait accompli* in the ongoing crisis over Formosa and Berlin though, at the same time, he also seemed to prefer to rely on American guarantees. He thus stressed that

we should continue to make a British contribution to the deterrent even if what we could afford was too small to be an effective deterrent by itself, there was merit in membership of the 'nuclear club'.[55]

He stressed that with limited wars now more likely, priority would have to be given to maintaining the minimum amount of conventional forces necessary to defend Britain's world-wide commitments. He hoped once these needs had been fulfilled there would be enough finances for a 'useful contribution' to the overall Western deterrent. He was adamant that while Britain should retain a capability to use the deterrent independently in self-defence it was not important for it to be independent for any other objective 'since a degree of interdependence would save a vast amount of money'.[56]

There are definite indications in the 1958 documents that in the context of a growing appreciation of 'nuclear sufficiency', increasing attention was paid to the option of what this study has termed British 'unilateral independence'. In an Air Ministry paper on fighter defences of the deterrent in November of that year, it was stressed that with the concept of 'fortress America' receiving greater American support, the Soviets could calculate that a rapid simultaneous assault on American peripheral bases outside the United States and in Britain might reduce the weight of an allied nuclear response, and with the United States directly under threat, the Americans might then be more likely to bargain. Consequently,

Because of this and with the approval of the Minister of Defence, on the advice of the Chiefs of Staff, the target policy for Bomber Command planning covers a situation in which the United Kingdom might be forced to retaliate alone.[57]

[55] DEFE 4/111, COS 77 (58) 1, 3 Sept. 1958.        [56] Ibid.
[57] AIR 8/2220, D (58) 26, 18 Nov. 1958. It is unclear whether such a plan was finalized in 1957 or 1958.

Furthermore, in a January 1958 COSC discussion, Sir Richard Powell indicated that a working party under the direction of the Cabinet Office was analysing the procedure for reaching a decision on the launching of the deterrent including the option of getting a decision regarding a launch of the purely British element of the deterrent.[58] In addition, in a discussion during November on a JPS paper on the political control of tactical nuclear weapons it was pointed out by a Ministry of Defence representative that the report went further than was desirable or necessary in stressing that British Ministers would always need to consult with the Americans before authorizing the use of nuclear weapons. This was believed so because

> Our intention was to maintain an independent deterrent and he saw no reason why the United Kingdom or United States Government should not make an independent decision to use nuclear weapons in limited wars in which the other partner was not concerned.[59]

Finally, and perhaps most significantly, in a meeting of the Defence Committee in November 1958 Minister of Defence Duncan Sandys informed the members that 'he could envisage circumstances in which the threat that we would use our nuclear deterrent independently of the United States would be the only method of preserving peace'.[60] These pronouncements on 'unilateral independence' need, however, to be placed in some perspective. For Sir Richard Powell's statement on independent launch control arrangements is revealing in the fact that nearly a year after the Sandys White Paper such arrangements were still not finalized. Moreover, Powell also maintained that discussions would proceed on the launch arrangements concerning the American forces based in Britain and that the object was to use this as a lever to move on to more general talks with the Americans on procedures for launch. Joint Planning with the object of enhancing 'independence in concert' thus continued to remain a primary objective.

At the same time, despite claims that Britain need not always consult with the Americans before initiating tactical nuclear

[58] DEFE 4/103, COS 6 (58) 2 discussion of JIC (57) 120 (Final), 17 Jan. 1958.
[59] DEFE 4/113, COS 95 (58) 2 discussion of JP (58) 89 (Final), 13 Nov. 1958.
[60] CAB 131/19, 24 (58) 1, 5 Nov. 1958.

weapons use, the amended JPS report approved by the COSC
was explicit that

Having reviewed all the circumstances in which United Kingdom
forces might use nuclear weapons, we cannot foresee any case in
which the Prime Minister would not consult the President of the
United States of America personally before authorising the initial use
of these weapons.[61]

The COSC went on further to stress that it was imperative to
secure combined planning with the Americans with regard to
the use of nuclear weapons in limited wars in all theatres
especially in the Far East. Combined planning should cover
both the selection of targets and means of attack.

It may be argued that Sandys's claim concerning the independence of Britain's deterrent certainly appears to be a major
departure from the statements made at the 27 February 1957
Defence Committee meeting in which it was maintained that it
was most unlikely for nuclear weapons to be used independently
of the United States. Yet in this 1958 case Sandys is clearly
referring to the 'threat' to use nuclear weapons and not to their
actual use to which the 1957 discussions refer. In any event, he
did not specify even to the Defence Committee what were the
circumstances in which Britain would threaten to use nuclear
weapons independently. Moreover, his statement must also be
viewed in the context of an attempt by the Treasury at the end
of 1958 to cut the defence budget including the cancellation of
Blue Streak and therefore Sandys may have purposely hardened
his position. Similarly to the other pronouncements made in
1958, this statement does not in itself indicate that the object
of 'unilateral independence' was taking precedence over the
objective of interdependent planning or that independence was
now more than very narrowly defined and constrained to very
limited circumstances.

In terms specifically of targeting, in the recently released
1957 papers it is possible to see an increasing interest in the
concept of countervalue attacks—an interest that is not so
strongly apparent in the documents available for the years
1955–6. Thus, in May 1957, the Air Ministry—in comparing
the merits of the Mark 1 and Mark 2 V-bombers—included in

[61] DEFE 5/86, COS (58) 255, 14 Nov. 1958.

its assumptions a potential set of targets in the Soviet Union consisting of 98 major centres of administration and industry with a population exceeding 100,000 within a radius of 2,100 nautical miles of the East Anglia air force bases.[62]

This focus on countervalue objectives seems also to have been reflected in a paper delivered to the Defence Committee by the Cabinet Secretary, Sir Norman Brook, on the subject of expanding Britain's capacity for the production of fissile material for nuclear weapons. In it he stated a requirement for 'about 100 megaton weapons for strategic use'.[63] (While 'strategic use' was not defined in Brook's paper, it is possible, in the light of the meaning attached to the word during the Second World War, to interpret it as counter-city targeting. In any event, megaton weapons seemed especially suited to this task.) Finally, in October 1957, the Air Ministry seems to have taken the next step when they presented a paper on the 'Strategic Target Policy of Bomber Command' in which—according to Mountbatten— the impression was given that in the event of the UK being forced to take unilateral retaliatory action against the Soviet Union 'we could quickly break the Russian will to continue war'[64]—indicating city targeting, at least in the context of this independent option.

Indeed, during 1957 it is possible to note a steady progression from a focus on counterforce attacks to an emphasis on an independent countervalue capability. The declaratory stress in the 1957 White Paper on an independent deterrent stance was

[62] AIR 2/14699, Memo by R. C. Kent, 23 May 1957. Participants at the Kings conference on the Sandys White Paper were adamant that 98 countervalue targets was in excess of anything that Britain was independently targeting at this time and that this target set was drawn up simply for heuristic purposes—a point supported by discussions of target numbers released in the 1958 papers.

[63] CAB 131/18, D (57) 14, 27 July 1957. In this paper Brook admitted that no precise estimate could be made as to Britain's ultimate requirement of fissile material 'partly because we do not yet know the amount or type (plutonium or U.235) of material which will be needed for each weapon and partly because we have not finally determined the total of nuclear weapons which will be needed to implement our defence policy'. This, however, did not prevent Brook from demanding the construction of a new diffusion plant because 'The effective measure of our authority as a world power, is, however, our stock of fissile material. At present we are still only a potential nuclear power. We shall not retain our influence in world affairs unless we go forward and turn potentiality into reality.' Here Brook was agreeing with Caccia's reasoning for seeking an independent nuclear capability.

[64] DEFE 4/100, COS 78 (57) 3 discussion of COS (57) 208 (closed) and COS 1546/8/10/57, 15 Oct. 1957.

by the end of the year apparently accompanied by an increasing emphasis on such an operational posture. This certainly helps support an interpretation that the declaratory focus on independence was more than simply a cloak for the less ambitious objective of 'independence in concert'.

Of course, the existence of targeting plans for 'unilateral retaliatory action' is not in itself surprising. It is to be expected that targeting planning for all sorts of contingencies existed and that unilateral independent action based on countervalue attacks was one of them. The question is whether this was thought the most likely contingency to which all else must be subordinated, and whether plans for such a possibility were determining the procurement and structuring of Britain's nuclear force.

Participants in the King's conference on the Sandys White Paper seemed agreed that a national targeting plan was in existence at this time—though exactly when one began to be laid out was unspecified. According to Sir Richard Way, this consisted of ten cities of which he mentioned Moscow, Leningrad, and Kiev. The point is, however, that there was concurrence with T. C. G. James's claim that the national targeting plan was a 'plan of last resort'. Indeed, according to James, 'We never had exaggerated ideas of what the deterrent could do to Russia. I don't think there is ever any question of the UK deterrent being capable of the total devastation of the Soviet Union.'[65] Despite the fact that there was as yet not the means to implement such a policy, it is possible that an independent national targeting plan based on counter city attacks had been in existence for some years before 1957 (thereby negating any claim that 1957 represented a turning point in this respect), but it appears that at no time was this considered the most likely contingency and the prime objective to which end British policy should be aimed. Indeed, in the October discussion of the paper 'Strategic Target Policy for Bomber Command', Mountbatten objected to the inclusion in this paper of the 'highly improbable' course of unilateral action and the impression that Britain could deliver a decisive blow against the Soviet Union. The CAS, Sir Dermot Boyle, remained adamant that Bomber Command's force should not be underestimated and

---

[65] King's conference on the Sandys White Paper.

even acting unilaterally would be able to inflict severe damage on the Soviet Union. Nevertheless, he admitted that this blow would not necessarily be decisive and he was anxious to continue planning with the Americans.[66] Thus, evidently, not only did the Navy object to independent action, but the Air Ministry appeared ready to subordinate such a contingency to the vital goal of co-ordination with the United States.

Indeed, in terms of targeting and war planning, joint operations remained the first priority. One of the first tasks Sandys undertook—even before he began work on the White Paper— was to ratify an agreement with the Americans on joint targeting. It was made clear at the King's conference on the White Paper that throughout 1957 Britain continued to work towards a joint targeting plan with the Americans.[67] Within the context of this planning, British independence was defined by her retention of a specific target set which would be attacked by British aircraft in the first wave of joint allied strikes on the Soviet Union.[68] Given that British aircraft would make up the first wave of a joint allied assault, it is not unreasonable to assume that targeting here was also suppressive in nature and included those types of targets most threatening to the United Kingdom. Although there is a dearth of direct evidence for this contention, in a discussion in November 1958 on the range of Blue Streak mention was made of 'the trend . . . for targets to move further east as time goes on'[69]—thereby indicating that military targets were still under consideration. In any event, it can be argued that Bomber Command could add little to SAC's capability for destroying urban-industrial areas and the problems of different targeting priorities between British and American planners remained independent of the size of Britain's nuclear deterrent, accuracy of her weapon systems, or the growth of Soviet air defences.

---

[66] DEFE 4/100, COS 78 (57) 3, Discussion of COS (57) 208, 15 Oct. 1957.
[67] King's Conference on the Sandys White Paper. Work was certainly slow and in August the Air Council reported that they were as yet unsure how many strikes the UK would have to make against Soviet targets as they were still waiting for progress in talks with the Americans. AIR 2/14699, Air Council Paper on V-Bomber Force, 16 Aug. 1957.
[68] King's Conference on the Sandys White Paper.
[69] DEFE 4/114, COS (58) 97, 28 Nov. 1958.

It is certainly clear that as joint planning proceeded in 1958 Britain remained concerned about targets that could provide a threat to the United Kingdom.[70] In a May 1958 COSC discussion of an Air Ministry Paper entitled 'Bomber Command—Strategic Target Policy', Sir Dermot Boyle informed the other Chiefs that two meetings had already been held between SAC and Bomber Command and that the co-ordination between the two nuclear strike forces was very pleasing and there was no major real differences in viewpoints.[71] He went on to state that although Bomber Command as yet did not have full knowledge of the complete United States nuclear strike plan, she was now acquainted with their intentions regarding any targets which could pose a threat to Britain. This clearly was still a major concern of the United Kingdom and their satisfaction could only but have indicated that these were being covered, at least in part, by SAC. Britain must have been assured by SAC's plans given that the amount of these targets clearly outnumbered Bomber Command's projected independently controlled capabilities (aside from Blue Streak which was still very much on the drawing board), which, as noted, had been reduced to 144 V-bombers.

Significantly, Boyle also rejected an attempt by Mountbatten to include for consideration with the Americans a specific set of naval targets, arguing that 'many of them would be found to be covered coincidentally in the existing plans, since they were located in cities which would in any case be subject to attack'. It is unclear from the document who in this case is doing the attacking of the cities but it should not be taken to imply that this was the United Kingdom, or if it was the United Kingdom that this represented the sole types of objectives targeted in a joint attack. For again, it would seem improbable that despite there being 'no real difference of view' between the two nuclear forces SAC was primarily concerned with attacking all targets Britain regarded as threatening; and it would seem illogical that even if SAC was prepared to follow such a plan, Bomber Command would be willing to leave it to the Americans while focusing the main thrust of their efforts on countervalue targets. Certainly there must, at the very least, have been a major Bomber

[70] See for example DEFE 4/107, COS 46 (58) 4, 30 May 1958.
[71] Ibid.

Command effort directed at these counterforce targets with countervalue targets also receiving attention. Boyle's rejection of Mountbatten's plans is arguably not a reflection of the subordination of counterforce to countervalue targeting but an indication of the broader and ongoing bureaucratic debate between the RAF and the Navy over the nuclear deterrent.

Yet, it cannot be denied that parallel to this interest in 'independence in concert' remained the sub-theme of a capability for unilateral independent action based on countervalue strikes. Its increasing prominence in 1957 is explained not only by some interpretations of the implications of the Suez crisis but also by the Air Ministry's recognition of the potential availability of megaton weapons, its growing appreciation of the decrease in accuracy that would follow from the ultimate replacement of gravity bombs with the Blue Steel stand-off missile, its decreasing number of V-bombers, the increasing number of Soviet counter-force targets,[72] and fear of improving Soviet anti-aircraft defences.[73] The three latter points underlined the difficulties of implementing a limited counterforce strike against even those targets judged to be most threatening to Britain, while the former opened up the possibility for highly destructive counter-city targeting.

Thus, in 1958, the need for a unilateral countervalue capability continued to receive growing attention with requirements being explicitly stated in minimum deterrence terms. Thus in the September 1958 COSC discussion on 'nuclear sufficiency' the Air Ministry stated that it had given great attention 'to the degree of threatened destruction which would deter Russia from attacking the United Kingdom'.[74] It was the Air Ministry's opinion that the destruction of 30 Soviet cities would be adequate, 'but it was not a matter that could be

---

[72] A Defence Research Policy Committee paper on Guided Weapons presented to the COSC in October 1958 warned that 'There is at present no evidence that the Russians have ceased building up their manned bomber strength', though there was also no indication that they were as yet intent upon producing ballistic missiles aimed at Britain. DEFE 4/113, DRPC (58) 82, 22 Oct. 1958. A brief from the Assistant Chief of the Air Staff for Air Defence on Fighter Defence of the Deterrent discussed at a Defence Committee meeting in November 1958 stressed the 'build up of the bomber force and the multiplication of the Russian bomber bases from which a surprise attack could be mounted . . .' AIR 8/2220, D (58) 26, 18 Nov. 1958.

[73] See AIR 2/14699, Memo by R. C. Kent, 23 May 1957.

[74] DEFE 4/111, COS 77 (58) 1, 3 Sept. 1958.

calculated and the ultimate decision would have to be based on political considerations'.[75] In conclusion the CAS stated that Britain must aim at the provision for a 'minimum deterrent contribution' whose control should solely be in the hands of the United Kingdom. While thirty Soviet cities was the present figure he admitted that the size of the force would have to be determined following an assessment of the extent of destruction to the Soviet Union which could be considered effective. He was resolute that conventional forces should be supplied from resources remaining in the budget after this minimum deterrent capability had been fulfilled and that the present 20 per cent of the defence budget allocated to the deterrent was insufficient. A memorandum would have to be put to the ministers and they would have to decide the measure of destruction in Russia that should be adopted. The importance of countervalue criteria in determining force size can also be noted in a memorandum by the Chancellor of the Exchequer presented to the Defence Committee in November 1958. In it he stated that

The Air Staff say that a V-bomber force of the strength at present planned could deliver successfully attacks on 30 to 40 out of 131 major centres of Russian industry and administration. This is in addition to the targets that could be destroyed, by any ballistic missiles under our control.[76]

The Chancellor went on to betray his own strong economic motivations and the ongoing lack of clarity as to the purposes of the nuclear deterrent when he stated that

Even if the number of targets that can be successfully attacked is not directly proportional to the size of the bomber force, is it really clear that a smaller force than 144 U.E. would not suffice to secure us the co-operation of the United States—if indeed that is the true aim of the independent deterrent?[77]

In returning to the theme of continuity and discontinuity across the 1955–8 period, it is possible to note that there are elements of both these tendencies in relation to British nuclear strategic planning. On the level of targeting, 1957 definitely saw a major shift towards countervalue objectives. Indeed by

[75] Ibid.
[76] CAB 131/20, D (58) 69, 17 Nov. 1958.          [77] Ibid.

September 1958 it appears that the force was being configured primarily on the basis of minimum deterrent countervalue considerations. On the other hand, on the more significant level of the purposes of that deterrent force in terms of the priorities accorded various strategic plans, it appears that continuity was the most persistent theme with 'independence in concert' remaining predominant over plans for unilateral retaliatory action. Here, the influence of Duncan Sandys is more acutely felt as the Minister of Defence, together with the Prime Minister, strongly emphasized the American nuclear strategic connection. It was, after all, in the wider context of British strategic planning that targeting had to be grounded and Sandys and Macmillan were adamant that Britain's defence in the post-Suez world should be inextricably bound up with the United States's nuclear capability. This attitude is further revealed in the progress of negotiations over the deployment of American Thor ballistic missiles in Britain.

### Independence, Interdependence, and Problems of Control, Procurement, and Production: The Thor and Blue Streak Missiles

Issues that were to become entangled with the ongoing negotiations over the revised McMahon Act, the as yet essentially unresolved and undefined issue of the independence of Britain's deterrent, were the associated problems of the control of the Thor IRBMs and the development of the Blue Streak missile. Indeed, the issues of US missile deployment in Britain and the future of Britain's indigenous surface-to-surface missile force were inextricably bound up with the purposes of Britain's nuclear deterrent power. The debate as it unfolded in 1957 revealed a measure of underlying tensions within the defence establishment over the degree of independence to be pursued and the role of nuclear weapons in the context of Anglo-American relations.

Discussions between the Americans and British on IRBMs had begun tentatively in 1954. The following year a Joint Scientific Advisory Board was set up with the aim of assisting Britain in securing the earliest possible operational capability in the missile field, with the first meeting of the board being held in 1956.[78] During that year the Americans expressed interest in establishing six or seven bases of IRBMs in the United Kingdom.[79]

Prior to Sandys's visit to Washington in January 1957, the Secretary of State for Air, George Ward, wrote the Minister a letter in which he expressed the basic dilemmas underlying the question of UK missile deployment. Ward was of the opinion that Sandys should aim at getting further American help in developing Blue Streak (in furtherance of the Sandys–Wilson agreement of 1953) but must insist on retaining both technical and operational independence. Technical independence would, of course, be compromised by the fact that it was technical assistance which was being requested from the Americans in the first place—though it was implied that this 'independence' could begin once the transfer was complete.[80] On the question of operational independence, Ward had addressed the central question of an independent British nuclear deterrent because without operational independence, 'unilateral independence' as well as the more limited 'independence in concert' was severely compromised.

When it came to the possibility of US Thor deployments in Britain Ward told Sandys that if the Americans offered him these missiles, they should be accepted but 'so far as any quid pro quo is invited, this should be limited to our agreement to making this country available as a base for their deployment'.[81] Ward was concerned that Britain should steer well away from agreements that would curtail the British right to use these weapons independently—though whether he was referring to 'independence in concert' or 'unilateral independence' or both is unclear.

Sandys, however, viewed the situation in a different light. It seems that for him, operational independence was far less important an issue than that of solidifying Anglo-American co-operation. He was not prepared to risk the chance of securing such an agreement over the issue of total independent British

[78] AIR 19/942, Brief for Secretary of State on Anglo/US Co-operation on the Medium Range Ballistic Missile, undated.
[79] See for example DEFE 13/216, Memo to Minister of Defence, 23 July 1956.
[80] AIR 2/14712, Ward to Sandys, 25 Jan. 1957.          [81] Ibid.

control—an issue that would have caused problems as a result of the McMahon Act's requirement that American nuclear weapons remain under American control. Indeed, while Secretary of Defence Wilson had given an impression that some formula could be found to give the custody of the warheads for these missiles to the British—thereby, in effect, circumventing the McMahon Act which forbade such a transfer[82]—this was soon to be neglected by the Americans.

Concurrence between Wilson and Sandys in January 1957 on American missile deployments in Britain was quickly translated into a draft agreement reached at Bermuda between Macmillan and Eisenhower. The plan was for the United States to deploy as fast as possible an experimental squadron of approximately five missiles at an American air base in the United Kingdom. These missiles would be completely under the operational control of the United States. Thereafter, four squadrons of 15 missiles each would be deployed and the experimental station closed down. The first two of the new squadrons would be under the operational control of American forces though they would later be transferred to the operational control of the British. The second two bases would, immediately on completion, be handed over to British personnel who would operate the missile systems. However, the draft agreement was explicit that

References to the IRBM missiles in this document do not include the nuclear warheads. The United States will store in the United Kingdom nuclear warheads for missiles made available to the United Kingdom and for United States missiles located in the United States. All nuclear warheads so stored will remain under full United States custody and control in accordance with United States law.[83]

Furthermore it was stated that the United States could maintain in Britain under its own operational control an amount of missiles (not exceeding the number transferred to British operational control) and that the United Kingdom would give sympathetic consideration to future requests for the deployment of more missiles in the United Kingdom. Most significantly, it

---

[82] AIR 19/942, Note for the Record, 13 Dec. 1956.
[83] AIR 19/942, Draft Agreement on Deployment of the United States Intermediate Range Ballistic Missile in the United Kingdom, 16 Apr. 1957.

was stressed that the operational use of the IRBMs 'would be the subject of joint determination between the two governments'.[84] Thus, the United States effectively exercised a veto over independent British control of the missiles. While questions of command and control had yet to be finalized, the trend seemed to be away from total British independence.

Indeed, Macmillan's interpretation of the agreement reflected his concern not for independence but for co-operation. On 24 March, when asked for his views on the significance of the agreement to deploy US missiles in Britain, he replied that it gave Britain the protection of the American deterrent. In addition,

it is a symbol of co-operation, because it allows us to turn some of our research, development, and production to other valuable defence projects instead of trying merely to duplicate and run along parallel with what the United States has already done. So that I think it is important in itself to harmonize our work together, and this is one of the first results of such harmonization.[85]

The emphasis here was on co-operation and economy not on total independence. Ward's advice seemed to have been roundly ignored.

Not surprisingly, the Air Ministry expressed ambivalence about accepting the Thors. On one level, they supported the plan to acquire the missiles because it was agreed that they would contribute significantly to the Western deterrent and give the RAF experience with the use of missiles. On the other hand, the Air Ministry had doubts about how effective these as yet untested weapons were. They were also worried about the costs which their budget would have to bear, the unresolved issue of the manufacture of British warheads and their relation to the issue of the independent use of these missiles, and the implications of the US deployment on the Blue Streak programme. The Air Ministry went on to question whether the Thor agreement would have a positive influence on the independence of the British deterrent.[86] Also, in view of the fact that the Thors would ultimately cost Britain £12 million, would require a manpower of 3,000 men, and 'would be useless to the Americans

[84] Ibid.          [85] PREM 11/1837, Press Conference, undated.
[86] AIR 2/14712, 3 May 1957.

if sited in the United States',[87] it was the opinion of Permanent Under Secretary of State for Air Maurice Dean that Britain should attempt to drive a hard bargain with the Americans over Thor deployments.[88] What would constitute a hard bargain was here left unstated, although possibly—given Air Ministry reservations over the Thor deployment issue—it included not just economic factors and the supply of advanced fighters but also issues of independent command and control. Certainly, there were those in the Air Ministry who argued that Thor should not be procured at any price.[89]

Arguably the problem reflected the different conceptions of the Air Ministry on the one hand and Sandys and Macmillan on the other over the significance of the deterrent in the context of Anglo-American relations. For, while Sandys and the Prime Minister sought as a prime objective the twin goals of solidifying the relationship through strengthening Britain's deterrent and strengthening the deterrent so as to solidify the relationship, the Air Ministry wished to maximize the degree of independence at all levels even if this caused difficulties with the Americans. Whether Britain primarily sought to pursue a policy of 'unilateral independence' or 'independence in concert', the Air Ministry seems to have recognized that at root rested the issues of independent command, control, and targeting.

Sandys certainly did not share to the same degree the Air Ministry's concerns. In a meeting with the service heads and Chiefs of Staff on 28 May, Sandys admitted the inequality of the agreement when he stated that

Whilst there would be political agreement between the two Governments that neither would use the missiles without the consent of the other the British would not have the same physical control over the Americans as they would have over us. Until such time as we can develop our own warheads, we would be entirely dependent upon the Americans who would physically hold the 'key' to the 'warhead cupboard'. We would, however, have no such physical control over the Americans and would have to rely entirely upon their word not

---

[87] AIR 19/856, 12 Mar. 1957. According to T. C. G. James, the RAF was also concerned that the Thor missiles were as yet not a fully tested weapon system. Interview, 30 June 1958.

[88] AIR 2/14712, Dean to Powell, 12 Mar. 1957.

[89] AIR 2/14712, Memo by Broadbent, 12 Mar. 1957.

to use the weapons under their control without first seeking our consent.[90]

But at the end of May in a meeting of a special Cabinet subcommittee on the British nuclear deterrent—GEN 570—the Minister of Defence stressed that the maintenance of the American veto over the use of the missiles, even if they were fitted with British warheads, was not of great importance since it was doubtful 'that we should in fact think it profitable to develop British warheads for American missiles which by that time would be regarded as obsolescent'.[91] In short, the Minister was willing to live with a situation which ran counter to the principles of total independence. His lack of concern reflected the fact that such a capability was never his primary objective.

Nevertheless, Sandys had, in his correspondence with the Americans, pushed the point of independent British control of the missiles once the United Kingdom had replaced American warheads for Thor with ones of her own manufacture. The Minister of Defence maintained that Dulles and Wilson had accepted such a British proposal and this had been written up in a letter, a draft of which had been sent to Wilson. Unfortunately, this letter had not been acknowledged. The subcommittee then agreed that

Since it was doubtful whether the Americans could now be persuaded categorically to agree that we could use any missiles supplied by them, whether of the present or of later types, except by joint agreement [it is concluded] that this issue should not be raised in the context of the main Agreement and that we should let the matter rest on the non-repudiation of the letter which had been sent.[92]

It is true that during this period the British were not uninterested in acquiring a batch of Thor missiles for totally independent control. But this was never pushed to the limit and was shelved in 1958 when the decision was made to continue with Blue Streak. Thor would never be a truly independent British force.

Thus, although discussions also focused on the advisability of seeking some form of control over the American Thor

---

[90] AIR 19/942 PS to CAS, 28 May 1957.
[91] CAB 130/122, GEN 570/2nd meeting, minute 2, 30 May 1957.
[92] Ibid.

squadrons (for example, the control of electrical power), Sandys continued to be sometimes more concerned with the appearance of independence than its actual substance. He agreed that if the position was challenged in Parliament, the answer would be that since the UK did not intend to develop her own warheads for the missile, the question of totally independent use was 'academic'.[93] On 21 June, the Minister of Defence replied to an American version of the Thor treaty (that sent to Sandys by Wilson on 18 April) by listing a number of disagreements which included the problem of independent control. But even this was not a strong challenge to the American draft and the Minister of Defence's expressed desire to discuss an arrangement concerning the control of missiles deployed by American forces in the United Kingdom was framed in terms of the need 'for the reassurance of [Britain's] public'.[94]

Not surprisingly, by the end of the year—just after the United States had secured NATO concurrence for the deployment of American controlled IRBM bases—Sandys had agreed that the transfer of the missiles could take place under the provision of Article 5 of the North Atlantic Treaty which stated that an attack on one signatory would be regarded as an attack on all. He thus implicitly subordinated national to alliance concerns. Such was the ambiguity of the agreement that, according to Botti, while the Americans appeared to get the assurance that the United Kingdom would fire the missiles if the Soviets attacked only the United States and not Britain, the British could maintain that they were not pledged to launch their IRBMs automatically.[95]

This ambiguity mirrored the ambiguity in the related issue of whether Britain could, if she so wished, use the missiles independently of the United States—a problem which, as noted, Sandys did not wish to tackle head on either. Botti maintains that during 1957 Britain was keen 'on a degree of independence with respect to targeting'.[96] Further clarification of what is meant by this 'degree of independence' is with the available

---

[93] CAB 130/122, GEN 570/2nd meeting, minute 2, 30 May 1957.

[94] AIR 19/942, Ministry of Defence London to British Embassy Washington, Draft Agreement for Deployment of IRBM in Great Britain, Note of Points Requiring Further Discussion, 21 June 1957.

[95] Botti, *The Long Wait*, 209.          [96] Ibid. 194.

documents unfortunately not possible. However, it is necessary to place such a phrase against the backdrop of Sandys's willingness to accept the joint decision mechanism. For by doing so, Sandys was in effect accepting that all targeting decisions would ultimately require American consent. Without totally independent control it was irrelevant what target plans British planners agreed to amongst themselves, for the Americans would, in the end, have to give their consent before these targets could be attacked.[97]

By the end of the year little had been done to address the Air Ministry's concern in April that 'Thor cannot be used without US consent. Therefore whether or not we make our own warhead, we shall have no power of independent action with this missile'.[98] The Defence Committee's conclusion at the end of December that

in practice, there might be little time for consultation between the two Governments. On the other hand, it would be undesirable that the nuclear retaliatory forces should be launched automatically, irrespective of the nature and scale of the aggression against a member of the North Atlantic Alliance . . .[99]

may be seen as possibly a form of reassurance concerning British independence, but it may also have been (or have solely been) an indication of the vulnerability of the system to an American launch without British permission. On another level, the Defence Committee may also have been seeking to distance itself from an interpretation of the Thor Agreement which committed Britain to launching the missiles if only Britain and not the United States was attacked.

In any event, by the beginning of 1958 the Americans had largely discounted the significance of her planned European IRBM deployments. Developing Soviet missile capabilities made Thor very vulnerable to attack, while the recent test of

---

[97] Botti's excellent analysis would have been further strengthened if the author had had access to British documents. Botti views Sandys's attempts to attain agreement on independent counterforce targeting as an example of Britain seeking an independent nuclear deterrent force (p. 194) when Sandys was here most likely only seeking a much more limited objective of 'independence in concert'. Moreover, if Sandys was attempting to bolster British 'unilateral independence' then his interest would have been not in independent counterforce but independent countervalue targeting.

[98] AIR 19/849, Memo, 2 Apr. 1957.

[99] CAB 131/18, D 14 (57) 3, 31 Dec. 1957.

the solid-fuelled Atlas missile underlined the relative backwardness of the liquid-fuelled Thor system. The difficulties surrounding the launch procedures of the Thor also highlighted the limitations of this weapon so that, according to Botti, the United States pushed on with the agreement mainly for political reasons.[100] Yet, also on the British side, the COSC were increasingly beginning to express their doubts about the deployment. Of great concern were reports of American interest in placing the IRBMs at the disposal of SACEUR[101]—arguably a back door to further American control. On 22 January 1958, the COSC agreed that if the missiles were placed under SACEUR's control it would be detrimental to British security because he might choose to use them in a tactical support role and not against strategic targets and that it might require fifteen nations to agree to a launch making them impossible to use.[102]

Of all the Chiefs, the most concerned about the Thor deployments during 1958 remained the CAS, Sir Dermot Boyle. On 28 January he addressed a memorandum to the COSC outlining his firm opposition to allowing the deployment of a weapon system which was expensive, of unproven reliability, highly vulnerable, and did little to increase Britain's independence. He stressed that 'The Air Ministry have always opposed being rushed into this commitment which in our view is designed to serve American ends more than British'.[103] Boyle insisted that they be accepted on the conditions that they be totally financed and manned by the US but only launched following a joint decision, or that the missiles be accepted under the existing arrangements provided that the whole system be under British control.

In a letter from Powell to the Americans on 31 January the points made by the RAF were raised. Specifically, what was stressed was the rejection of SACEUR control over the IRBMs, the unease over the operational reliability of Thor, the suggestion that perhaps more advanced missiles be supplied later, and the need '[f]or political reasons' to state that all the squadrons

[100] Botti, *The Long Wait*, 208.
[101] DEFE 4/103, COS 7 (58) 1, 21 Jan. 1958.
[102] DEFE 5/81, COS (58) 12, 22 Jan. 58.
[103] AIR 19/942, American IRBMs, 28 Jan. 1958.

would be British from the start and that if operational orders for firing were given these should be made through British channels.[104] Moreover, the British appeared once more to be backing away from any language which suggested that they would have to launch their missiles if only the USA was attacked. Not surprisingly, the Americans were dismayed that Britain appeared to be reneging on her earlier agreements. Powell was soon informed that the Americans were doing everything they could to get the missiles ready but they could not replace Thor with a more advanced system as this would represent an open-ended commitment and be contrary to American law. It was pointed out to the British that the Americans did not wish to man the first two IRBM sites but would have to as British personnel would not be as yet ready trained. These American units would have to come under the American chain of command but an attached British officer at each base would have full power of veto over any launch.[105]

By the third week of February, the United States had agreed not to demand the deployment of more IRBM bases. Nor did they demand that reference to SACEUR's operational control of the missiles be made, that the RAF would from the outset man the first missile base, and that the wording of the draft memorandum of agreement which implied that the weapons would be fired automatically if any member of NATO be attacked be amended to underline that the decision to launch was a joint British–American one. However, a secret letter accompanying the agreement still promised a sympathetic British response to a US request at a later stage to deploy additional bases which could be manned by Americans.[106] Furthermore, the Americans were adamant that while they would not demand that the UK squadrons be committed to SACEUR, they were not opposed to a future request by him for operational control of these systems.[107] It should also be noted that the wording of the relevant paragraph in the final memorandum on a future launch decision still contained the statement

[104] AIR 19/942, Draft Message to Mr Quarles, appended to Telegram from Hood to Powell, No. 242, 4 Feb. 1958.
[105] AIR 19/942, Telegram No. 242, 2 Feb. 1958.
[106] CAB 129/91, C (58) 40, 11 Feb. 1958.
[107] AIR 19/942, Telegram No. 242, 2 Feb. 1958.

that it would be made under Article 5 of the North Atlantic Treaty—though this was now rendered more ambiguous by being preceded with the sentence underlining the joint nature of the decision.[108] With these issues agreed upon and the fact that 'All nuclear warheads so provided shall remain in full United States ownership, custody and control in accordance with United States law', Sandys was forced to admit to the Cabinet,

These American missiles cannot, of course, be regarded as an element of independent British nuclear power; but they represent a valuable addition to the combined strength of the allied strategic deterrent . . .[109]

In the light of the primary objective of strengthening the nuclear alliance with the United States this lack of independent control could readily be tolerated. The agreement with the Americans was concluded on 22 February 1958. The plan was for the first squadron to be deployed between June and December 1958, the second by mid-1959, and the last two by March 1960. During his visit to Washington in June 1958 Macmillan joined Eisenhower in signing an agreement concerning the employment of nuclear weapons under joint control. With regard to the American bases in Britain this agreement '[replaced] the loose arrangement made by Attlee and confirmed by Churchill'.[110] Interdependence thus received another formal boost.

As noted, throughout the year the RAF remained very ambivalent about the programme, with Sir Dermot Boyle not wasting any opportunity to rail against 'a commitment which was designed to serve American rather than British ends'.[111] It is important to recognize that part of this circumspection related to the perceived implications of Thor deployment for the true future symbol and instrument of Britain's independently controlled deterrent, Blue Streak. In a meeting of the Air Council on 30 January 1958 Deputy Chief of the Air Staff Sir Geoffrey Tuttle said that 'If the [Thor] project were to succeed, the dangers of pressure to abandon our independent I.R.B.M.

---

[108] CAB 129/91, Annex B to C (58) 49, 24 Feb. 1958.
[109] CAB 129/91, C (58) 40, 11 Feb. 1958.
[110] Macmillan, *Riding the Storm,* 294.
[111] DEFE 4/106, COS 36 (58) 5, 24 Apr. 1958.

deterrent, Blue Streak, would increase'.[112] While the Secretary of State for Air George Ward replied that the decision with regard to Blue Streak would be made by ministers on the basis of their assessment of the value to Britain of an independent deterrent which Thor could not provide, from a point of view of finance and manpower, the RAF could never be really sure.

Clearly, the implications of the subordination of independent British action with the Thor missiles for independent British deterrence could have been offset with a greater emphasis on Blue Streak deployment. As pointed out in Chapter 4, the Blue Streak missile—at least after research and development assistance from the United States had been secured—would be an entirely British missile with command and control completely under British auspices. The question then to be addressed is what attention did this project receive as negotiations over Thor deployment progressed?

During 1957 the Air Ministry evinced a certain degree of concern over the government's slowness in proceeding with Blue Streak. Indeed, already during the 1957 White Paper discussions, the Air Ministry seems to have felt that the Minister of Defence was intent upon slowing down the Blue Streak programme. Thus, in March 1957, Permanent Under Secretary of State for Air, Maurice Dean, wrote to George Ward and informed him that the abandonment of Blue Streak would result in the deterrent becoming dependent on obsolete V-bombers, obsolescent Thor missiles, and such weapons as the United States chose to supply to Britain. Clearly, this would have dangerous implications for the future independence of Britain's deterrent and Dean expressed uncertainty as to whether the full implications of this were appreciated by the Cabinet.[113]

Certainly, the Cabinet expressed insensitivity to Air Ministry concerns. On 28 March, the Chancellor of the Exchequer, Peter Thorneycroft, said that in view of the recent agreement with the United States about the supply of ballistic rockets, it would be important to avoid giving the impression in the forthcoming defence debates that Britain was intent upon manufacturing her own version of the weapon.[114] A month

[112] AIR 19/942, Air Council Meeting, 3 (58) 30 Jan. 1958.
[113] AIR 19/856, Dean to Ward, 4 Mar. 1957.
[114] CAB 128/31, CC 26 (57) 1, 28 Mar. 1957.

earlier, Macmillan had told the Defence Committee that based on the assumption that the US offer of Thor missiles would be accepted,

> we need not plan to produce ourselves a medium range ballistic rocket, but we should continue a modest programme of research so that we could still make a contribution to the United States development programme.[115]

This ambivalence about the future of Blue Streak received further expression with Sandys's proposal to cut the suggested research and development budget for 1958/9 by £20 million to £190 million. Such a reduction would have made a shift in the focus on the Blue Streak programme difficult to avoid. At the beginning of April, Sandys was informed by the Air Ministry that one of the main arguments for the change in defence policy outlined in the White Paper was the continued existence of a British contribution to the deterrent. To have any value this contribution would have to be independent and operationally effective. Consequently, until control was secured over Thor (and the weapon actually tested) it would be wrong to give up Blue Streak—what Sandys appeared to the Air Ministry to be doing.[116] It was the view within the Air Ministry that 'if we wish to retain power of independent action when the V-bombers run out, we must retain Blue Streak'.[117] The Air Ministry had certainly overcome its earlier hesitations about the Blue Streak project, a situation made possible, no doubt, by the decision to terminate the development of the supersonic bomber.[118]

The 1958 White Paper stated unequivocally that 'A British ballistic rocket of a more advanced type is being developed on the highest priority, in close co-operation with the United States.'[119] Yet, by the end of the year Britain was considering moving away from the missile even before the future of an alternative was secure. On 8 September 1958, Sandys presented a memorandum to the Defence Committee in which it was stated that it was necessary to reconsider the plan to develop Blue

---

[115] CAB 131/18, D 2 (57) 1, 27 Feb. 1957.
[116] AIR 19/849, Memo by Broadbent, 3 Apr. 1957.
[117] AIR 19/849, Memo, 2 Apr. 1957.
[118] See AIR 19/849, Air Ministry (unsigned) to Powell, 15 Mar. 1957.
[119] *Report on Defence, 1958*, Cmnd. 363, Feb. 1958.

Streak. In it Sandys stated that although the weapon was estimated to cost £200 million for development alone and that by the time it was employed it would be technically inferior to comparable American systems, the decision was to proceed with the project because: (1) in order to maintain an independent British deterrent there was a need to possess nuclear capable rockets under unrestricted control; and (2) on scientific and industrial grounds it was desirable for Britain to invest in rocketry. However, following the amendment of the McMahon Act, Britain was now promised information concerning the manufacture of lightweight megaton warheads as well as the possibility of acquiring American rocket tails. Consequently, Sandys stated that Britain should now investigate the possibilities of either suspending development of Blue Streak, helping the US develop a medium range rocket tail of a more advanced type, exploring the option of partnership with Western European countries in developing a rocket tail or using the new information to design a lightweight warhead for this new rocket. So as to avoid a gap between the time of the obsolescence of the V-bombers and the introduction of a new rocket, the life of the V-bomber should be extended through deploying the bombers with the Blue Steel Mark 2 or acquiring Thor without constraints.[120]

However, by early November Sandys was again shifting his position on Blue Streak. In a memorandum to the Defence Committee on 3 November he stated that it would be possible in the next few years to develop a missile far mor advanced than Blue Streak was at present. Moreover, possible Western European partners would remain dependent on the Americans and would, in any event, require a much shorter range missile. While the Americans had also now provided Britain with information on the Thor warhead which was suitable for Blue Streak they did not wish to continue producing Thors indefinitely and could not be relied on to supply a successor to Thor. Sandys also went on to state that Polaris development was not sufficiently advanced for it to be considered a replacement for Blue Streak and 'for us to stake everything upon it'. Moreover Polaris would not have the accuracy of a land-based missile, nor would its warhead be as inexpensive. It would also be necessary to build six or eight

[120] CAB 131/20, D (58) 47, 8 Sept. 1958.

missile-launching submarines. Consequently Sandys was now adamant that

if we wish to maintain an independent British contribution to the nuclear deterrent after the mid-sixties, we must proceed with the development of BLUE STREAK and aim to be in a position to start deploying these weapons in 1965.[121]

This was not a view supported by the Chancellor of the Exchequer, who in November stressed that 'the development of Blue Streak should be abandoned, even if this meant that at some time in the 1960s we should cease to have an independent nuclear deterrent'.[122] The Treasury was concerned that the development and use of Blue Streak would cost £400–600 million and that if the missiles were deployed underground the costs would be considerably higher. In discussion it was agreed that a study should be carried out on the cost of buying Thor and of developing a later British rocket if Blue Streak was not procured. Furthermore while no decision could yet be taken on Polaris, it was also agreed that in conditions of 'nuclear sufficiency' 'it might become less important to have all the three elements of the British deterrent—bombers, THOR, and BLUE STREAK—at present envisaged for the next ten years'. In discussion it was stated that bombers had flexibility and that 'Renewed consideration should therefore be given to the development of a supersonic bomber as the main British contribution to the deterrent in the late 1960s.'[123]

Yet, by 17 December Sandys was extolling the virtues of Polaris including its mobility and its comparative invulnerability, while at the same time demanding that development proceed on Blue Streak.[124] This did not prevent the Minister from agreeing to some reduction in expenditure on Blue Streak and thereby deferrring the acceleration of the programme.[125] Indeed, despite the Minister's apparent commitment to this centrepiece of Britain's independent deterrent, by the end of the year its future was still unclear. His willingness to continue with Blue

[121] CAB 131/20, D (58) 57, 3 Nov. 1958.
[122] CAB 131/19, 24 (58) 1, 5 Nov. 1958.
[123] CAB 131/19 D 24 (58), 5 Nov. 1958.
[124] CAB 131/20, D (58) 63, 17 Nov. 1958.
[125] CAB 131/20, D (58) 87, 19 Nov. 1958 and CAB 131/20, D (58) 86, 20 Dec. 1958.

Streak seemed to be framed in negative terms. While he stated that it would perhaps be wiser to await developments in the Polaris programme,

We have already spent or committed £50m on BLUE STREAK. It would obviously not make sense to stop the project now and then quite likely start it up again in a few years' time, having lost much valuable time and wasted a great deal of money.[126]

Furthermore, in a Defence Committee discussion on the defence estimates the warning was given that if a further saving on top of the planned £5 million for 1959/60 was taken off the Blue Streak project, it would make the missile operational not in 1965 but rather in 1969–70. Indeed, the point was made that 'It was for consideration therefore, whether if savings greater than £5 millions were to be sought in 1959–60, it should now be decided to abandon BLUE STREAK altogether.'[127] Nevertheless, it was pointed out that it would be unwise to take a decision to abandon the missile until further analysis had been completed over the form the deterrent should take from the late 1960s. Significantly, Macmillan concluded the meeting by pointing out that the Defence Committee faced some drastic decisions on policy particularly as it effected the deterrent. His preference for the time being to defer major decisions indicated that this central pillar of Britain's independent deterrent was far from secure.

## The Army's and Navy's Nuclear Ambitions and Anglo-American Interdependence 1957–1958

In October 1957 the Army put forward a requirement for four types of atomic weapons: an 8-mile atomic shell, a 30-mile atomic rocket, a 180-mile atomic rocket, and a nuclear armed mobile anti-aircraft missile.[128] Similarly to the other two services, the Army saw its independence being facilitated through interdependence with the Americans. It was stressed that Britain should aim at securing an agreement whereby the Americans would supply her with tactical nuclear weapons with as few

---

[126] CAB 131/20, D (58) 63, 17 Nov. 1958.
[127] CAB 131/19, 31 (58) 22 Dec. 1958.
[128] DEFE 7/1682, Nuclear Army Weapons, 21 Oct. 1957.

restrictions on employment as possible and that efforts be directed towards co-ordinating research programmes on tactical nuclear weapons. The Army pointed out that the 30-mile guided rocket was a promising weapon which the United States was not working on and that British research into such a project could be used as a bargaining tool for information and supply of other systems.[129]

The Army indicated that the emphasis on policy would still be directed towards interdependence with the Americans. It was stated that in the NATO and SEATO theatres the Americans would most probably provide Britain with tactical nuclear weapons while in independent British internal security operations and imperial policing tactical nuclear weapons would not be appropriate. Concomitantly, in the context of the Baghdad Pact theatre from which the Americans maintained their distance, it was pointed out that since Britain was not planning to deploy land forces, the question of the Army deploying nuclear weapons there did not arise.[130]

Yet, the Army still envisaged the possibility of independent British employment of tactical nuclear weapons. Indeed, the Army maintained that

since future events cannot be foreseen with certainty, it would be unwise to base our whole policy on the assumption that the Army will never need nuclear weapons except for operations in conjunction with the U.S.[131]

It was considered possible that Britain could find herself fighting in a local war with a country supplied with Soviet small yield nuclear weapons. In addition, in the long term, it was possible that many countries would be armed with tactical nuclear weapons and that Britain could not be left behind in this area of development.

As was to be expected, the Army's interest in various scenarios in which independent employment would be considered did not go down well in all quarters. The War Office's response to a Macmillan request for an outline of the reasons why the Army

---

[129] DEFE 7/1682, Nuclear Army Weapons, 21 Oct. 1957. The Army was at this stage expressing interest in a nuclear shell that the Americans were developing and in a 155 mm. nuclear capable gun. It was assumed that Britain would receive the 180-mile replacement missile for Corporal which was being developed in the USA.
[130] Ibid.                          [131] Ibid.

required tactical nuclear weapons led Deputy Secretary at the Ministry of Defence, Richard Way, to state that it was his belief that the Army should acquire nuclear weapons

less because we can specifically foresee circumstances in which they will be required, as because the consequences of not doing so would be unacceptable. I do not believe that the War Office paper approaches the question in the right way. It is full of dubious conceptions like 'winning' and 'ensuring success' in the land battle, whereas I should have thought they could more profitably have based their case on the consequences of a decision not to have tactical nuclear weapons for the Army.[132]

If the Russians and the Americans had these types of weapons, the British would have to have them too. Clearly, thinking here was that status and equality in the eyes of friends and enemies was more important than emphasis on scenarios of independent employment.

A description of a mention of winning and success as 'dubious conceptions' underlines the contention that the Ministry of Defence under Sandys was less interested in the military efficacy of tactical nuclear weapons for war fighting than it was in the overall deterrent effect of the strategic allied nuclear force. Certainly by the end of 1958, deployments of tactical nuclear weapons on the Continent were still not being undertaken in a manner that was tightly linked to the reduction of the British Army on the Rhine.

On 9 August Foreign Secretary Selwyn Lloyd had in fact written to Sandys warning him of the large gap between NATO requirements for the deployment of United Kingdom missile units (Britain was to deploy eleven surface-to-surface and four surface-to-air units by 1963) and the actual plans for deployment. In reply to NATO's Annual Review Questionnaire, the United Kingdom had stated there was no possibility of forecasting an increase beyond the two existing Corporal regiments, although the issue was under examination. Lloyd did not stress the military consequences of this problem but pointed to the political problems that would arise in Western Europe should Britain not deploy more units. As a result of this brief, Sandys told the War Office to investigate the problem—an investigation

[132] DEFE 7/1682, Way to Powell, 20 Sept. 1957.

which at the end of 1958 resulted, with the COSC's approval, in a suggestion that involved the formation of three Honest John units by 1960.[133] This measure still indicated that the United Kingdom would be two units short of the NATO requirement and it certainly appears—even as the size of BAOR ran down—that political rather than military considerations determined Sandys's interest at the end of 1958 in considering an increase in tactical nuclear deployments.

The desire of the Royal Navy to send large numbers of personnel to join the American nuclear submarine project had given rise to much friction between the head of the American naval nuclear project, Admiral Rickover, and the British. As noted, these difficulties were to give way to a much improved climate once Rickover had suggested that Britain procure a nuclear submarine reactor from the American Westinghouse firm.

The dependence of the British navy's nuclear programme on the Americans had been recognized by Mountbatten. On 29 January at the First Sea Lord's weekly meeting he stated that he had become convinced that failure to agree to the procurement of a propulsion plant would result in the end of Britain's plans to develop the nuclear powered Dreadnought. 'On the other hand, agreement would constitute the first step in interdependence and could be expected to be welcomed by the Government.'[134]

The agreement to make the purchase from Westinghouse was supported by the Defence Committee on 5 February.[135] A memorandum outlining the details of the Admiralty's ideas was sent to Washington and agreed to by Dulles in a letter on 2 June. Rolls-Royce was nominated as the British firm to deal with Westinghouse. The passage through Congress of the McMahon treaty allowed for a supply contract (covering sale

---

[133] DEFE 5/87, COS (58) 278, 8 Dec. 1958. Existing British projects at the end of 1958 for surface-to-surface missiles involved the Corporal programme, the Blue Water programme, and a programme for medium artillery with an atomic capability. Two Corporal units were already deployed in Britain which would soon be moved to Germany and the War Office planned to have two Blue Water missile units in the Strategic Reserve in the UK by 1965. Figures on the proportion of BAOR artillery to be given an atomic capability were not as yet available.

[134] ADM 205/177, First Sea Lord's Weekly Meeting, 29 Jan. 1958.

[135] CAB 131/19, 2 (58) 4, 5 Feb. 1958.

of machinery, training, and some maintenance) and a licensing
contract (under which Rolls-Royce would be allowed to manufacture the relevant equipment) to be set up. As a result of this
agreement Britain was certain that it would now be able to
commission Dreadnought by 1960 at the latest.

Yet, Mountbatten also reaffirmed his desire for independence
and his ambivalent attitude towards so much dependence on
the Americans when he stated that Britain's second and subsequent nuclear submarines should be totally constructed in
Britain. Certainly, Britain continued development—though at
a slower speed—at Dounreay of a shore-based prototype reactor
for a totally British nuclear submarine.[136] However, by the end
of the year it was being stated that consideration would have to
be given to the expenditure at Dounreay which appeared to be
escalating. Moreover, it was stressed that a

British nuclear deterrent of the POLARIS type would require a different
submarine hull but its propulsion machinery would be identical with
that in DREADNOUGHT. There was little risk, therefore, that the present
proposal would represent nugatory expenditure if it was eventually
decided to develop a British nuclear deterrent of the POLARIS type.[137]

The greater dependence on American know-how was certainly
becoming more apparent and as Eric Grove has pointed out,
'As the Americans had intended, the national British nuclear
program suffered from this U.S. purchase'.[138]

Indeed, one of the issues that came to dominate discussions
in 1958 was clearly that of the Polaris missiles themselves and
the evolving naval attitude towards the deterrent. For despite
the Navy's focus throughout the 1957 White Paper negotiations
on maintaining the strongest conventional order of battle
possible, Mountbatten was also not prepared to let the RAF
retain their monopoly of the independent deterrent.

This had already been manifested in 1954 when First Sea
Lord Mcgrigor had speculated on the possibility of sea-launched

---

[136] ADM 205/176, Board Minutes 5216–17, 27 Mar. 1958.

[137] CAB 131/19, 28 (58) 1, 26 Nov. 1958.

[138] Grove, *From Vanguard to Trident* (London, 1987), 233. The British were able to buy
the Skipjack reactor system rather than the Skate system that Rickover initially wanted
to sell. The Dreadnought was only finally commissioned in 1963 while HMS *Vulcan*
became operational in 1965 and HMS *Valiant* in 1962.

missile systems replacing the RAF bombers and Mountbatten had since kept in contact with the US Polaris programme through his contact with Admiral Burke. On 27 May 1957 the First Sea Lord raised the possibility with Sandys of Polaris as an alternative to the Thor or Jupiter missiles then under consideration for Britain's IRBM force. The Ministry of Supply was, however, strongly opposed to this idea at the present stage and warned that Polaris was not an alternative to Thor or Jupiter in performance or in time and that it involved a far greater degree of technical risk. While the US Navy planned to introduce the weapon in 1965, the Ministry of Supply regarded the whole programme as technically ambitious, as attention would have to be given to solid propellants, a two-stage system, and megaton warheads of reduced weight. Nevertheless, it was suggested that the Navy approach the American Navy on a service-to-service basis and keep contact with the project to see how it developed.[139]

An Admiralty Working Party was assigned to investigate the operational and strategical implications of arming Britain's submarines with Polaris missiles. It recommended that Britain deploy eight nuclear submarines armed with Polaris missiles. In discussion on the Admiralty Board it was pointed out that at most times six submarines would be in commission or made rapidly operational. If the submarine-based force was used, three of the vessels would be in place at the beginning of war with three others being capable of reaching positions from which to fire their missiles in a short period. In terms of lethality, the first version of Polaris would have a yield of 75 per cent of Blue Streak but the later versions would be of equal lethality to Blue Streak. The Board were confident that 'the strategical advantages of substituting such vessels for the BLUE STREAK missile were so overwhelming that the policy advocated in the memorandum should be adopted as a major naval objective'.[140] Unofficial exchanges with the US Navy appeared to indicate that the required information and possibly even the missiles themselves would be supplied by the Americans. The impending changes in the McMahon Act made this all possible. However, it was agreed that it would be best not to

---

[139] AIR 19/942, Ministry of Supply to Duncan Sandys, 29 May 1957.
[140] ADM 205/176, Board Minutes, 5216–17, 27 Mar. 1958.

push the project too strongly but rather to await the outcome of a Ministry of Defence enquiry into the potentialities of Polaris. In this decision

> the Board were influenced not only by the bitter opposition which the Air Ministry must be expected to offer to the substitution of the seaborne POLARIS for the land-based BLUE STREAK; but also by the risk that if too great an enthusiasm were shown prematurely for the POLARIS project, the Admiralty would be pressed to realise it without any addition to Navy votes to pay for it. On the other hand, if time were allowed for the great advantages of POLARIS over BLUE STREAK to sink in, the idea that the savings on the one should accrue to Navy Votes to pay for the other would begin to seem quite natural.[141]

Certainly throughout the period the Navy remained intent upon convincing Sandys that the nuclear submarine project should not be followed at the expense of conventional forces,[142] thus reflecting once more its interest less in a 'New Look' force posture than in one of multiple capabilities. By September this concern was still very much with the Navy. At the First Sea Lord's weekly meeting on 17 September Mountbatten stated that the present Admiralty's policy was that due to its own lack of funds it would be better not to bid for Polaris, but rather to await a government decision on the project and hope that it would then supply additional finance. He also indicated that any emphasis on Polaris would undercut the Navy's arguments on nuclear sufficiency[143]—which demanded additional conventional forces. The previous week Mountbatten had stated that 'he detected the first signs that Ministers were beginning to have doubts about the deterrent policy' and that 'it was not too early for us to start re-thinking in this light'; and 'He suggested that thought should be directed to placing more importance on conventional forces . . .'.[144]

The Navy was not of course intent upon moving out of the nuclear deterrent business. Her first three Red Beard bombs were to be received in January 1959[145] and on 10 September Sandys informed the First Lord of the Admiralty that production

---

[141] Ibid.

[142] ADM 205/172, First Sea Lord's Meeting, Item 2, 26 Mar. 1958.

[143] ADM 205/172, First Lord's Weekly Meeting, 17 Sept. 1958.

[144] ADM 205/172, First Sea Lord's Weekly Meeting, 11 Sept. 1958.

[145] DEFE 7/679, The Implications of the Admiralty Proposals to Stow Nuclear Weapons in Aircraft Carriers, 8 Oct. 1958.

of the NA 39 could proceed.[146] Moreover, in 1958 a British naval officer was appointed as a liaison with the US Polaris missile project[147] and towards the end of the year, following the decision to carry on with Blue Streak, Mountbatten expressed optimism about the government agreeing in the future to fund Polaris. This optimism was not ill founded as at a Defence Committee meeting on 17 December Sandys had stated that a submarine-based deterrent offered Britain major advantages:

> If, therefore, the rocket-launching submarine materialises as the Americans hope, it is quite conceivable that we may come to the conclusion that this is the best way in which Britain can make her limited contribution . . .[148]

Throughout, the Navy's logic appears to have been that in nuclear matters it wished to wrest control of the deterrent from the RAF but it would have to play its cards very carefully so as not to overly antagonize the Air Force in the process. In the meantime, in an era of 'nuclear sufficiency' and economic pressures on its fleet, it did not foreclose the option of convincing the government that it should not place too much emphasis on Britain's independent deterrent—especially if this came at the expense of its conventional forces. These contradictory impulses —resolvable only by a massive though, arguably, impractical financial input into the Navy—indicate that the Navy's guiding principle often remained not nuclear independence so much as her own bureaucratic aggrandizement.

On 16 April 1957, Minister of Defence Duncan Sandys informed the House of Commons that

> So long as large American forces remain in Europe, and American bombers are based in Britain, it might conceivably be thought safe— I am not saying that it would—to leave the United States the sole responsibility for providing the nuclear deterrent. But, when they have developed the 5000 mile intercontinental ballistic rocket, can we really be sure that every American Administration will go on looking at things in quite the same way?[149]

---

[146] ADM 205/172, First Sea Lord's Weekly Meeting, 11 Sept. 1958.

[147] Grove, *Vanguard to Trident*, 234.

[148] CAB 131/20, D (58) 63, 17 Nov. 1958. As noted, the Minister was, however, also adamant that the feasibility of Polaris was not yet proved and that there could be no question of immediately deciding on the sea-launched missile.

[149] House of Commons, vol. 568, cols. 1760–1, 16 Apr. 1957.

The logic of this pronouncement was that it was incumbent upon Britain to provide herself with a final guarantee should 'nuclear sufficiency' undermine the possibilities of American support for Europe in the face of some future Soviet aggression. This, as noted, expressed itself in Britain's thermonuclear test programme, the growing size of her V-bomber force, the procurement of the Thor IRBMs, the continued development of Blue Streak, and the Navy's interest in the Polaris missile.

Yet, the question is not whether Britain was interested in developing and improving its nuclear deterrent—a process that had long been underway—but whether from 1957 it is possible to note that independent nuclear deterrence defined as the ability to deter and engage in nuclear war unilaterally became the *prime* objective of British defence policy to the detriment of other goals including most importantly a nuclear production and planning relationship with the United States.

If in 1957 and 1958 the major objective of British policy was primarily to develop a unilateral means of deterring and waging war against the Soviet Union, this is not always reflected in Sandys's approach to the questions of command and control of Thor, his arguable ambivalences towards Blue Streak manifested in 1957 (though later giving way to stronger support), or as noted in the previous chapter, his approach to the number of V-bombers to be procured and the defences of the V-bomber bases. Here his willingness to subordinate issues of control to the goal of US missile deployment and strategic co-ordination and his strong and consistent sensitivity to economic considerations point to Sandys's and Macmillan's inclination to continue to place trust in SAC's deterrent power. Inconsistencies abounded with concern about 'nuclear sufficiency' and its implications for American guarantee going hand in hand with Army and Navy claims that more money should be spent not on Britain's independent deterrent but on conventional forces. Ministry of Defence fears of 'nuclear sufficiency' and the perceived decline in the reliability of the United States, too, reflected itself in a contradiction, in that the case for strategic co-ordination was pushed harder than ever. On the other hand, it can be argued that there was no inconsistency here and the perceived decline in the credibility of American guarantees made it more than ever necessary to push forward with co-ordinated planning and information exchange—both as a hedge against future American isolation and also as a means for limiting the American ability to retreat from a relationship of strategic nuclear concert.

This, of course, is not to imply that plans did not exist for independent nuclear action against the Soviet Union. Certainly these were extant and became increasingly apparent during 1958. However, these were both in 1957 and 1958 contingencies of last resort, subordinated both in preference and planning to the option of nuclear concert with the United States. This was a situation evidence by explicit statements to that effect by both Macmillan and Sandys throughout the period in question, and by their overwhelming desire to improve the Anglo-American relationship on all levels.

While the Air Ministry and the RAF often expressed confused notions of nuclear independence—reflecting an area where little had changed since the pre-Sandys period—they were certain that it required as much independent control as attainable, as large a force as possible, a future force that was technologically advanced (that is, including Blue Streak) and credible, and the retention of manned fighters. Conversely, when Sandys and Macmillan (who, too, were often and perhaps deliberately ambiguous) made statements on the independence of Britain's deterrent, they were in the final analysis primarily concerned not with the most unlikely contingency of unilateral action but the more immediate goal of 'independent deterrent influence'—specifically the possession of a nuclear force as an incentive to the United States to include Britain in her strategic plans and her deterrent orbit.

According to the documents that have been made available, in terms of force planning by 1958 both the RAF and the Ministry of Defence were certainly in agreement that V-bomber force structuring needed to be determined by explicit minimum deterrence terms and this, in turn, was naturally based on the countervalue targeting. Nevertheless, this does not necessarily imply that in terms of the contingency of independence in concert, Britain would have totally shifted away from counterforce assaults on targets most threatening to her. While there is no direct evidence of specific counterforce targets, logic seems to suggest that she must have still been keen on destroying these types of targets. Thus, across the 1955–8 period there are areas of strategic continuity as well as, if not new points of departure, then a degree of shifts in emphasis.

It was argued in the previous chapter that the reduction in manpower was the central focus of the Ministry of Defence's 1957 efforts and plans and, indeed, this appears to have had the greatest impact on actual planning both in 1957 and 1958. In contrast, as noted in this chapter, the British were in 1957 and 1958 not much interested in moving away from the major goal of nuclear strategic concert with the United States—a goal that was already present in the pre-1957 discussions on the structure and purposes of Britain's nuclear power—at least in terms of making it a secondary strategic preference.

The Americans were certainly given this impression. In November, a senior (though unnamed) official in the British Ministry of Defence informed American officials at their embassy in London:

UK nuclear weapons production was largely for political reasons, both in terms [of a] desire to give [the] UK increased stature as a nuclear power and in [the] hope [that] UK possession [of] these weapons would give [her] greater leverage in dealing with [the] US.[150]

Nuclear interdependence with the Americans therefore remained the key objective of British security policy throughout the period under study.

[150] NA, RG 59, 741.5/11, No. 2972, 9 Nov. 1957.

# Conclusion

THE 1956 Suez campaign and the resulting political crisis forced defence policy in general and nuclear strategy in particular into the forefront of the British political debate. By stripping bare the political illusions of post-war foreign policy and by underlining the limitations of its conventional military might, the Suez crisis helped push the Conservative government into articulating a strategic vision that upheld Britain's world power pretensions through an emphasis on all-powerful nuclear weapons.

The sensitive issue of the future of Britain's national service programme and the size of the armed forces provided another, albeit indirect, means whereby both government and non-government supporters found themselves addressing the balance between conventional and nuclear forces and thereby the question of the significance of nuclear weapons in the context of British force posture and strategy. In 1958 the decision was to be taken whether the politically unpopular legislation allowing for conscription was to be renewed. If it was not, then some means of replacing this loss of conventional fire-power would have to be secured. Here, issues of nuclear strategy, economic savings, and political pressures combined to underline the importance of developing a coherent strategic posture that integrated nuclear weapons into Britain's planning for war in Europe and in extra-European theatres.

Thus the British 'New Look'—similarly to its American predecessor and to the earlier Global Strategy Paper—was a policy characterized not only by the threat of massive nuclear response, but also by the search for economies through the replacement of conventional with nuclear fire-power. Two points are of note here. The documents certainly reveal that analogous to the American variant of the 'New Look' economic motivations were central to British thinking—certainly throughout the 1955–8 period. Indeed, this economic theme represents a major continuity across the period under study. The second point is that the documents covering the 1955–8 period lend support to the view expressed in the writings of Pierre, Groom,

Malone, and Clark and Wheeler that a growing appreciation of the strategic implications of nuclear and thermonuclear weapons informed upon a willingness to consider the replacement of conventional with nuclear forces. Ministers of Defence, Chiefs of Staff, and service heads were throughout these years agreed that nuclear weapons had altered the character of war and that this would have to be taken into account in contingency and force planning. Thus, *continuity* in economic motivations was mirrored by a *continuity* on the level of broad strategic concepts.

Continuity, however, should not solely be assessed on the level of motives and generalities, but also on the more relevant level of force programming and resulting policy outcomes. Certainly, the more significant level is that of programming and results and not intentions and theoretical speculations. For it is on the latter level of policy where ideas are actualized and general theoretical formulae are translated into procurement decisions. Because this process involves direct costs in terms of forces and capabilities (as opposed to theoretical speculation where the costs are more indirect and long term) it is the more interesting and important level—certainly as far as the question of policy continuities is concerned.

The progress of the 1955 Long Term Defence Programme and the 1956 Policy Review revealed that on a broad level, definitions of 'organizational essence' militated against acceptance of large cuts in budgets and manpower. On a more specific level, the Army's and Navy's attachment to global war forces made the adoption of a coherent strategic posture which reflected a match between, on the one hand force deployments and capability procurement, and on the other, an appreciation of the possible consequences of thermonuclear war, difficult to achieve. Recognition of the horrors of thermonuclear war sometimes did not go hand in hand with a willingness to recognize that long war strategies may be of dubious value. With the Army's view of its role as including the provision for a large scale ground war in Western Europe, the Navy's perception of its task as including support of a large battle fleet and reserves for operations during and after a thermonuclear exchange, and the RAF's attachment to a substantial Fighter Command, economic savings through force and capability reductions remained difficult to secure.

The tediousness and repetitiveness of the cost-cutting exercises of 1955–6 highlighted the slow pace of progress of these programmes and demonstrated that while the direction of planning pointed towards the Sandys White Paper, the speed at which decisions were being made and cuts secured did not suggest its irrevocable expression in 1957. The former Permanent Secretary at the Ministry of Defence, Sir Richard Powell, for one, is adamant about this point. Indeed, the services appeared incapable of generating a force posture of the type outlined in Sandys's first Defence White Paper. At the same time, it was not only service attitudes that militated against the evolution of British defence policy to the point reflected in the 1957 White Paper but also the organizational setting which allowed these forces to come into play. After all, it does not appear that during the negotiations surrounding the 1957 White Paper or following its publication, service definition or defence of their 'organizational essence' altered radically. For example, in 1958, while Sandys remained optimistic over recruitment figures,[1] many remained opposed to the total termination of national service and reliance on only 165,000 men.[2] The RAF continued to express its interest in manned bombers and in the need for fighter aircraft beyond the P. 1—demands totally at variance with the 1957 White Paper.[3]

Sandys's achievement, then, is that through force of personality and a shift in the balance of power within the decision-making process the ability of the services to defend what they perceived to be their essential interests was greatly weakened. It was these changes which helped generate the 1957 revolution in the nuclear–conventional force balance. From the start, Sandys had recognized that for the purposes of strengthening the central direction of defence planning, the organizational changes heralded in 1955 represented a false new dawn. The January 1957 directive and the later 1958 White Paper on defence organization had at their centres the object of subordinating service predilections to national objectives— defined, that is, by the Ministry of Defence. The fact that inter-

---

[1] NA, RG 59, 741.5/6-458, No. 7013, Whitney to Dulles, 4 June 1958.
[2] See Anthony Head's speech in the House of Commons in House of Commons, vol. 951, cols. 988 ff., 28 July 1958.
[3] NA, RG 59, 741.5/5-858, No. 6424, Embassy in London to Dulles, 8 May 1958.

service rivalry was to increase further during 1957–8 reaffirms the point of the cathartic nature of Sandys's first year in the Ministry of Defence and underlines the revolutionary implications of his policy in terms of force planning.

The *discontinuity* between the pre-1957 and 1957–8 force plans is most clearly reflected in a comparison of the force projections at the end of 1956 and at the end of 1957. While, of course, following the end of the Korean rearmament programme there was a decline in manpower and capabilities, the decline in 1957 was extremely sharp. The difference between cost projections for the end of the decade made in 1955 and those in 1957 is also marked.[4] Moreover, the shift of pronouncements to a stress on balanced collective forces in NATO underlines the significance of these changes for the manner in which British power was now to be deployed.

Consequently, while it may be claimed that the British stress on a strategy of massive retaliation in 1957 and 1958 reflected the culmination of trends present since at least the Global Strategy Paper of 1952, a review of the 1955–8 documents reveals that in terms of progress towards the 1957 'New Look' it was more strongly a culmination of declaratory trends. Ultimately, of course, economic realities would have impinged upon a force posture similar to that announced by Sandys, but the momentum and direction of policy in 1955–6 does not indicate that this would necessarily have taken place at the beginning of 1957 had not Macmillan and Sandys intervened as strongly as they did. Whether Britain could have espoused such a strategy so forcefully and explicitly in the context of the retention of large conventional forces and funding is questionable as the inconsistencies between declaratory and procurement policy would have been apparent for all to see. The 1957 White Paper was a public document—which the 1952 Global Strategy Paper was not—and therefore it had to pay far more attention to consistency, at least in terms of the relationship of forces to economy.

Viewed from this angle, the force posture drawn up in 1957 represented more of a revolution than a culmination. This is a

---

[4] While Selwyn Lloyd's 1955 projections pointed to an end of the decade level of defence spending averaging around £2,000 million, actual spending for 1959/60 stood at approximately £1,475.7 million. See A. Pierre, *Nuclear Politics* (London, 1972), 344.

perspective that is clouded not only by a tendency to compare declaratory policies across the 1950s, but also by the then government's proclivity to stress policy continuity with the earlier period. Both Sandys and Macmillan were always at pains to emphasize that Britain continued to attach great importance to ground forces in Europe and that she still retained her ability to meet all obligations. Obviously—and especially in the light of criticisms from the opposition, government back-benchers, and Britain's allies—Sandys did not wish to bolster the perceptions of decline in power that were prevalent in the wake of the Suez crisis.

The effect of the Suez crisis on British strategic planning in 1957 was both direct and indirect. Not only did it bring to power Macmillan, whose desire for military cost-cutting was well-known, and Sandys, whose penchant for military economies was even more notorious, but it created the environment which made the translation of declaratory into action policy a reality. Thus, although it was a mixture of organizational and personality changes that accounted for the success of the Minister of Defence in shifting the balance between conventional and nuclear forces, that this shift was initiated when it was is not unrelated to the flux in perceptions concerning the basis and purposes of British power that had accompanied the débâcle at Suez. Moreover, the failure in October 1956 did not leave service reputations untarnished, with the result that the new Prime Minister was presented with a somewhat weakened target. Again, as has been argued in the secondary literature, while a reduction in conventional forces would have inevitably come about at some point in time, the timing, speed, and finality with which the termination in conscription and other cutbacks were announced is strong circumstantial evidence that they were connected with the shock of Suez. If Suez and the perceived shifting strategic environment were not sufficient conditions for change then they were certainly necessary ones.

The lessons drawn from the crisis by Macmillan and Sandys reflected their concern for broad economic and political considerations above narrow military ones. Thus, service concerns for the procurement of capabilities and manpower necessary for Britain to sustain and improve independent military action was subordinated to the objectives of economic savings and the

Anglo-American partnership. On one level, this took the form of a stress on balanced collective forces—a means both for redressing and legitimizing reductions in British conventional forces. On another level, it took the form of a stress on Britain's independent nuclear contribution. The impression was given that what would be lost in terms of conventional independence would be made up with nuclear independence. Ostensibly, Suez served to reinforce a tendency long prevalent in British defence thinking—that the American guarantee could not in crisis be relied upon and that in an age of nuclear parity Britain would need her own capability unilaterally to deter her greatest enemy, the Soviet Union.

However, it has been argued in this study that while the Sandys White Paper does reflect a continuity as to the purposes of British nuclear power, it is not a continuity reflecting a move to a truly independent force posture. From the available documentation it appears that the parameters of the mainstream debate in 1955–6 did not include a great emphasis on the requirement for unilateral independence. The major question was whether to achieve a capability for destroying those targets most threatening to Britain in the context of a combined allied mission or to rely partly for even this limited objective on the American Strategic Air Command. Defence Committee discussions in 1957 reflect that the Minister of Defence located his position within the confines of this debate—at least in terms of the primary objective of policy which was viewed as some form of strategic concert with the United States. While during 1957 and increasingly in 1958 the contingency of unilateral nuclear response received growing attention, this was always considered a contingency of last resort and, for the purposes of policy and planning, subordinate to the main goal of deterrence in alliance and independence in concert with Strategic Air Command. Thus, while the documents reveal the concept of independence to have been an essentially contested concept, they also point to a continuity in terms of interdependence in planning with Sandys coming down primarily on the side that stressed greater integration with the Americans.

Despite growing questions concerning the credibility of American nuclear guarantees, Britain's policy-makers were intent upon viewing nuclear weapons chiefly in the context of those guarantees. The 1958 White Paper (which the Americans described as a progress report on the 1957 White Paper[5]) was unequivocal when it stated that war in Europe could be prevented almost indefinitely. It was stated that 'There is thus no military reason why a world conflagration should not be prevented for another generation or more through the balancing fears of mutual annihilation.'[6] While it was also stated that Western 'overall superiority' would increase because of the deployment of land-based missiles in Europe this was admitted to be so only because the Soviets could not then or in the future be confident of destroying all US strategic air bases on the American continent. Thus, while those who wished Britain to be rid of her deterrent capabilities did not address the question of American credibility, neither did those who sought to integrate the British nuclear deterrent with that of the United States. Both sides of the debate held implicit optimistic assumptions with regard to US intentions and very pessimistic assumptions regarding Britain's ability to survive such a nuclear conflict, or perhaps, placed great trust in Britain's declaratory statements that global war was a most unlikely contingency. In this sense too, there is continuity over the 1955–7 period.

To explain the discrepancy between declaratory and action policy, between the rhetorical stress on independence—a focus, admittedly, sometimes qualified with statements regarding the merits of interdependence—and the private search for interdependence, one is forced to return to issues of crisis and its implications for prestige and politics. The economic and political benefits of terminating national service were accompanied by the perceived domestic political necessity of reaffirming Britain's continued world power status—even if this meant an actual gap between Britain's commitments and her capabilities. Through its cost-cutting measures and termination of conscription the Macmillan government achieved financial savings and public support; through its emphasis on Britain's independent status the administration placated those who saw Suez as a failure of military capabilities and political will rather than a true reflection of Britain's reduced power. Arguably, the ad-

---

[5] NA, RG 59; 741.5/2-1958, No. 2775, Shullaw to Department of State, 13 Feb. 1958.
[6] *Report on Defence, 1958*, Cmnd. 363, HMSO, para. 5.

mission of financial and political weakness and the translation of that admission into a new economic force posture would have been difficult to achieve without the declaratory umbrella of national vigour and resilience embodied in the focus on independent deterrence—even if this belied a real gap between national commitments and national resources.

Therefore, while it can be claimed that from the Global Strategy Paper until the end of 1956 there was an inherent contradiction between a growing declaratory stress on nuclear deterrence and actual reliance on multiple capabilities, by the end of 1958 this inconsistency was represented by a continued declaratory focus on independent world power status and procurement and deployment policies which reflected irrevocable retraction.

As a special Foreign Office steering committee set up to assess the Anglo-American relationship reported in January 1958:

To adopt interdependence as a policy is to recognise interdependence as a fact and to decide to promote it as the only means of progress and safety. It involves taking a process which is happening anyway and turning it to advantage by extending, accelerating and proclaiming it.[7]

This did not mean that the relationship of interdependence to independence was—or arguably, could have been—made fully explicit. This often led to a continued measure of strategic confusion as to the purposes of Britain's nuclear power. For example, as late as the end of 1958 the Chancellor of the Exchequer asked the Cabinet

Even if the number of targets that can be successfully attacked is not directly proportional to the size of the bomber force, is it really clear that a smaller force than 144 U.E. would not suffice to secure us the co-operation of the United States—if indeed that is the true aim of the independent deterrent.[8]

As Wheeler's doctoral study of the Chiefs of Staff Committee and decision-making for nuclear strategy in the first decade of British nuclear strategy indicates, the importance of purely

[7] FO 371/132330, Steering Committee, Planning Paper on Interdependence, 27 Jan. 1958.
[8] CAB 130/20, D (58) 69, 17 Nov. 1958.

strategic criteria in the development of British defence policy was by the mid-1950s in decline. It was in decline because pressing economic imperatives were beginning to push strategic considerations to the side. That study is supported by the findings of this thesis to the extent that it is demonstrated here that in the first year of Duncan Sandys's leadership in the Ministry of Defence, nuclear strategic thinking was very much a secondary consideration in a larger formula that sought major financial savings. The strongest evidence of this is found in the Minister's almost single-minded focus on manpower reductions and the concern expressed in the Air Ministry over Sandys's approach to the deterrent.

In question then is Sandys's role as a strategic thinker. According to Clark and Wheeler, 'the erosion of British nuclear strategy was to coincide with the articulation of a public doctrine of independence, as in the White Paper of 1957'.[9] Certainly Sandys's apparent willingness to subordinate all to economic requirements and his style of achieving quick results with the minimum of discussion points to a technocratic mind rather than that of a broad strategic conceptualizer. Therefore, it can be argued that the decline in the importance of strategic considerations was exacerbated by placing defence policy in the hands of someone who was 'a doer rather than a thinker', more sensitive to immediate economic and political factors than to requirements of British nuclear deterrent strategy.

However, to claim that Sandys was less than responsive to the requirements of an independent nuclear strategy is not to say that he neither understood nor cared for sound strategic formulae. Indeed, his actions point to a far broader conception of strategy—a strategy which recognized the importance of a firm economic base and made a realistic assessment of Britain's position relative to her main ally and her main enemy. The conclusion was therefore reached that economically and militarily Britain's security interests were best served through conventional integration with NATO and nuclear integration with the United States. This was not the abdication of strategic thinking but its inevitable manifestation in a period of growing economic and political constraints.

---

[9] I. Clark and N. J. Wheeler, *The British Origins of Nuclear Strategy 1945–1955* (Oxford, 1989), 16.

That Sandys was prepared to place trust in American guarantees in a period of increasing American vulnerability to Soviet nuclear attack is therefore not necessarily an indication of the poverty of his strategic thought as much as it is an indication of the poverty of Britain's resources. Strategic choices, after all, are not always made between the good and bad, but often between the bad and the far worse. On the one hand, the Minister could have attempted to procure nuclear capabilities primarily on the basis of a totally independent counterforce capability but this would, in the face of the increasing Soviet target set, have ultimately cost substantial amounts. Alternatively, he could have assigned the force first and foremost to countervalue targets on the basis of a unilateral British strike against the Soviet Union, but it seemed hardly realistic for Britain to wage unilateral nuclear war—though there was no harm in making declaratory statements to this effect or developing contingency plans for such a scenario.

On the one hand, he could have continued to rely on the Americans—a reliance which had so far paid off in terms of successful deterrence—and to influence the use of SAC as much as possible through the possession of a nuclear capability. His tendency towards the latter option therefore was not strategically unreasonable. Yet, the problem with this analysis is that the papers do not indicate the Minister privately arguing in such explicit terms. The impression then still remains that Sandys was overly beholden to economic factors and more interested in quick results than in strategy. The strategic analysis outlined above was more implicit than explicit and in that sense not subject to a reasoned cost–benefit analysis. Indeed, the Minister may have reached strategically prudent choices for essentially a-strategic reasons. Consequently, it is difficult to ascertain from the perspective of motivations the quality of Sandys's strategic thought. The perspective of results, however, helps provide a more positive interpretation.

Another approach towards assessing Sandys's contribution to British security policy is to look at the legacy of the 1957 White Paper for British strategic planning in the late 1950s and early 1960s—especially in terms of the conventional–nuclear force balance and the purposes of Britain's nuclear deterrent power. With regard to the former, Sandys's imprint appeared soon to be undermined. While the 1957 White Paper had afforded a saving of £100 million on the 1956 defence projections, and while the 1958 White Paper announced a slight reduction in expenditure,[10] by 1959 increased expenditure had caused a rise of £20 million in planned defence spending.[11] Indeed, while Sandys could cut defence spending, he could do little to reduce costs—and with commitments held relatively constant, the gap between capabilities and demands had to be closed. Intimations of a growing shift towards conventional forces could already be noted in the 1959 White Paper in which no mention was made of Britain's deterrent doctrine and in the 1960 White Paper (Sandys was now no longer Minister of Defence) where it was stated that nuclear power

is only one component of the deterrent. Because of the need to meet local emergencies which could develop into a major conflict, conventionally armed forces are a necessary complement to nuclear armaments.[12]

As noted, the size of the Army was soon increased to 180,000 and in 1960 the new Minister of Defence, Harold Watkinson, stated that BAOR would not be reduced below 50,000 men and the 2nd TAF would not be cut back any more. The 1962 White Paper took the declaratory shift even further when it stated that

We must continue to make it clear to potential aggressors, however, that we should strike back with all the means that we judge appropriate, conventional·or nuclear. If we had nothing but nuclear forces, this would not be credible. A balance must be maintained, therefore, between conventional and nuclear strength.[13]

Three points can be gleaned from these developments. The first is that the radical nature of the 1957 Macmillan government's conventional force plans are underlined, because service resistance again manifested itself most strongly in this area.

---

[10] Report on Defence, 1958, Cmnd. 363 HMSO, para. 78. The defence estimates for 1957/8 were £1483 million, but with aid from the United States and Germany savings of £63 million could further be secured. To this had to be added Admiralty and Ministry of Supply supplementary estimates of £42 million. The defence estimates for 1958/9 amounted to £1465 million, but when taking into account receipts for local costs, the total was £1418 million.

[11] *Progress of the 5 Year Defence Plan: 1959*, Cmnd. 662, HMSO, para. 48.

[12] *Report on Defence 1960*, Cmnd. 952, HMSO, para. 3.

[13] *Statement on Defence 1962: The Next Five Years*, Cmnd. 1639, HMSO, para. 8.

Secondly, the significance of Sandys's personality is reinforced because once the Minister was out of the way (or on his way out) the old forces could again begin to reassert themselves. Thirdly, and perhaps most importantly, despite these latter forces, the 1957 White Paper's revolutionary import remained in place because, as Groom puts it,

The decision that had been taken was in many ways irrevocable, for only a crisis of great magnitude could give any Government the political courage to reverse national priorities and demand the support of the nation in the sacrifices that the rebuilding of Britain's conventional forces would entail.[14]

In other words, despite the loosening of Sandys's hold on budgeting and manpower levels, the cuts he had initiated in 1957 were so far reaching—especially that of manpower reductions—that a return to the pre-1957 force posture was simply out of the question. Indeed, the next major revolution in British defence policy came in the 1960s when commitments were radically cut rather than capabilities increased.

With regard to the question of the independence of Britain's deterrent, British actions in the early 1960s are more easily explainable by Sandys and Macmillan's private thoughts than by their declaratory rhetoric. The decision to give up the Blue Streak project in 1960 and to rely first on the American Skybolt missile and later on Polaris represented, in a sense, a willingness to integrate more fully with American strategic nuclear power —at least in terms of production. This does not seem so surprising when viewed against the background of the statements to the Defence Committee in February 1957 that Britain would in no circumstances use nuclear weapons independently of the United States' or Sandys's 1958 hesitations over Blue Streak. If, as argued, Sandys's and Macmillan's strategy was to secure greater US strategic co-operation and to place Britain's nuclear future firmly in alliance terms, then the decade following the 1957 White Paper saw the fruition of their schemes.

The first year of Duncan Sandys at the Ministry of Defence was therefore in some ways a turning point and in some ways a period characterized by a reaffirmation of existing trends. Viewed as a totality, it resulted in an integration of the various

[14] A. J. R. Groom, *British Thinking about Nuclear Weapons* (London, 1974), 249.

aspects of policy which made up strategy in a more systematic manner than had previously been achieved. Organizational and personality changes combined to take advantage of weakened service positions. This led to the adoption of a more coherent strategy—defined in terms of the relationship between conventional and nuclear forces—and the most credible deterrent posture that was economically feasible, politically effective, and strategically realistic.

# Bibliography

## 1. Primary Material

### (a) *Unpublished*

#### THE MAIN BRITISH ARCHIVAL MATERIAL
#### (PUBLIC RECORDS OFFICE)

For a good survey of relevant Public Records Archival material as it relates to British nuclear strategic policy-making see Clark and Wheeler, *The British Origins of Nuclear Strategy*, 243–7. Clark and Sabin provide an extensive survey of British nuclear studies resource material in *Sources for the Study of British Nuclear Weapons History* (Nuclear History Project, 1987). Briefly, Cabinet and Cabinet sub-committee papers relating to British nuclear weapons policy and planning in the 1950s can be found in CAB 128, CAB 129, CAB 130, and CAB 131. DEFE 4 and 5 contain the minutes and memoranda of the Chiefs of Staff Committee. Memoranda of the Joint Planning Staff are located in DEFE 6. Documents relating to the 1955 Long Term Defence Programme are filed in DEFE 7. Papers of the RAF pertaining to British nuclear planning and policy-making during the 1955–8 period can be found mainly in AIR 2, AIR 8, and AIR 19. Much information on the 1957 White Paper may be gleaned from ADM 205/114. Information on the manpower question and national service can be found in WO 32. Papers covering the Foreign Office approach to the subject matter are located under the general FO 371. PREM 11 contains useful documents from the Prime Minister's File that have a bearing on the subject.

#### AMERICAN ARCHIVAL MATERIAL

For this book research was undertaken at the National Archives in Washington where RG 59 General Records of the Department of State must stand as the best starting block for research into this period of British defence policy; at the Library of Congress; and at the Eisenhower Library in Abilene Kansas where Papers of Dwight D. Eisenhower as President, Ann Whitman File revealed much interesting information as did the John Foster Dulles Papers 1952–9.

#### COLLECTIONS OF UNPUBLISHED PAPERS

Liddell Hart Papers (held at the Liddell Hart Centre for Military Archives, King's College London).

Mountbatten Papers (held at the University of Southampton).

The Unpublished Memoirs of Duncan Sandys (Private Copy of Lady Duncan Sandys).

The Unpublished Memoirs of Sir William Dickson (Mountbatten Papers, NA/99, University of Southampton).

The Unpublished Memoirs of Sir William Davis (Private Copy of Dr S. Forgan).

INTERVIEWS/CORRESPONDENCE

Private interviews were conducted with:

Colonel K. G. Post (in 1957 a personal adviser to the Minister of Defence), 1 Mar. 1988.

Sir Richard Powell (in 1957 the Permanent Secretary at the Ministry of Defence), 18 June 1987.

Mr T. C. G. James (in 1957 an Assistant Secretary in the Air Ministry and later an official air historian), 15 Dec. 1987.

In the context of an oral history seminar conducted on 1 July 1988 in the Department of War Studies on the subject of the 1957 Defence White Paper, the following additional people were interviewed:

The Rt. Hon. Julian Amery (in 1957 a Parliamentary Under Secretary of State in the War Office).

Sir Arthur Drew (in 1957 an Under Secretary at the Ministry of Defence).

The Earl of Selkirk (in 1957 First Lord of the Admiralty).

Sir Richard Way (in 1957 a Deputy Secretary at the Ministry of Defence).

Correspondence was exchanged with:

Sir Dermot Boyle (former Chief of the Air Staff), 28 May 1987.

Sir Patrick Dean (in 1957 an Under Secretary of State in the Foreign Office), 19 February 1988.

Sir Nigel Fisher (a former Under Secretary of State for Colonies who served under Sandys in the early 1960s), 23 February 1988.

Air Chief Marshall Sir David Lee (in 1957 Secretary to the COSC), 20 March 1988.

Sir Richard Powell, 2 June 1988.

Sir Edward Playfair (in 1957 a Permanent Under Secretary of State in the War Office), 27 May 1987.

General Sir Dudley Ward (in 1957 Commander in Chief of the British Army on the Rhine), 22 February 1988.

In preparation for the oral history conference correspondence was also exchanged between Professor L. Freedman and:

Sir Dermot Boyle (in 1957 Chief of the Air Staff), 10 June 1988.

Rt. Hon. Aubrey Jones (in 1957 Minister of Supply), 18 May 1988.

## (b) *Published*

### OFFICIAL GOVERNMENT PUBLICATIONS

*Central Organisation of Defence*, Cmd. 6923, HMSO, 1946.

*Statement on Defence, 1955*, Cmd. 9391, HMSO, 1955.

*Statement on Defence, 1956*, Cmd. 9691, HMSO, 1956.

*Defence: Outline of Future Policy*, Cmnd. 124, HMSO, 1957.

*Central Organisation for Defence*, Cmnd. 476, HMSO, 1958.

*Report on Defence, 1958*, Cmnd. 363, HMSO, 1958.

*Progress of the 5 Year Defence Plan: 1959*, Cmnd. 662, HMSO, 1959.

*Report on Defence 1960*, Cmnd. 952, HMSO, 1960.

*Statement on Defence 1962: The Next 5 Years*, Cmnd. 1639, HMSO, 1962.

*Hearings before the Subcommittee on Agreements for Cooperation of the JCAE.*
Amending the Atomic Energy Act of 1954—Exchange of Military Information and Material with Allies, 85th Congress, 2nd Session 1958, 104, 187, 196, 229–30, 298.

*Agreement . . . For Co-operation on the Uses of Atomic Energy for Mutual Defence Purposes*, Cmnd. 537. Treaty Series No. 41, 1958.

*Amendment to Agreement between the Government of the United Kingdom of Great Britain and Northern Ireland and the Government of the United States of America for Cooperation on the Uses of Atomic Energy for Mutual Defence Purposes*, Cmnd. 859, Treaty Series No. 72, 1959.

### PARLIAMENTARY DEBATES

Hansard, House of Commons Debates (1954–8).

### OTHER COLLECTIONS OF OFFICIAL DOCUMENTS

*Foreign Relations of the United States*, Vol. iv, 1955–7, Western European Security and Integration, US Delegation to NATO Heads of Government Meeting in Paris to Department of State, 17 December 1957.

*NATO Facts and Figures*, North Atlantic Treaty Organisation, information Service, Brussels, October 1971.

## 2. Secondary Material

*Books*

ALLISON, G. T., *The Essence of Decision* (Boston: Little Brown, 1971).

ARNOLD, L., *A Very Special Relationship: British Atomic Weapons Trials in Australia* (London: HMSO, 1987).

BARTLETT, C. J., *The Long Retreat: A Short History of British Defence Policy* (London: Macmillan, 1972).

BAYLIS, J., *Anglo-American Defence Relations, 1939–84* (London: Macmillan, 2nd edn., 1984).

BLACKETT, P. M. S., *Atomic Weapons and East-West Relations* (Cambridge: Cambridge University Press, 1956).

BOTTI, T., *The Long Wait: The Forging of the Anglo-American Nuclear Alliance, 1945–58* (Connecticut: Greenwood, 1987).

BRODIE, B., *The Absolute Weapon* (New York: Harcourt Brace, 1946).

BROOKES, A., *V-Force: The History of Britain's Airborne Deterrent* (London: Jane's 1982).

BULL, H., and LOUIS, W. R. (eds.), *The Special Relationship: Anglo-American Relations since 1945* (Oxford: Oxford University Press, 1986).

CLARK, I., and WHEELER, N. J., *The British Origins of Nuclear Strategy 1945–1955* (Oxford: Oxford University Press, 1989).

CLOAKE, J., *Templer, Tiger of Malaya: The Life of Field Marshal Sir Gerald Templer* (London: Harrap, 1985).

DARBY, P., *British Defence Policy East of Suez 1947–68* (London: Oxford University Press, 1973).

DEIGHTON, A. (eds.), *Britain and the First Cold War* (London: Macmillan, 1990).

DIVINE, R., *Blowing in the Wind: The Nuclear Test Ban Debate 1954–1960* (New York: Oxford University Press, 1978).

DUKE, S., *US Defence Bases in the United Kingdom* (London: Macmillan, 1987).

EDEN, A., *Full Circle: The Memoirs of Anthony Eden* (London: Cassell, 1960).

EDMONDS, M., *The Defence Equation: British Military Systems —Policy Planning and Performance Since 1945* (London: Brasseys, 1986).

EPSTEIN, L., *British Politics in the Suez Crisis* (Chicago: University of Illinois Press, 1964).

FREEDMAN, L. D., *Britain and Nuclear Weapons* (London: Macmillan, 1980).

—— *The Evolution of Nuclear Strategy* (London: Macmillan, 1981).

FREEMAN, J. P. G., *British Nuclear Arms Control Policy in the Context of Anglo-American Relations, 1957–1968* (Basingstoke: Macmillan, 1986).

FULLICK, R., and POWELL, G., *Suez: The Double War* (London: H. Hamilton, 1979).

GOWING, M., *Britain and Atomic Energy 1939–45* (London: Macmillan, 1964).

—— *Independence and Deterrence: Britain and Atomic Energy, 1945–52* (London: Macmillan, 2 vols., 1974).

GRAY, C., *Strategic Studies and Public Policy: The American Experience* (Lexington: University of Kentucky Press, 1982).

GROOM, A. J. R., *British Thinking about Nuclear Weapons* (London: Frances Pinter, 1974).

GROVE, E., *From Vanguard to Trident: British Naval Policy Since World War II* (London: Bodley Head, 1987).

HALPERIN, M., *Bureaucratic Politics and Foreign Policy* (Washington, DC: Brookings, 1974).

HOBKIRK, M., *The Politics of Defence Budgeting* (London: Macmillan, 1984).

HORNE, A., *Macmillan, 1891–1956* (London: Macmillan, 1988).

—— *Macmillan, 1957–1986* (London: Macmillan, 1989).

HUNTINGTON, S., *The Common Defense: Strategic Programmes in National Politics* (New York: Columbia University Press, 1961).

KAHAN, J. H., *Security in the Nuclear Age: Developing US Strategic Arms Policy* (Washington, DC: Brookings, 1975).

KAPLAN, F., *The Wizards of Armageddon* (New York: Simon and Schuster, 1983).

KISSINGER, H., *Nuclear Weapons and Foreign Policy* (New York: Harper and Brothers, 1957).

LIDDELL HART, B. H., *Defence of the West* (London: Cassell, 1950).

—— *Deterrent or Defence* (London: Stevens, 1960).

LIDER, J., *British Military Thought after World War II* (London: Gower, 1985).

MACMILLAN, H., *Riding the Storm* (London: Macmillan, 1971).

—— *Tides of Fortune* (London: Macmillan, 1969).

MALONE, P., *The British Nuclear Deterrent: A History* (London: Croom Helm, 1984).

MENAUL, S., *Countdown: Britain's Strategic Nuclear Forces* (London: Hale, 1980).

OSGOOD, R., *NATO: The Entangling Alliance* (Chicago: Chicago University Press, 1962).

—— *Limited War* (Chicago: Chicago University Press, 1957).

PIERRE, A., *Nuclear Politics: The British Experience with an Independent Strategic Force 1939–70* (London: Oxford University Press, 1972).

RHODES, R. J., *Anthony Eden* (London: Weidenfeld & Nicolson, 1986).
ROSECRANCE, R. N., *Defence of the Realm: British Strategy in the Nuclear Epoch* (New York: Columbia University Press, 1968).
SCHILLING, W., HAMMOND, P., and SNYDER, S., *Strategy Politics and Defence Budgets* (New York: Columbia University Press, 1962).
SELDON, A., *Churchill's Indian Summer: The Conservative Government: 1951–55* (London: Hodder & Stoughton, 1981).
SIMPSON, J., *The Independent Nuclear State: The United States, Britain and the Military Atom* (London: Macmillan, 1983).
SLESSOR, Sir J., *Strategy for the West* (London: Cassell, 1954).
—— *The Great Deterrent* (London: Cassell, 1957).
SNYDER, W. P., *The Politics of British Defence Policy, 1945–62* (Columbia: Ohio State University Press, 1964).
STEINBRUNER, J., *The Cybernetic Theory of Decision: New Dimensions of Political Analysis* (Princeton: Princeton University Press, 1974).
WILLIAMS, F., *A Prime Minister Remembers* (London: Heinemann, 1961).
YOUNGER, A. J., *Britain's Economic Growth, 1920–1966* (London: Allen & Unwin, 1970).
ZIEGLER, P., *Mountbatten* (London: Collins, 1985).

## Articles and Theses

BETTS, R. K., 'A Nuclear Golden Age? The Balance Before Parity', *International Security*, 2, No. 3 (1986/7).
BLACKETT, P. M. S., 'Thoughts on British Defence Policy', *New Statesman*, 5 Dec. 1959.
BLUTH, C., 'Nuclear Weapons and British–German Relations', in R. O'Neill and B. Heuser (eds.), *Securing Peace in Europe, 1945–1962: Thoughts for the 1990s* (forthcoming).
BUCHAN, A., 'Towards a New Strategy of Graduated Deterrence', *The Reporter* (1 Dec. 1955).
BUZZARD, A., 'Massive Retaliation and Graduated Deterrence', *World Politics*, 32, No. 2 (1956).
——, SLESSOR, J., and LOWENTHAL, R., 'The H-Bomb: Massive Retaliation or Graduated Deterrence—A Discussion', *International Affairs*, 32, No. 2 (1956).
CLARK, I. and SABIN, P., *Sources for the Study of British Nuclear Weapons History* (Nuclear History Project, Maryland, 1987).
CROSSMAN, R. H. S., 'The Nuclear Obsession', *Encounter*, 11, No. 1 (July 1958).
CROWE, W. J., 'The Policy Roots of the Royal Navy, 1946–63' (Ph.D. Thesis, Princeton University, 1965).

DEVEREUX, D. R., 'Between Friend and Foe: The Formulation of British Defence Policy Towards the Middle East 1948–56 (Ph.D. Thesis, King's College London, 1988).

EDMONDS, M. and GROOM, A. J. R., 'British Defence Policy Since 1945', in Higham, R. (ed.), *The Sources of British Military History* (London: Routledge & Kegan Paul, 1972).

FISHER, N., 'Minister who Ruled with a Rod of Iron', *Observer*, 29 Nov. 1987.

FREEDMAN, L., 'British Nuclear Targeting', in Ball, D., and Richelson, J. (eds.), *Strategic Nuclear Targeting* (Ithaca: Cornell University Press, 1986).

GORDON, C., 'Duncan Sandys and the Independent Nuclear Deterrent', in Beckett, I., and Gooch, J. (eds.), *Politicians and Defence* (Manchester: Manchester University Press, 1987).

GREENWOOD, D., 'Defence and National Priorities Since 1945', In Baylis, J., *British Defence Policy in a Changing World* (London: Croom Helm, 1977).

HOWARD, M., *The Central Organisation for Defence* (London: Royal United Institute for Defence Studies, 1970).

KISSINGER, H. A., 'Military Policy and the Defence of the Gray Areas', *Foreign Affairs*, 33, No. 3 (1955).

MARTIN, L., 'The Market for Strategic Ideas in Britain: The "Sandys Era" ', *American Political Science Review*, 56, No. 1 (1962).

NAVIAS, M., 'Strengthening the Deterrent: The British Medium Bomber Force Debate, 1955–6', *Journal of Strategic Studies*, 2, No. 2 (1988).

NITZE, P., 'Atoms, Strategy and Foreign Policy', *Foreign Affairs*, 34, No. 2 (1956).

POWELL, J. E., 'Lord Duncan Sandys', *Independent*, 27 Feb. 1987.

POWELL, R., 'The Evolution of British Defence Policy', in *Perspectives on British Defence Policy* (Southampton: University of Southampton, 1978).

REES, W., 'The 1957 Sandys White Paper: New Priorities in British Defence Policy', *Journal of Strategic Studies* (June 1989).

ROSENBERG, D. A., 'The Origins of Overkill: Nuclear Weapons and American Strategy, 1945–60', *International Security*, 7, No. 4 (1983).

—— 'A Smoking Radiating Ruin at the End of Two Hours', *International Security* (Winter 1981/2).

SAUNDBY, R. H. M., 'The Royal Navy in the Atomic Age', in *Brassey's Annual, 1955* (London: RUSI, 1955).

SCHILLING, W. R., 'US Strategic Nuclear Concepts in the 1970s', *International Security*, 6, No. 2 (1981).

SLESSOR, J., 'British Defence Policy', *Foreign Affairs*, 35, No. 4 (1957).

TORLESSE, A. D., 'The Role of the Aircraft Carrier', in *Brassey's Annual, 1955* (London: RUSI, 1955).

VENABLES, M., 'The Place of Air Power in Post-War British Defence Planning, and its Influence on the Genesis and Development of Nuclear Deterrence 1945–52' (Ph.D. Thesis, Dept. of War Studies, King's College, London, 1985).

WALKER, J., 'British Attitudes to Nuclear Proliferation, 1952–1982' (Ph.D. Thesis, University of Edinburgh, 1986).

WHEELER, N. J., 'British Nuclear Weapons and Anglo-American Relations 1945–54', *International Affairs*, 62, No. 1 (1985/6).

—— 'The Roles Played by the British Chiefs of Staff Committee in the Development of British Nuclear Weapons Planning and Policy-making 1945–55' (Ph.D. Thesis, Dept. of Politics, University of Southampton, 1988).

WOHLSTETTER, A., 'The Delicate Balance of Terror', *Foreign Affairs*, 37, No. 2 (1959).

# Index